D0086173

We Mean Business

BOWLING GREEN STATE UNIVERSITY
DISCARDED
LIBRARY

We Mean Business

Building Communication Competence
in Business and Professions

WILLIAM I. GORDEN
Kent State University

RANDI J. NEVINS
Michigan State University

HarperCollinsCollegePublishers

BOWLING GREEN STATE
UNIVERSITY LIBRARIES

Acquisitions Editor: Daniel F. Pipp
Project Editor: Diane Rowell
Design Supervisor: Dorothy Bungert
Adapted Text Design: Molly Heron
Cover Design: John Callahan
Cover Photo: COMSTOCK INC. / COMSTOCK INC
Production Manager/Assistant: Willie Lane/Sunaina Sehwani
Compositor: Digitype, Inc.
Printer and Binder: R. R. Donnelley & Sons Company
Cover Printer: The Lehigh Press, Inc.

For permission to use copyrighted material, grateful
acknowledgment is made to the copyright holders on pp.
317–319, which are hereby made part of this copyright page.

We Mean Business: Building Communication Competence
in Business and Professions
Copyright © 1993 by HarperCollins College Publishers

All rights reserved. Printed in the United States of America.
No part of this book may be used or reproduced in any
manner whatsoever without written permission, except in the
case of brief quotations embodied in critical articles and
reviews. For information address HarperCollins College
Publishers, 10 East 53rd Street, New York, NY 10022.

Library of Congress Cataloging-in-Publication Data

Gorden, William I., 1929–
    We mean business : building communication competence in business
  and professions / William I. Gorden, Randi J. Nevins.
        p.   cm.
      Includes index.
      ISBN 0–06–500048–X
      1. Business communication.   2. Communication in organizations.
    3. Interpersonal communication.   I. Nevins, Randi J.   II. Title.
    HF5718.G665   1992
    651.7—dc20   92–18520
                                                            CIP

92 93 94 95   9 8 7 6 5 4 3 2 1

To Gloria and Gay Lin
William I. Gorden

*To the Nevins, Perry, and Cooper families,
and my best friend, Tom Stanulis*
Randi J. Nevins

Contents

CHAPTER 2   **LISTENING AND THE COMMUNICATION PROCESS IN THE WORKPLACE   24**

CHAPTER 3   **INTERPERSONAL COMMUNICATION IN THE WORKPLACE   40**

Preface

Our aim in writing this text is to communicate closely and directly with our audience about current issues in communication for business and professions. This book is targeted for the growing number of people who are or will be members of an organizational setting. *We Mean Business* is meant for:

- People who are interested in understanding the power and complexities of an *organization's culture*, including dimensions of commitment, norms, ritual, and significant symbols.
- People who are interested in learning more about *voice and ethics* in the workplace, including issues of business ethics, principled reasoning, and employee voice.

- People who are interested in learning more about different forms and functions of *interpersonal communication*, including communication apprehension and uncertainty, listening, nonverbal communication, and special problems that require interpersonal competencies.
- People who are interested in developing confidence and competence in *public speaking*, including information about organizing and delivering different types of business presentations, adapting to different audiences, and supporting arguments with evidence.
- People who are interested in *group dynamics and team building*, including issues of running meetings, group creativity, group cohesiveness, and team building.
- People who are interested in learning more about the various forms of *written communication* within the workplace, forms and preparation for *interviewing*, and using *audiovisual* materials.

BUILDING COMMUNICATION COMPETENCIES

Because this text focuses on building communication competencies in writing, speaking, and listening, we are certain that readers will find it a valuable resource. We believe that *We Mean Business* has value not only for the classroom, but also for one's professional library. Throughout the text there are numerous illustrations that support claims about topics such as nonverbal, written, interpersonal, and public communication. Rich examples are also included to supplement points about aspects of organizational life such as organizational culture, voice, ethics, and persuasion.

The text is written in a clear, personal manner that several reviewers have called "entertaining." Our intent is to talk with the readers, and help them feel confidence in building competencies so necessary for success in organizational life.

"WE MEAN BUSINESS" AND "SKILLBUILDERS"

Two unique features of this text that will benefit readers are the inclusion of "We Mean Business" prompts within each chapter and "Skillbuilders" at the close of each chapter.

The "We Mean Business" inserts probe the reader's thinking while considering issues and dilemmas put forward by the text. We hope that by raising questions about the material, readers will be more critical and have more ownership of the information. These probes can provide a springboard for discussions.

The "Skillbuilders" placed at the close of each chapter are activities that are designed to synthesize and provoke thought about the content of each chapter. The central theme of our text is building communication competencies. The "Skillbuilders" provide an opportunity to practice the competencies described, and are designed to encourage creativity and thoughtful responses.

We hope we have provided a forum for readers to engage in conversations with others about communication issues and competencies.

ACKNOWLEDGMENTS

We want to express our gratitude to those instructors and students who read early drafts of this text and provided numerous helpful suggestions. We would also like to thank the following reviewers: Samuel Edleman, California State University at Chico; Pamela Edwards, University of Northern Iowa; Karen Foss, Humboldt State University; Ethel Glenn, University of North Carolina at Greensboro; Suzanne Hagen, University of Wisconsin at River Falls; Julie Ham, New Mexico State University; Paul Harper, Oklahoma State University; Martha Haun, University of Houston; J. Daniel Joyce, Houston Community College; Sandra Ketrow, University of Rhode Island; Gary Kreps, Northern Illinois University; Jerry Mays, Murray State University; Charles Newman, Parkland College; and Tyler Tindall, Midland College. We are grateful to Judith Anderson, Dan Pipp, Diane Rowell, and Cynthia Bailie for all the editorial detail so necessary to make this an attractive textbook.

No manuscript gets to print before many eyes have seen it and many hands have edited and typed it. Kerry Belitz and Kim Hutchison, former students at Northeast Missouri State University, helped tremendously with the researching and editing of Chapters 7 and 10. Kerry Belitz (NMSU) and Maureen Ambler (Kent State University) typed and retyped the manuscript. Ruth Nevins carefully proofread and edited the manuscript. Jill Thurston did much of the work in creating and typing the first draft of the glossary. Erica Nagel helped with permissions and indexing. We thank them all.

William I. Gorden
Randi J. Nevins

Organizational Culture: It Is the Workplace

Concepts for Discussion

- Language
- Communicating quality
- Communicating organizational commitment
- Communicating corporate culture

- Norms
- Rituals
- Significant symbols
- Theory applications

When asked to define what quality on the job meant to them, members of a metropolitan ballet company said, ''Quality is . . .

GENERAL MANAGER: A level of perfection that cannot be lessened in any way . . . it must be consistent, wherever it is performed.''

OFFICE WORKER: It's reaching for that excellence, trying to perfect everything you do and everything you feel. Striving for a kind of perfection and yet allowing for error.''

PERFORMER: Quality is dedication, being determined to work things out. Doing a good class . . . everything ties together.''

The definition of quality has become increasingly important to major corporations. As organizations make the move to achieve quality products and service, people entering the job market also must begin to define their own sense of quality. You, as young adults beginning your careers, are concerned about what it will be like in the place where you will work. You want to feel pride in what you accomplish and to feel that the company where you work cares about you.

There are measures you can take to understand better the environment where you work or would like to work. The total environment of a workplace is known as a corporation's culture. Analysis of such areas as quality, rituals, shared meanings, organizational commitment, critical incidents, and language can all help us to discover "the way the place is."

The purpose of this first chapter, therefore, is to enable the student to talk about and communicate intelligently in an organization's work culture. Those who become well acquainted with the information in this chapter will increase their corporate culture I.Q. We will talk about cultures in which you will work, for some will work in for-profit private enterprise and others in the not-for-profit public organizations. Wherever you work, communication will reflect and shape the culture.

The topics that are addressed are: communicating quality, communicating commitment, and communicating culture. Lastly, we will suggest steps one may take to learn firsthand about an organization's culture.

> *Culture*: shared values, traditions, norms, preferences, and practices. These components together total more than their parts. They form webs of meaning and significance that those who interact have spun. Culture does not determine behavior, but it influences choices with respect to what is acceptable, preferred, probable, and possible.

COMMUNICATING QUALITY

The Language We Use Reflects and Shapes Corporate Attention to Quality

To compete and survive, corporate America appears to have jumped on the "talk quality" bandwagon. So it is that consumers are told that: "At Ford, Quality is Job #1." The Rockefeller group promotes the slogan "I make the difference." McDonald's stresses "Quality, Service, Cleanliness, and Value." Not to be outdone, Anheuser-Busch boasts that they are the "Somebody who cares about quality," and Coors's motto is "Quality in all we are and all we do."

Many of these slogans are familiar to you. You may see them in the media or encounter them where you work. Why do you think that so many

Box 1-1 ## Is Quality "Job No. 1"?

One individual wrote to the editor of *Fortune* magazine. Because her letter was published, millions of readers heard her complaint: "Quality may be Job No. 1, but zero defects are not." She was distressed that her Taurus had a window shatter, a defective trunk light, and a digital speedometer that was erratic.

The woman said "The dealer doesn't understand why I get upset when my car doesn't work. I get answers ranging from, 'we just sell 'em, we don't make them' to 'these things' still happen to American cars, not Japanese ones."

Source: Adapted from Elizabeth A. McKaigney, *Fortune*, February 15, 1988, p. 25.

companies in America are proclaiming quality as their number one concern? Obviously, it is an appeal for quality to and from consumers. It is also an appeal to employees. Most employees want to produce high-quality goods and service. They do not want to be part of fraudulent and sloppy workmanship. These voices urge America to instill quality within its own culture, or else Americans will "buy" quality somewhere else.

Language reflects and shapes attitudes. Quality work is linked to corporate language proclaiming and pledging quality. Intensified attention to product quality can be traced to intensified language of quality. This is a time of Japanese and Pacific Rim challenge to "Made in the U.S.A." This is also a period of competition for markets in the European Economic Community. Hopefully, the current concern for quality is good news for you as future employees in the workforce!

What does this mean specifically to you as future employees? J. C. Bowles, author of a series of articles pertaining to quality efforts published in *Fortune* magazine, stated that "A measure of excellence is achieved by making the improvement process a permanent part of a company's culture." American companies realize the notion of quality must extend beyond their advertising slogans. By "talking quality into action," they are making the future look brighter and more fulfilling for corporate America.

WE MEAN BUSINESS

How do you define quality, commitment, and culture?

When we asked our classes, we received responses such as: expensive, the best, no flaws, a Porsche, excellence, and reliable. Were these close to your definitions? Would you feel good working for a company that defined quality in a similar way? Wouldn't we feel pride in working for an organization that is trying to strive to "be the best that it can be?" Review the quotes at the beginning of the chapter that described how several people from a ballet company defined quality. Are their definitions similar? What does it tell you about their feelings for their organization?

When the authors studied this ballet company, we found that each member of the organization, regardless of position, used precisely the same word to describe their work. The word they used was perfection. We found that this ideal of perfection is also alive in less artistic enterprises. For example, the United States Army slogan suggests that you should "Be the best that you can be." Ordinary people, like each of us, have within them the drive to do quality work and to produce quality products. And we also deserve to be recognized for this quality. So how do we find a company that will recognize us for our accomplishments and will motivate us to reach our potential? Look at the corporate culture. There's our answer. Quality can also be communicated nonverbally. One company that is making an effort to send messages of equality and openness is a large financial institution, The Mortgage Corporation, in Washington D.C. One of the authors was invited into the boardroom of that institution and asked for a reaction to the boardroom table, which was a triangular-shaped table with slightly rounded corners. The vice president said that the chief executive did not sit at any of the corners but in the middle along one of the sides. There was unique symmetry in that boardroom, not unlike King Arthur's roundtable.

The open office landscaping on the floors below likewise had a triangular design. Separated by head-high partitions, cubicles were arranged so that each employee had an equal amount of space walled on two sides with an opening on an aisle. Only the top executives were situated in more spacious corner offices with a bit more privacy and windows.

Muted by deep carpets and music, these work areas were comfortable and decorous. An art consultant periodically changed the collection of paintings and sculpture for everyone's enjoyment, just as a contracted florist cared for and changed the plants.

"So what do you think about this table?" asked the vice president. It fit and reflected an effort on the part of the organization to break from traditional authoritarian administration. The vice president, charged with corporate communications, then said that he was thinking of diagramming the organizational chart differently for the next annual report, perhaps in the form of overlapping circles instead of the traditional chain of command, and "What do you think of that? Or might overlapping pyramids be better?"

The vice president was thinking in organistic rather than mechanistic terms about his organization's structure. Yet while this financial institution had tried to break from tradition, had it really gotten away? The reality of hierarchy still existed. There was a chief executive, five executive vice presidents, more vice presidents, directors, and managers. Much specialization and differentiation existed within the walls of that corporate headquarters

and in its several branch offices. There were controls over the expenditures in the various divisions and departments, and with rapid growth had come specialized integrative functions such as a vice president charged with various communication tasks.

The delta shape of the boardroom table, indeed, was quite appropriate. An organization, wherever it is located and regardless of efforts to treat everyone equally, is nevertheless pyramidal in its structure and does treat some more favorably than others. Even in this financial institution, which had gone to such extraordinary effort to partition open space equally and fit it with like furnishings, favored treatment could be seen in the larger and more private accommodations assigned its officers. Yet it serves as a good example of corporate attention to employees and the quality of the organizational culture.

Attention to a concept must be articulated loudly and forcefully, as the three principles presented above from Bowles's series of articles in *Fortune* illustrate. They also demonstrate that in order to turn words into action, structures such as Kodak's suggestion system must be put in place and attended to routinely. They also illustrate that one cannot order a culture, but that culture is what is present in a place. It has grown to be what it is by talk and action.

Are you beginning to get a feel for the importance of defining quality? The examples we have presented so far point to three meanings of quality: (1) quality of product and service, (2) quality of work life, and (3) quality of attitude. These three meanings overlap and interact, but for a moment let's examine them separately.

Quality of Product and Service

Lee Iacocca, chief executive officer of Chrysler, wrote in *Talking Straight* that quality is a "fuzzy concept" but in its simplest terms "means products that work well and last long." It is the customer, of course, who is the referee, who decides whether one product is best for the money. Sources such as *Consumer Reports* provide independent testing and comparisons of goods and services. Such agencies help consumers make informed judgments.

Learning to use language accurately is especially important to one's career effectiveness and success. So let us apply the scalpel to a particularly significant symbolic term like quality. An effective communicator in the workplace uses the word quality in very precise ways. The language of quality, like all language, is made up of words, numbers, pictures, and sounds that stand for something else. A symbol is defined as that which stands for something else.

When consumers or employees speak of a product or service as one of "high quality," they are describing its fitness for use. Joseph Juran, in the *Quality Control Handbook* defines fitness for use in reference to:

Box 1-2 **The Renaissance of American Quality**
Several Principles Crucial to Developing Quality in
Corporate America

PRINCIPLE ONE: QUALITY BEGINS AT THE TOP

Sanford N. McDonnell was elected chairman and chief executive officer of McDonnell Douglas Corporation in 1980. He believed that to prosper in the future they had to dramatically change McDonnell Douglas's culture. He stated:

> We decided that we wanted to bring every McDonnell Douglas employee, every department, every function, into active participation in a renewed quality effort.

McDonnell began by stressing five interrelated management initiatives, which he called "The Five Keys to Self-Renewal." He identifies those keys as: strategic management, participative management, human resource management, ethical behavior, and, finally, productivity.

PRINCIPLE TWO: EMPLOYEES MUST BE INVOLVED

Gene Little faced unusual circumstances when he took over as plant manager of Rockwell International's electronics manufacturing facility in the West Texas border town of El Paso: Little's work force was multiethnic, representing minorities, the handicapped, and people from 15 nations. He decided that his goal for this very diverse labor pool would be the creation of a common culture about quality.

Little and his supervisors spent hours talking to employees, telling them how important their jobs were. When problems arose, he sat down with the employees involved and asked them to solve them.

- Technology — e.g., hardness, inductance, acidity
- Psychological — e.g., taste, beauty, status
- Time-oriented — e.g., reliability, maintainability
- Contractual — e.g., guarantee provisions
- Ethical — e.g., courtesy of sales personnel, honesty of service shops.

It is necessary to be able to qualify what is meant by technologically, psychologically, time-wise, contractually, and ethically fit for use so we can more tangibly measure the definition of quality. It is relatively easy to measure and put into words and numbers technological, chronological, and contractual indicators of quality. Defending psychological and ethical indicators, however, necessitates more abstract terminology.

The Joint Commission on Accreditation of Health Care Organization specifies that each department should have indicators of health care. An indicator is a measurable variable relating to the structure, process, or out-

''Within 18 months, output at the El Paso plant was up 55%, factory test yields up 80%, parts quality had improved 40%.'' Commenting on that, Thomas C. McDermott Jr., vice president of quality and reliability assurance, said: ''Absenteeism and employee turnover had all but disappeared.''

PRINCIPLE THREE: QUALITY IS A NEVER-ENDING PROCESS

Even though Eastman Kodak has held a reputation for quality since 1880, the company recently launched a major new quality drive called ''Quality—The Kodak Edge.''

''Unlike many companies for whom a renewed emphasis on quality is a matter of survival, we have historically enjoyed a reputation as a quality leader in our industry—and we still do,'' reported Kay R. Whitmore, president. ''However, we felt there was work to be done. We were attracted to the idea that quality is an umbrella subject, rather than simply a matter of how well you make the things you sell. We're trying to approach quality now as something that's important in everything we do—quality of communication, of financial analysis, of market research. We've simply broadened a topic that's always been important to us and expanded it to everything we do.''

Kodak's reputation for continuous quality and improvement is revealed also by its record of good labor relations. The company has always been a leader in the field of job enrichment. Founder George Eastman firmly believed that nobody had a monopoly on good ideas and in 1898 he started a system for rewarding employees who came up with a better way of doing things. The Kodak Suggestion Program, the forerunner of them all, began with a $2 reward to a worker who pointed out the advantage of washing the windows in a production area. In 1984, Kodak men and women submitted 89,051 suggestions and the company paid nearly $3.7 million for the 28,437 that were adopted.

Source: ''Renaissance of American Quality,'' Jerry Bowles, *Fortune,* October 14, 1985, pp. 165–188.

come of care. Structures refer to resources, equipment, or numbers and qualification of staff. So an emergency trauma center, according to the criteria specified by the Joint Commission, should have certain resources, equipment, and qualified staff in order to qualify as providing good or excellent care. When the Commission inspects, it also evaluates the processes of the care: how well patients are interviewed, tested, and treated. And most importantly, it evaluates indicators of outcomes such as quickness and thoroughness of recovery in light of the inquiry or illness. Delivering quality health care is a complex process of communication and treatment.

A review of a medical facility by the Joint Commission is almost as traumatic as being taken to an emergency ward! One of the authors visited a Veterans Administration regional medical center. Nationwide VA health care had recently been reviewed by the Joint Commission. The report had targeted a number of areas that were deficient in health care. Such an accreditation report serves as strong motivation for attention to quality. In order not to lose accreditation, that organization needed a systematic approach to structuring, processing, and assessing indicators of quality care.

The same kind of impetus for precision in technology and in management decision making resulted from the Challenger disaster. The whole shuttle lift-off went haywire because of a minor design flaw and a poor decision-making process. The engineers warned that the weather was too cold for the 0-rings. NASA pressured Morton Thiokol managers to approve the launch; consequently, the engineers' warning was overridden.

After the shuttle explosion, after Congressional hearings, and after the halt of subsequent rocket launches, quality in technology and management decision making was more rigorously defined.

Quality control is a process that employs precision language. Each material and process is analyzed to determine the key input variables that are essential for fitness for use. Suppliers are told specification and tolerance limits. Measuring instruments and gauges are certified and synchronized. Sampling and inspection procedures and decision rules are spelled out for rejection and/or correction for nonconformance to specifications. Formulas must be followed explicitly. A Merck Pharmaceutical Company quality control manager told one of the authors that operators must complete a noncompliance form that details any deviation from prescribed processing of a product, and then tests must be run to determine if the batch must be dumped or can be reconstituted. The Food and Drug Administration insists upon careful records filed for years, for if something should go wrong they could more easily trace the cause. As you can see, precision in the definition of what constitutes quality tells a lot about a workplace's culture.

Quality of Working Life

Quality of working life has become an important umbrella term for talking about the work environment: pay and benefits; equipment; safety and cleanliness within the work area; job training and enrichment; morale; and corporate commitment to employee rights. Quality of worklife criteria is enforced by law in Scandinavian countries. The Norwegian Work Environment Act, Section 12, specifically states:

> Employees shall be afforded opportunities for personal development and the maintenance and development of their skills. Monotonous, repetitive, machine or assembly work that does not permit alteration of pace shall be avoided. Jobs shall be designed to allow some possibility for variation, for contact with other workers . . . and for information and feedback to employees concerning production requirements and performance.

Except for safety, most Quality of Working Life (QWL) matters in the United States are at the discretion of the employer. This by no means implies that QWL is a minor concern. Employers realize that the better QWL conditions are, the easier it is to keep highly capable employees and gain employee loyalty.

Richard Huseman and John Hatfield, two professors in business administration whose graduate work was in organizational communication, reason that employees base what they give upon what they get. They call this the "equity factor." In their book *Managing the Equity Factor or "After All I've Done for You . . ."*, the authors say that about 53 percent of managers and 83 percent of hourly workers feel underrewarded. Have you ever felt similarly in jobs that you have held?

What do employees who feel underrewarded do? They have three alternatives: to reduce the energy and conscientiousness they put into their work, to look elsewhere for work, or to try to persuade their superiors to increase the rewards. Employers who shortchange employees are likely to find that their workers will get even by lowering effort, increasing absenteeism, turnover, sabotage, or stealing. Thus it is imperative that as future employees and employers you consider QWL in the workplace culture.

There is a quid pro quo. Quality work is given when employees get quality of worklife. Robert Levering, in his text *A Great Place to Work: What Makes Some Employers So Good (And Most So Bad)*, argued that great places and bad places differ in at least nine ways: rights, responsibilities, rewards, consistency, patience, openness, accessibility, commitments, and fairness. When employees are treated fairly, trusted with responsibilities, rewarded for performance, and assured that everything possible will be done to provide a quality working life, they give in return quality work and corporate loyalty.

Levering and his colleagues who studied the *100 Best Companies* reported that these companies that provided high QWL over a ten-year period were "more than twice as profitable as the average *Standard and Poor* 500." That outperformance was acknowledged by the stock-buying public, for the *Best 100*'s stock price grew at nearly three times the rate of the others.

Quality of Attitude

Quality also is defined by attitude. We mentioned attitude in our examples of ballet personnel and musicians who said they were striving for perfection in their work. What a far cry that is from the people Studs Terkel interviewed for his book *Working People Talk About What They Do All Day and How They Feel About What They Do*. Many of the people he interviewed (cab drivers, assembly-line workers, janitors, policemen) worked in dirty, boring, dangerous jobs. Dull and demeaning work dulls the spirit.

Yet almost everyone wants to do a good job and would like to have a job that she or he could love. In a very real sense, we are all lovers of quality. We want to do work that is meaningful—that brings satisfaction and happiness to those who use the goods we make and the services we provide.

Quality is an attitude that is linked to the call within each of us to do good, to do well, to do better, and even sometimes to do best. Striving for quality is akin to a religious experience. Quality is an icon that makes life meaningful. It is the essential fair social exchange and trust between employer and employee and between producer and consumer. This discussion of quality should make it clear that its definition embodies both precision and passion.

If a culture is to have a central theme such as quality, that theme entails articulating mission statements and symbols, programs, rewards, heroes, and villains. In this next section we will discuss how that process works.

Commitment:
1. a strong belief in the goals and values of the organization,
2. a willingness to devote considerable effort to the organization, and
3. a strong desire to remain within the organization

COMMUNICATING ORGANIZATIONAL COMMITMENT

The Language Used Reflects and Shapes Corporate Commitment

One way we can begin to analyze the culture of an organization is to examine the level of commitment that members feel toward their corporation. Even if you are not employed full-time at the moment, take a few moments to fill out the organizational commitment questionnaire on pages 12 – 13. Focus your responses based on ONE position that you have held. Score your results. How much commitment did you feel toward that job? Ask yourself what it is about the culture of that workplace that you liked.

Most organizational communication scholars agree that commitment has three characteristics: (1) a strong belief in the goals and values of the organization, (2) a willingness to devote considerable effort to the organization, and (3) a strong desire to remain within the organization.

Each of us has a need to belong. It is important to us to be a part of an organization, and to be accepted. To some extent, being a part of a workplace culture fulfills this need. Therefore, an employing organization has a hold on us!

Most people spend an average of 40 years in the workforce. Unfortunately, many feel alienated from the products they make and the companies for which they work. Each morning some suffer "the edge of the bed blues."

Just why do organizations exert such power over us? Geert Hofstede, an intercultural researcher and director of personnel of a multinational corporation based in the Netherlands, says that the common experiences that make up a people's social and political history result in customs, traditions, norms, and preferences that a culture of people share. These values are firmly planted in each of us. Hofstede's text *Culture's Consequences* discusses his massive study of workers in 40 different nations to find their work-related values.

The four dimensions tapped were:

- Power distance — the degree to which a society accepts the fact that power is unequally distributed in it (remember the "boardroom" example above?).
- Uncertainty avoidance — the extent to which a society feels threatened by ambiguity.
- Individualism — the sense of independence versus collective identity and interdependence one has within one's group or clan.
- Masculinity — the collection of aggressive, performance, object-centered traits in which in almost all societies males score higher than females.

How might such dimensions or clusters of cultural values influence organizations or the process of organizing? Hofstede refers to national cultures as either lions or foxes. Nations with both large power distance and large uncertainty avoidance he labels lions (Latin American, Mediterranean, and Islamic countries, and Japan). Lions favor organizations that are full bureaucracies and in which, if employee participation occurs, it is imposed from above. At the other pole, nations holding values of relatively small power distance and with little uncertainty avoidance, he labels foxes (the Scandinavian countries and the Netherlands). Foxes favor organizations with implicit structures and subordinate-initiated employee shop floor participation.

The U.S. cultural map reveals that Americans want only a moderate power distance between superiors and subordinates. That is, they know that someone must be in charge, but that individual should not be bossy. Therefore, management and supervision had best be consulting and collaborative rather than ordering and telling employees what to do. The results also showed that Americans can tolerate uncertainty. Americans are the most individualistic of all peoples. Therefore, wise managers will attend to individual identity, to role-making more than role-taking, to protection of employees' private lives, to task autonomy, to employees' pleasure, and to providing meaningful work.

This map tells us Americans value achievement, aggressive performance, money, and things. The carrot is more motivating than the stick — both the intrinsic pull of wanting to achieve and the extrinsic pull of needing the tangible payoff of work to purchase "the good life" are factors. Therefore, effective management builds upon these motivations.

The impact of conflicting national values is keenly illustrated when joint USA-Japanese business ventures fail (for example, Singer, Kraft Foods, TRW, and Union Carbide). Those who have studied these failures tell us the most crucial contributing factor is different cultural managerial perspectives. American managers typically gather information, seek relevant counsel, and then make a decision. Japanese managers instead focus on a harmonious process of decision making; focusing on problem identification and circulation of proposals, and more indirect processes designed to save face

---

Box 1-3 **Organizational Commitment Questionnaire**

A P W C M

Check the blank if true for you:

_____ 1. The way I feel is "you can take this job and shove it."

_____ 2. Hard work offers little guarantee of success.

_____ 3. Our society would have fewer problems if people had less leisure time.

_____ 4. I feel very little loyalty to where I work.

_____ 5. I talk up my employing organization to my friends as a great place to work.

_____ 6. When asked about a foul-up, I just say, "Don't ask me, I just work here."

_____ 7. Getting along with friends is more important than working hard.

_____ 8. Most people who don't succeed in life are lazy.

_____ 9. I could just as well be working for a different employer as long as the type of work is similar.

_____ 10. I am willing to put in a great deal of effort beyond that normally expected in order to help my employing organization succeed.

_____ 11. "The edge of the bed blues" is what I get before I leave for work.

_____ 12. Life would be more meaningful if we had more leisure time.

_____ 13. Anyone who is able and willing to work has a good chance of succeeding.

_____ 14. It would take very little in my present circumstances to cause me to leave where I am employed.

---

and generate consensus. Yet in Japan, as compared to America, there is much greater respect for authority.

The cultural differences of extreme American individualism clash with Japan's unique mix of authoritarian and collective values. To speak one another's language, as important as that is, is not sufficient for a successful joint venture.

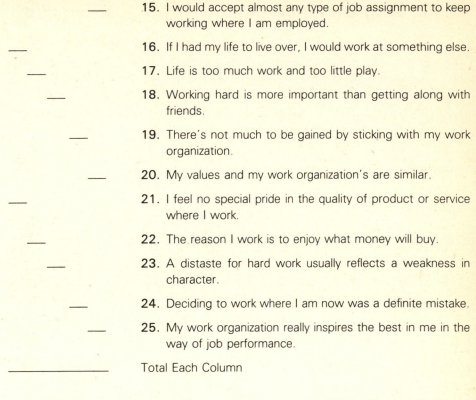

_____ 15. I would accept almost any type of job assignment to keep working where I am employed.

_____ 16. If I had my life to live over, I would work at something else.

_____ 17. Life is too much work and too little play.

_____ 18. Working hard is more important than getting along with friends.

_____ 19. There's not much to be gained by sticking with my work organization.

_____ 20. My values and my work organization's are similar.

_____ 21. I feel no special pride in the quality of product or service where I work.

_____ 22. The reason I work is to enjoy what money will buy.

_____ 23. A distaste for hard work usually reflects a weakness in character.

_____ 24. Deciding to work where I am now was a definite mistake.

_____ 25. My work organization really inspires the best in me in the way of job performance.

_____ Total Each Column

Self-score by adding A, P, W, C, and M columns. The highest number of items in each column that you could have checked as "True for you" is five. The higher the number, the higher you are indicated to be

A = alienated
P = personality motivated
W = work ethic motivated
C = calculating whether another job would be better
M = committed deeply to the mission of your workplace

Source: Scale by William I. Gorden.

WE MEAN BUSINESS

Think of your best and worst jobs held. Describe how you felt about each job. Compare this to the definition of organizational commitment.

Box 1-4 **Moment of Truth**

A ''moment of truth'' is an episode in which a customer comes in contact with a company representative—a chance meeting with a janitor in an elevator, a complaint issued at a service desk—that leaves a vivid impression customers remember for a long time.

This is a crucial concept for service businesses: Because they can't base their reputations on the quality of tangible products, their future is built on the quality of their moments of truth.

COMMUNICATING CORPORATE CULTURE

The Language Used Reflects and Shapes Corporate Culture

Employees' job satisfaction and organizational commitment hinge upon whether they share beliefs within the culture. Almost every scholar, when talking about culture, refers to shared meanings. Action becomes collective when members of organizations develop shared meanings for events, objects, words, and people.

Norms

Every organization has a set of unwritten rules and guidelines that are standards for appropriate behavior. In order to be accepted as a member of the organization, each member is expected to comply with these **norms**. Workers are usually taught in subtle ways how to conform to these norms. Ralph Kilmann, author of *Quick Fix: Managing Five Tracks to Organizational Success*, asserts that organizational members are taught to accept the norms of a culture without questioning. Consider organizations where you have been employed. Think about why you have to wear a certain uniform. Why promptness is so important. Why your superior wants you to address him as Mr. Smith instead of Bill, or Ms. Wright instead of Ruby.

Each of us, to some degree, has a need to fit in, and wants to be considered part of the ''group.'' Observe cultures of which you are a part. See how quickly ''new'' members conform to the norms set by the members. This conforming process occurs rapidly! Those who do not choose to conform to the norms usually pay a price. Perhaps they are reprimanded, given less responsibility, passed over for promotion, or fired.

Critical Incidents

Employees take note of critical incidents that occur within the organization. Events such as the time when Fred stood up to the boss and was fired, and when Harriet told the boss about her personal problems and was passed over

---

Box 1-5   **Sing Sing**

Konosuki Matsushita, founder of Matsushita Electric Industrial, believed that the ultimate aim of production was to eliminate poverty and create prosperity. He introduced the practice of employees singing company songs, a practice that became a tradition in Japan. He also published a monthly magazine called *PHP (Peace and Happiness through Prosperity)*. It became a best seller.

Source: Adapted from ''God of Management,'' *Fortune*, May 22, 1989, p. 14.

---

for a promotion, paint a picture of a work culture that cannot tolerate criticism. New hires learn how their workplace works, what the management wants, what really counts there to get along, to keep out of trouble, and to get ahead.

WE MEAN BUSINESS

Can you think of any ''critical incidents'' that have become a part of the folklore where you have worked?

Rituals

To understand and interpret an organization's culture effectively, you must observe the company's traditions, customs, and rituals. Some areas to observe include:

> Celebrations — Do they celebrate birthdays? What special events are celebrated?
>
> Time — What is the pace like? How much time is wasted?
>
> Breaks — Do people take coffee/lunch breaks? For how long? At designated times?
>
> Talk — To whom do you talk? How much? For how long? How do you/they greet people (first/last name)?
>
> Meetings — Who sits where? Who sides with whom?
>
> Dress — Is there a formal or informal dress code?
>
> Artifacts — How are offices decorated? With personal artifacts or power symbols?

Box 1-6   **You Can't Steal Snow White**

The Walt Disney Company sued the Academy of Motion Picture Arts and Sciences for doing a parody of Snow White as a feature of their Oscar awards in 1989. The parody, performed without permission, was not flattering and Disney management was not pleased. Disney dropped the suit after the academy apologized. Disney also sued three Florida day care centers to remove unauthorized painted likenesses of Mickey Mouse, Goofy, and Donald Duck from their exterior walls.

Logos and creations that are products of one's business are worth money. They are not free. It is not safe or honest to steal others' creations.

Those whose words are used without attribution have a right to object. When a speaker quotes another, she or he should be sure to attribute that quote to that source —even if it is Snow White.

Source: Based in part on Harris Collingwood, ''Heigh-ho, Heigh-ho, It's off to court we go,'' *Business Week*, May 15, 1989, p. 42.

Touching—Is it permissible? To whom? How much? Is there sexual harassment?

Recognition—How are achievements rewarded? What trophies and certificates are visible?

Significant Symbols

Another area to observe is specific language used by employees and consumers to describe the organization. The study of how people talk about a company can provide a lot of insight about "the way the place is" and help you determine if it is indeed an organization in which you would feel comfortable. When we studied the ballet company, we observed the routines of the members of the organization, interviewed various employees and a member of the board of trustees, read critical reviews of their performances, and attended practices and an actual performance of the ballet company. In this way we could observe the organizational culture from a variety of perspectives. We specifically focused on the language used in these contexts. You can do this too, when you are searching for a job (although probably on a much smaller scale!). Students can learn a great deal from such information —seeking informal informational interviews, even when not seeking a new job.

The language of metaphor conveys what is important to an organization. The language used is very often handed down through time. So, this gives you an indication of what values the company may hold dear. For example:

- Disney considers all its employees members of a "cast" with the consumer being the "audience." (See Box 1-7.)

Box 1-7   # The Metaphor of "Family"

At Disneyland, two dominant metaphors have arisen in the language and culture of the organization. The philosophy of Disneyland at its beginning was one of making the park a "drama" and its employees "cast members." In planning the park, the parking lot was thought of as the "outer lobby" and the ticket booths were theater "box offices." The organization still uses terms such as "guests" instead of customers, "casting" rather than personnel, and "onstage" and "backstage" areas of the park.

Disney employees also use language depicting their company as a happy, close-knit family. This began with Walt Disney, who was seen as a caring employer and insisted all members of the organization use first names.

Said one Disney ride operator, "These people are like my brothers and sisters." Another employee said, "The people who work here treat each other as a family, there seems to be a common cause. . . . We're a family presenting family entertainment; it's like we're inviting someone to our home to entertain them."

In the 80s, with increasing economic pressure on the park to make money, employees become offended by changing management policies they saw as against the "family" feeling of Disney.

"It used to be, 'let's try to make the employees as happy as possible so that they make the public happy' and now it's 'let's save as much money as we can and make a buck,'" said a ride operator.

Employees had gotten so used to being a family they seemingly forgot Disneyland was a business. "It's getting more like a business . . . I don't think the park should be run like a business," said an employee.

"My family wouldn't treat me the way they [management] do," said another Disney worker.

This discontent led to a strike by Disneyland workers in 1984. Managers felt their actions were justified by economic realities, but employees saw the underlying issue as a threat to the Disney "family" by management.

The strike brought about drastic changes in the way employees perceive the culture of Disneyland. Most feel much less part of the family. Instead, they feel that management, and even some other employees, are now adversaries.

The strike also shows how important corporate culture can be. Because Disney employees saw the organization as a "family," and management saw it more as a "drama" and a business, management made changes which were unacceptable to employees, and it led to a strike. These seemingly compatible views of the company were held so strongly that it took a strike to force the two to a compromise.

Source: From Ruth C. Smith and Eric M. Eisenberg, "Conflict at Disneyland: A root-metaphor analysis," *Communication Monographs*, Vol. 54, December, 1987, pp. 367–380.

- The Limited plays the role of hostess or host of a party, and caters to its guests. It helps them experience shopping as fun. Employees can host a good or a bad party depending upon how well they prepare for it, how well they attend to their guests, and even how careful they are after hours when the party is over.

- Goodyear Rubber — Beyond the corporate slogan "Protect our good name," an employee explained that his task was to "enhance" the company image. . . . Not a facade but by being a good human being. . . . It's communicating with spirit. . . . Letting people know you care."

Language reflects beliefs that are an everyday part of life for these organizations and more. For each of these companies, certain language employed in their rituals, folklore, and critical incidents was endowed with significance.

Leaders in both the private and public sectors want to create a workplace culture committed to quality, yet no matter how eloquent their rhetoric, they cannot order a new culture. Cultural values are strong and pervasive. They are rooted in corporate history. Even with concerted effort, significant cultural change and organization-wide improvement will take five to ten years, the experts tell us. They also suggest that leaders who would change the corporate culture cannot do it directly, but must live the culture they want. They must "walk" the talk.

Fortune reporter Brian Dumaine says creating a new corporate culture is "like a Confucian principle: Cultural change must come from the bottom, and the CEO must guide it." Chief executives cannot simply encase and distribute a new mission statement pledging quality in Plexiglas and expect change. But they can engage their managers and workforce in finding new ways to accomplish their tasks. They can demonstrate their concern for integrity of their products and an equally important concern for the quality of working life. They can reject those self-privileged perks (executive parking spaces, limousines, and corporate jets) and instead make profit-sharing a genuinely company-wide reward for working as a team. They can build trust by being trustworthy.

Those at lower levels, working from the bottom up, can make real contributions to creating the kind of work culture of which they can be proud. They can act as Robert Townsend described in *Up the Organization: How to Stop the Corporation From Stifling People and Strangling Profits*: to "make every decision (from your first job as a receptionist or file clerk on up) in the light of this question: 'How would I do this job if I owned the company?' And then do it that way, to the extent you can." Asking such a question, he asserts, is far more important than trying to please the boss.

Remember, corporate culture is not something somewhere else. It is you. By your responsible actions and speech, or lack thereof, you are it. By taking the roles assigned you and making those roles better, you are shaping the culture toward quality of product and quality of working life. That's the

---

Box 1-8 **Keys to Change in an Organization's Culture**

- Study the old culture.
- Provide critics of the workplace time to develop their ideas for creating a better culture.
- Find the most effective work unit and use it as an example of the norms you want.
- Plan on five to ten years to make an organization-wide improvement.
- Actions speak louder than words.

---

underlying purpose of improving your communication skills, and that's what this book is all about.

WE MEAN BUSINESS

Describe the culture where you currently work, where you held a summer job, or at your university. Use the elements listed above.

THEORY APPLICATIONS

Learning the Ropes

Above we have described many methods of analysis for uncovering the culture of an organization. Understanding the norms, shared meanings, commitment level, critical incidents, language, and how members define quality are all important methods of inquiry. We suggest that you begin this process NOW, where you work or attend college. Your instructor may assign you to deliver a speech that describes a workplace culture. Our own classes have found this assignment beneficial and enjoyable. Here is a list of suggestions that will help you to learn more about the culture of an organization:

1. Research the company. Read annual reports and corporate literature. Find the corporate motto. Look at pictures. (These tips are particularly helpful in preparation for the interviewing process!)
2. Ask for an informational interview. This will allow you to gain entrance to the organization without the "pressure" of an employment interview. Be professional, and plan your questions in advance. Ask for a tour. OBSERVE, LISTEN, LOOK!!
3. Observation—There is no better tool than observation. Study how employees talk, act, dress, move, etc. Once you are working for an organization, this is your BEST method for quickly learning what's "right" and "wrong." Try to observe before you ask. Each time you

ask a question, it signals to the rest that you are not yet a part of the group.

There is no doubt that cultures create meaning. We must do all we can to learn about the culture of the corporation of which we wish to be a part. As Ralph Kilmann, a professor who has specialized in organizational culture said, "The organization itself has an invisible quality—a certain style, a character, a way of doing things—that may be more powerful than the dictates of any one person of any formal system." Culture is the totality of the way of living. Morality is what it means to live, work, and play the way one does, and whether that national, regional, or particular workplace culture enhances the good, the true, the beautiful for those who live it. That is the deeper meaning of quality.

SUMMARY

A communications major summarized the issues presented very well. She told us that the concept of speaking of the workplaces as cultures for her represented a new metaphor for understanding organizations. The ultimate usefulness of looking at a workplace culture will depend in part on one's ability and willingness to grapple with its ambiguities and dwell upon its richness until an organization's symbols take on meaning. Members attempt to adapt to most of the components of a culture. However, if these factors strongly conflict with an employee's inner value system, he or she will most likely leave. Throughout this chapter, many examples have been given of how language reflects and shapes an organization's culture. We hope this information will be helpful to you in your quest for a satisfying career.

This chapter has proposed a number of benefits to those who score high in Corporate Culture Intelligence Quotient. A high CCIQ should pay off in a high quality of working life:

- better job interviews and career choices
- knowing what to look for during the organizational socialization process
- helping one to work with others interpersonally, one on one and on project teams
- improving one's knowledge of corporate vocabulary and valued symbols
- joining in collective efforts to create a corporate culture that facilitates employee loyalty and commitment to quality
- knowing how to tell the company's story when given an opportunity to represent it

We have traveled together through organizational culture in this chapter. You are reading the words we wrote, conferred over, researched, and polished in hopes that you might better understand how language and communication reflect and shape corporate culture.

This communication course in which you are enrolled and that has selected *We Mean Business* also is a culture. You are in it and part of it. You and those sitting next to you, your instructor, the department, and college or university make up that culture.

Our experience is that a class culture can be one committed to quality and a quality learning environment. We in this text have done our best to provide a quality learning experience for you. That experience is a process. We have faith you will contribute your best to making your class culture one committed to quality work. That means a place where it is safe to do well and safe to make mistakes and to try again to do better.

That is our wish for you. Please drop us a note to let us know if and what we have brought to this text works for you, or what we might do better. We will answer your letters. We are in this together.

SKILL BUILDER: ORGANIZATIONAL CULTURE

Divide the class into three groups. Each of the groups should be assigned to a type of company. The three companies are: an accounting firm, a hospital, and a construction company.

Directions to Class

You are a member of a(n) accounting firm, hospital, or construction company. Discuss the elements of culture that are present within this culture. Be prepared to discuss your answers to the following questions.

1. Describe the physical environment. (where located, office space setting, environment)
2. How do coworkers address each other? How do subordinates address their superiors? (first name, title, greeting)
3. How is the language unique to your culture?
4. What are the rules about dress or uniform?
5. Is there a formal or informal time structure? How is time used on the job?
6. Is there job autonomy?

SKILL BUILDER: ATTENTION! THE CULTURE OF THE U.S. ARMY

The scene: Sergeant Keith Gudehus is seated at his office desk. Lieutenant Gregg seeks permission to enter. He enters and immediately stands to attention and salutes. Sgt. Gudehus gives permission to stand at ease. Both are in uniform.

The conversation: "As you know, Lt. Gregg, the company will be traveling to Camp 1000 for an FTX this weekend. Tell me what your patrol's mission is and how you'll accomplish it."

"Sir, my patrol will leave at 2130 hrs. to conduct a recon mission near the south end of the lake. The patrol will give several personnel a chance to perform in leadership positions, as well."

"Very good, Lt. Gregg. Did you shave this morning, lieutenant?"

"Yes, sir."

"Then you must have missed a few spots. Why don't you do some push-ups while I go over my notes."

Lt. Gregg then completes 10 push-ups and returns to the position of attention in front of the desk.

"You're doing a good job, lieutenant. Report back here tomorrow at 0900 hrs. Dismissed."

Lt. Gregg then salutes, and Sgt. Gudehus returns a salute. Lt. Gregg does an about-face and leaves.

Discussion Questions

From the brief scenario above, what elements of culture were evident?

1. language _____

2. dress _____

3. power _____

4. time _____

5. rituals _____

RESOURCES

Bowles, J. C. (1987, September). "Quality: The competitive advantage." *Fortune*, 129–186. (See also *Fortune* 1985, 1986 for this theme.)

Deal, Terry E., and A. A. Kennedy. (1982). *Corporate cultures: The rite and rituals of corporate life.* Reading, MA: Addison-Wesley.

Dumaine, Brian. (1990, January 15). "Creating a new company culture." *Fortune*, 127–131.

Frost, Peter J., Larry F. Moore, Meryl Reis Louis, Craig C. Lundberg, and Joanne Martin. (1985). *Organizational culture.* Beverly Hills, CA: Sage Publications.

Gorden, William I. (1984, May–June). "Organizational imperatives and cultural modifiers." *Business Horizons*, 76–83.

Gorden, William I., and Randi J. Nevins. (1988). "The language and rhetoric of quality: Made in the U.S.A." *Journal of Applied Communication Research*, 15(1–2), 19–34.

Haragan, Betty L. (1977). *Games mother never taught you: Corporate gamesmenship for women.* New York: Warner Books.

Hofstede, Geert. (1980). *Culture's consequences.* Beverly Hills, CA: Sage Publications.

Huseman, Richard C., and John D. Hatfield. (1989). *Managing the equity factor or "After all I've done for you . . ."* Boston: Houghton Mifflin.

Iacocca, Lee. (1989). *Talking straight.* Boston: G. K. Hall.

Juran, Joseph M., Frank R. Grynam, and R. S. Bingham. (Eds.) (1951). *Quality control handbook.* New York: McGraw-Hill.

Kanter, Rosabeth Moss (1977). *Men and women of the corporation.* New York: Basic Books.

Kanter, Rosabeth Moss, and Barry A. Stein. (Eds.) (1979). *Life in organizations: Workplaces as people experience them.* New York: Basic Books.

Kilmann, Ralph H. (1985, April). "Corporate culture." *Psychology Today*, 62–68.

Levering, Robert. (1988). *A great place to work: What makes some employers so good (and most so bad).* New York: Random House.

Levering, Robert, Milton Moskowitz, and Michael Katz. (1985). *The 100 best companies to work for in America.* New York: New American Library.

Ouchi, William G. (1981). *Theory Z.* New York: Avon Books.

Peters, Thomas J. and Robert H. Waterman. (1982). *In search of excellence.* New York: Warner Books.

Sathe, Vijay. (1985). *Culture and related corporate realities.* Homewood, IL: Richard D. Irwin.

Schrank, Robert. (1978). *Ten thousand working days.* Cambridge, MA: MIT Press.

Terkel, Studs. (1972). *Working people talk about what they do all day and about what they feel about what they do.* New York: Avon Books.

Townsend, Robert. (1970). *Up the organization: How to stop the corporation from stifling people and strangling profits.* New York: Fawcett Crest.

——— (1984). *Further up the organization.* New York: Knopf.

Waterman, Robert H. (1987). *The renewal factor.* New York: Bantam.

Whyte, William H. (1956). *The organization man.* New York: Anchor.

Chapter 2

Listening and the Communication Process in the Workplace

Concepts for Discussion

- Characteristics of the communication process
- Listening
- Feedback

- Paraphrasing
- Obstacles to effective listening
- Strategies for improving listening
- Listening and the grapevine

Contract negotiations broke down. Suddenly, more than 25,000 employees of an automobile assembly plant in the Midwest "hit the bricks." They set up picket lines; they carried placards.

A newspaper reporter appeared on the scene. His assignment: talk to some strikers, write a feature story on their reasons for striking. The reporter approached a placard-bearing striker and asked his question: "What are YOUR reasons for being on strike?"

"Man," the striker said, "if you only knew. NO one in there ever listens to us. So—we give them a strike."

William F. Keefe
Listen, Management

Are you listening? This question may seem like a simple one. Unfortunately, the answer has far more ramifications than the average person realizes. Listening mistakes can be very costly in personal and professional relationships. For example, the chief executive officer of Sperry Corporation (manufacturers of computers and equipment), J. Paul Lyet, said that business relies on communication and that when a communication breakdown occurs, there is also a price to pay. Corporations pay for these mistakes by taking in fewer profits, and consumers pay for these listening errors by having to pay higher prices.

Think about it. If you are a poor listener, you are making your job twice as difficult and twice as long. Letters may have to be retyped, instructions given more than once, and phone messages may be given inaccurately. If productivity suffers, then so may your chance for a promotion!

What can you do to increase the effectiveness of your listening? An important place to start is by understanding the basic communication process and how it affects daily interactions. Then it is advantageous to explore feedback, listening and paraphrasing; discuss why members of the general public are not competent listeners; and examine strategies to help become more successful listeners in the workplace.

THE COMMUNICATION PROCESS

"Janet, what are your views about the new proposal?"

"Well, I am impressed, but I can tell that you have some reservations. What's the matter?"

"I'm just not sure that Mr. Raffold will agree to invest this much money. And with all the paperwork already stacked on his desk, who knows if he'll even find the proposal!"

A conversation such as the one above may seem typical to you. Indeed, each of us is involved in many similar transactions daily. But have you ever taken the time to analyze exactly what is occurring? Let's take a look step by step at the process by which these two humans communicated. It's a miracle that we take for granted every day.

The components listed above are the basic elements that appear in nearly every interaction. The SOURCE refers to the person sending the message; the RECEIVER is the listener. Your MESSAGE can be sent through a variety of CHANNELS such as telephone, person-to-person, or written communication. If there is a disruption, or something that prevents the message from arriving accurately to the receiver, this is called NOISE. Noise can be characterized as physical, psychological, or semantic.

Physical noise refers to some type of outside environmental distraction such as hearing banging, sirens, or railroad trains outside; sitting in a room with an uncomfortable temperature; or hearing loud voices from the next room. Preoccupation with personal problems or being lost in a daydream instead of listening are examples of psychological noise. Problems in under-

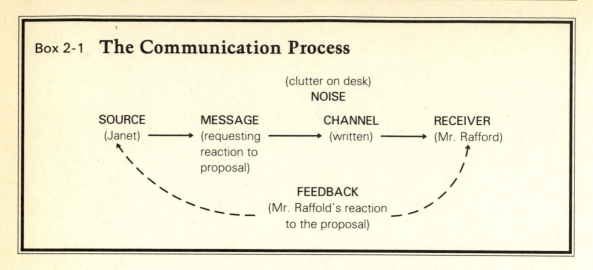

Box 2-1 **The Communication Process**

standing due to word choice, articulation, or speech impediments are called semantic noise.

Characteristics Governing the Communication Process

Even though every transaction is unique, there are some characteristics that govern all communication situations. Included in such principles of communication are the notions that communication is transactional, irreversible, a matter of perception, and inevitable.

When a conversation begins, two things are happening simultaneously. Each person is defining him/herself to the other person. We may be conveying messages such as "he/she seems snobby, inconsiderate, and rude" or "he/she seems charming, intelligent, and caring." These messages are communicated through our actual verbal language, but are more dominantly "spoken" through our nonverbal language (a more detailed discussion of nonverbal communication can be found in Chapter 5). At the same time that this is occurring, we are also responding to the other person's definition of her or himself with an interpretation such as "he/she seems really bored" or "he/she seems really interested and enthusiastic." The instantaneous sending-receiving/receiving-sending process is what makes communication a transaction. Transactional communication implies that both parties are interdependent—that what I say affects you and what you say affects me.

The second universal characteristic of communication is that it is irreversible. Have you ever watched an episode of "L.A. Law" or "Perry Mason" and heard the judge say to the jury, "The jury will dismiss that comment. Strike it from the record." Does this make the comment "unheard"? No. Once something is said, we cannot take it back. So it is especially important in business to carefully plan your thoughts BEFORE they leave your mouth. How many chances would you give an interviewee or an employee if he/she

Box 2-2   **The Power of Music**

Music is a multibillion-dollar industry. Our modern environment is immersed in music. In-car radio, elevator, dentist's office, home stereo, and individual Walkman, we turn it on or move in on it. Music in a store increases the amount of time shoppers stay and the amount of money they spend. People listening to up-tempo music eat faster than when listening to slower music. Usually we select music to reinforce our moods. Sometimes we choose music to change our mood.

Why is music so important to our daily lives? What is there about it that resonates with the human condition? What can we learn about communication from studying how music affects us? Music is entwined with how the brain and society function, such basic functions as perception, memory, and language. Perception, of course, refers to how sound is processed. The same mathematical formulation that characterizes music has been discovered in nature — the ocean waves, the wobbling of the earth's axis, and the beat of the human heart. The ear and body as a whole sort the sounds in each of our environments — the hum of a refrigerator, a bird's song, a voice.

Some sound is random noise. Some is so repetitious that it is boring. Music is a combination of the random and the predictable. The ear can perceive sounds as low as a rumbling train and as high as a screaming siren. Most cultures divide these sounds into about five to seven note scales. That organization of sound enables the brain to know patterns.

Those who wish to communicate with others would be wise to learn what music others prefer. Also those who would communicate might wisely remember that a spoken or written message like music should be an interesting mix of regular and random sound.

Source: Based in part on William F. Allman, ''The Musical Brain,'' *U. S. News and World Report,* June 11, 1990, pp. 55–62.

repeatedly said, "Oh, I didn't mean that. Let me rephrase that," or "I didn't mean for that to come out, I wasn't thinking."

A third characteristic that governs every interaction is perception. A message may be received by any one of the five senses, but its interpretation is a matter of individual experience. Perception is a process of becoming aware of the external world through our various senses: sight, smell, taste, touch, and hearing. Perception is an active rather than a passive process. It is a "lens" that we bring with us to every communication situation. Perception is the basis for forming impressions and, in essence, influences how the communication process works. Semanticists have said, "Meanings are in people, not in words." We create our own unique meanings, verbally and nonverbally, through perception.

The final characteristic is that communication is inevitable. You may be familiar with the phrase "One cannot *not* communicate." This axiom simply means that communication of some sort is *always* occurring. Whether the channel be written, oral, or nonverbal, we are always sending some sort of message about ourselves to our viewers. Can you think of a career that does not use communication skills?

LISTENING

As mentioned earlier, different worlds of meanings in each of us color the words we use, and psychological noise may distort the messages we send and receive. Words, in addition, must compete for the attention of others in a sea of words, sounds, and noises.

Listening is a skill that develops from infancy. Similar to nonverbal communication, babies first communicate primarily by attending to cues in their environment. This includes listening. Language acquisition and development occurs by listening. Most of our instruction takes place while listening. We learn the norms of our culture by visual and auditory channels.

Listening, as defined by Joe DeVito, author of many communication texts, is the active process of receiving aural stimuli. The most important word in this definition is ACTIVE. We choose whether to listen or not. And because listening requires a conscious effort, it is a skill often neglected, for listening does not mean merely staying silent while the other person speaks.

One common problem associated with listening is that this skill is often confused with hearing. Hearing is an automatic process, whereas listening is voluntary. We hear many stimuli simultaneously, and we choose which of these stimuli we attend to.

Perhaps the biggest mistake we make is to assume that we have communicated. When we assume we have communicated, we fail to check to see what meanings our target listeners have assigned the words we utter. We never really know what we have said until we hear another's response to our words.

We can be better communicators if we operate under the premise that misunderstanding may be the rule rather than the exception. If we live by the belief that "misunderstanding is the rule" then we will be more attentive to how we form and send messages. Messages have a better chance of being understood when the volume is up, when they are sent in more than one channel, when they are redundant, and when there is an opportunity for feedback.

Feedback

Another feature of the communication process is feedback. Feedback is a response or reaction one gets or gives to a message. Feedback, whether verbal or nonverbal, is constantly occurring during an interaction. Feedback can show approval or disapproval. The more feedback received during an interaction, the more accurate the message transmission is likely to be.

The receiver of a message determines to some extent how a message is received. The receiver may feel hurt, guilty, elated, or thankful. However, the manner in which the feedback is delivered verbally and nonverbally also "colors" the message. Senders can never determine exactly what the reaction will be.

Common sense tells us it is impossible to improve without feedback. Responsible feedback, whether positive or negative, can lead to growth in your professional career.

In order for feedback to be effective, there are five criteria to keep in mind:

- Immediate — Feedback should be given as soon as possible after the communication event.
- Appropriate — Though feedback should be immediate when possible, it should also be given at a time when the receiver will be receptive. Too much feedback can harm as well as help!
- Honest — Feedback should be given directly, and with a strong foundation of trust.
- Clear — Good, clear, specific examples of behavior should always be provided. Describe the behavior carefully. The clearer the message, the less chance for misinterpretation.
- Informative — Feedback should be descriptive of behaviors, not judgmental of the person's self.

Most employees and employers desire feedback. So, how do you get it and how do you want it? These two questions have a lot to do with employee communication satisfaction. The kinds of feedback include:

oral	written
personal	impersonal
immediate	delayed
private	public
positive	negative

What kinds are preferred? Most people like positive oral f͏ cause face-to-face positive feedback is emotionally satisfy͏ firming. That is, "When you tell me I've done well, ͏ OK!"

Employees also want positive feedback ͏ notes of congratulations for good work ͏ and written positive evaluations in t͏

Negative feedback is usually not l͏ usually is preferred over written. Negat͏ often necessary for growth. Keep in mind͏ is more permanent and therefore more da͏

Positive feedback generally is apprecia͏ and in public. Public praise, however, may be͏ it smacks of favoritism.

Immediate feedback tends to be used more for children, but is especially important for anyone when learning a task, particularly a potentially dangerous one or one that might damage the organization's reputations or sales. Delayed feedback is a way of evaluating long-term goal accomplishment. It is better not to overpraise if one must evaluate another over a long period.

Employees, whether they are superiors or subordinates, want to know how well others think they are doing. If you are not voluntarily given feedback, you may discreetly ask for some.

Andy Grove, author of the 1987 text *One-on-one with Andy Grove: How to Manage Your Boss, Yourself and Your Coworkers*, said that not only do employees need feedback, they are *entitled* to it. He said employees should set up regular, face-to-face, meetings with their boss.

After watching employees stick their heads in to ask a question of a boss, he said, "I knew beyond a shadow of a doubt that most of these interruptions could be avoided if the manager adopted a practice of regular one-on-one meetings."

Especially if you are a "boss," ask your subordinates periodically how well you are doing. Also ask your own "boss" how well you are doing. But don't overdo it and seem to beg for compliments. Everyone needs some strokes, but to appear overly hungry for positive feedback gives an impression of insecurity. It's normal to want feedback.

Paraphrasing

Asking for feedback is important even when we think we are understood. It is particularly important when we have an impulse to criticize, to disagree, or to reject. It is equally important when we are being asked to commit ourselves. At times like these, it is important for each of us to check out what we think we said and heard. Herein rests the value of the skill of paraphrasing. One of the most valuable interpersonal communicative behaviors is to paraphrase what we think we've heard or what we think was said and when we are unsure and need more information, ask.

Paraphrasing is a restatement of another person's ideas in our own words. This restatement is accompanied by a "tag," such as "is that it?", "it seems like," or "am I on the right track?"

Paraphrasing is a skill that takes concentration and a little extra time up front, but the rewards can be numerous. When a listener restates or "checks" that the message has been heard correctly, it helps the speaker see whether the message sent was actually the message received. Thus the listener "mirrors" the speaker's words to check accuracy. The speaker can then restate the message if necessary. Paraphrasing also sends a message of confirmation to senders that what they have to say is important and has been heard. Think of the benefits when consumers feel that sellers are listening and to employees when they feel supervisors are listening.

We need to recognize that it is impossible to paraphrase if we are preparing our own message at the same time. We must listen closely in order to be able to effectively put what we have heard into our own words.

In our professional transactions we can also show that we are attending to another's message by following a few simple nonverbal rules. According to Sharon Ratliffe and David Hudson, authors of the 1988 text *Skill Building for Interpersonal Competence*, we can show that we are attending to a speaker by:

- Facing the talker directly, so that you are physically accessible to them. Sitting or standing squarely in front of the talker helps avoid what is sometimes interpreted as "giving the cold shoulder."
- Maintaining an open posture so as to communicate acceptance for what is being said and encouragement to share more. An open posture is most clearly demonstrated by open, unfolded arms.
- Leaning slightly toward the talker to show interest and involvement.
- Maintaining direct eye contact to indicate that your attention is focused on the talker. The eyes are often thought of as the "windows to the mind and soul." Most people assume that your attention is focused where your eyes are. In fact, a visual bond tends to create a mental bond between people when they communicate.
- Using appropriate facial expressions to show the other person when you understand his or her message and when you may be confused or have questions about the content. In addition, you can use facial expressions to demonstrate empathy for a person. A smile during disclosures of sadness or depression would be inappropriate, just as a frown would be inappropriate when a person speaks of a pleasant experience. In either case, the person would probably be discouraged from continuing to speak openly and honestly.

WE MEAN BUSINESS

Keep a journal for one week of all the hours and minutes that you spend speaking, and the same for listening. Include one weekend in this journal

Obstacles to Effective Listening

Perhaps one of the largest problems that stands in the way of effective listening stems from parents and educators. Because listening is a skill in which we are all involved for a large part of our day, and because it seems to require very little effort, many assume that listening skills develop naturally.

Obstacles to listening exist in various forms and contexts. On the next page is a list of some reasons why we don't listen effectively. Can you see yourself in any of these examples?

Box 2-3 **Listening While Talking**

Listening while talking will show you how to follow up when negotiating points that are important to you. A murmur of approval, a groan of incredulity, a sigh of relief, or a mutter of disagreement will give you valuable information that you can use later in the negotiations.

- Rehearsing response — Think of times that you have been sitting in class or at a meeting, and the speaker says something that goes against one of your core values. Do you sit there for the rest of the speech and form a rebuttal to this one argument? Do you raise your hand, and keep it raised for the next twenty minutes waiting to be called on so that you can refute that statement? Haven't you tuned out a large segment of the speech? The speaker may have addressed the issue or answered your question, but you weren't listening.
- Prejudging — Often we enter a listening situation with the determination that this is going to be dull, boring, and not at all worthwhile. We may feel that we know enough about the topic and therefore do not need to listen, or we simply dismiss the topic as uninteresting and "tune out" the speaker. Have you ever gone to class and thought, "We just covered this in Management yesterday. I don't want to listen to this again. What should I do Friday night? I really want to go. . . ." This is a typical example of prejudging and tuning out listening.
- Avoid difficult listening — It takes much more effort to learn something new and different. It takes concentration; more concentration than the average person is willing to exert. How many of you have volunteered to attend panel discussions or presentations by speakers? Hopefully the answer is many, but if you are like most people, much difficult listening is avoided.
- Defeated — Many times, if you do attend functions that require difficult listening, you may get the feeling that the message is "over your head" and tune out the speaker. Instead of trying to comprehend at least part of the message, many give up in defeat.
- Focusing on something else — Sometimes, instead of listening to the verbal message, we tend to focus on something else involved in the transaction. Examples would include self-focus, or controlling the conversation without attending to the needs of the other speaker; and delivery-focus, in which we focus on a person's dress, appearance, or delivery habits (counting the number of "um's") instead of listening.

WE MEAN BUSINESS

Provide examples where you have been a poor listener using the five obstacles above.

Successful Strategies for Improving Listening

> Nature gave us two ears and only one mouth so that we could listen twice as much as we speak.
>
> Proverb

Possibly you were skeptical as you began reading this chapter on listening. Since it is a subject that receives very little attention in the classroom, you may have taken listening for granted. Hopefully, we have persuaded you otherwise. The first step to improving listening skills is recognition of the obstacles that most often block our listening. The problem cannot be remedied without diagnosis first. Once we recognize the typical "traps," several measures can be taken. For instance, we can focus on finding the main ideas of the speaker, take notes, and write down difficult words that may need to be defined. Try to put aside biases that may cause a brewing rebuttal to stop the listening process.

Some people have even gone so far as to say that managers and executives have been "walking on one leg." William Keefe, author of *Listen, Management*, declared that professionals tend to concentrate so much on speaking skills that listening skills have been virtually ignored. He claimed that a manager should be two parts listener and one part speaker.

Supervisors can increase listening effectiveness in the workplace. Along with establishing eye contact, forward lean, and the other nonverbal attending behaviors mentioned earlier, they can:

- separate personal from work-related problems
- discuss what is the most important problem to attend to now?
- the employee and supervisor can work together to identify and isolate the problems
- make sure time will be made for feedback on the progress of the plan

Bosses should understand the situation from the employee's perspective. Through careful listening and paraphrasing, the supervisor and employee should enjoy the benefits of accurate, constructive, and enjoyable communication.

You can get the jump on other professionals by attacking this problem now, before you enter the workforce. The first step to accomplish is to analyze your listening deficiencies. Use the answers to the "We Mean Busi-

Box 2-4 ## Am I Listening?

Andrew Wolvin surveyed students in the basic speech communication course at the University of Maryland—College Park. These students were of varying ages, grade levels, and majors. They had completed a unit on listening, so they were aware of their own listening behavior. The students' responses shown below profile college student listeners.

When asked to estimate the percentage of time they spent listening each day, responses ranged from 20 percent to 100 percent, and the typical response was 75 percent. Thirty-seven percent of the students responded that listening to lectures was their primary listening.

Students also listed their strengths as listeners as:
10%—concentration/comprehension
 9%—ability to maintain attention
 8%—ability to identify the main point
 7%—ability to have interest in the subject
 2%—ability to listen objectively

Students identified areas in which they needed to improve as listeners as:
20%—attention
15%—listening to lectures
14%—concentration
(also listed lack of interest and inadequate note-taking abilities as areas for improvement)

Focusing only on lectures, students identified useful techniques for improving listening comprehension:
24%—taking notes
23%—concentration
11%—identifying main points
 7%—maintaining eye contact with the speaker
(also responded with strategies for outlining, staying awake, motivation, and preparation)

A final question asked students to complete the sentence "I can best improve my listening by. . . ." Students responded with answers consistent with the others they had given.
28%—better concentration
11%—attention
 5%—experience
(other: additional courses in listening, staying awake, motivation, and preparation for listening)

Source: Adapted from Andrew Wolvin, "Improving Listening Skills," in *Improving Speaking and Listening Skills*, ed. Rebecca Rubin.

ness" question above, or the questionnaire included in the "Skill Builders" section to help identify bad listening habits.

It is vital to become aware of your own listening strengths and weaknesses. Another helpful hint is to keep a journal of your listening experiences and link these to the ineffective and effective listening behaviors described in this chapter. Analyze the example journal entry below, which appeared in Rebecca Rubin (editor), *Improving Speaking and Listening Skills:*

> December 7: Today I listened to a lecture in American history about the bombing of Pearl Harbor. I had visited Pearl Harbor memorial two years ago, and I kept thinking about the tour I had there. I guess it's still too easy for me to daydream unless the professor is really organized (p. 20).

WE MEAN BUSINESS

What obstacles to effective listening were apparent in the above example?

Following is a list of strategies aimed at those serious about improving listening habits. Good listeners put others at ease, remove distractions, are patient, go easy on criticism and argument, ask questions, and stop talking.

Gary Hunt and Louis Cusella conducted a field study of listening needs in organizations. They randomly sampled 250 organizations chosen from the *Fortune* 500 largest U.S. industrial firms. Their results indicated that most listening problems occurred during meetings, performance appraisals, and superior-subordinate communication. Two of the major causes of problems related to listening were attributed to a lack of feedback about listening skills and a lack of employee motivation to practice effective listening skills. The commitment to become an effective listener is an active, rigorous commitment. Will you accept the challenge?

Listening and the Grapevine

Now that you have your listening skills "tuned in," it is time to discuss another important source of information in the workplace. You are probably familiar with the raisins who for several years danced across our television screens to the tune "I heard it through the grapevine." Well, this popular song tells an age-old tale. The grapevine is one of the places to which employees turn for information. In fact, according to a study of 1300 companies completed by Michael Cooper, 70 percent of corporate information is received through the grapevine.

Informal communication is an important part of organizational life. Grapevines exist as a means of informal information exchange and interpersonal relationship development among many members of the corporation. Organizations that have friendly communication climates and effective upward and downward communication channels usually do not have a need for a powerful and pervasive grapevine. On the other hand, organizations that do not have effective upward/downward communication, and have a distrusting culture, often will have a very strong, thriving, and powerful grapevine. Grapevines can be beneficial as a way to circulate information quickly, but can have detrimental effects if the "rumors" are misrepresented as facts. Beware of placing too much stock in the accuracy of messages transmitted through the vine. Always verify a message with the original source if possible.

Keith Davis, mentioned above in relation to his ten commandments for effective listening, is known especially for research on the corporate grapevine. The first characteristic Davis discovered was speed. The informal network generally processes information more rapidly than formal channels do. Speed is one of the main reasons for the existence and success of the grapevine.

Somewhat surprisingly, Davis found that 90 to 95 percent of the information that was passed along the grapevine actually was accurate, although it may have been slightly distorted. Perhaps the reason for this accuracy is the selectivity of the vine. Because some people involved in the informal network selectively choose to pass information to more than one and to bypass some people, the chain is usually fast and can at times be accurate.

Informal communication patterns tend to be affected by the location of the people in the workplace. People who come into daily contact with each other are more likely to be included in the chain.

A study completed by Harold Sutton and Lyman Porter revealed three types of people involved in organizational communication. They categorized the people as

- Isolates — Those who typically ignored grapevine information.
- Liaisons — Those who generally passed on information.
- Dead-enders — Those who could not always be relied upon to pass on information.

Liaisons were the most interactive employees. Dead-enders concentrated on work tasks and isolates preferred to perform duties by themselves.

Grapevines, sophisticated or rudimentary, exist in almost every organization. The grapevine handles information that formal communication channels are not designed to handle. For example, information about acquisitions or mergers or management personal problems may not be accessible to all employees. When information is "hidden" from employees, they are more likely to be reliant on the grapevine. Wise employers provide employees with desired and relevant information so that they do not feel the need to resort to informal channels.

Another reason the grapevine often becomes powerful is that it helps the people within an organization develop interpersonal relationships and sat-

---

Box 2-5 **Rumors Cost Money**

McDonald's spent almost a year fighting a false report that it had put red worms in its hamburger meat to increase the protein content. General Foods launched a full-page newspaper advertising campaign solely to counter stories that their tongue-tingling, carbonated candy called Pop Rocks had been exploding in children's stomachs, while Squibb spent about $100,000 to correct the notion that its Bubble Yum gum contained spider eggs.

Back in the '50s, Du Pont experienced a rumor that floated around for years. A machinist supposedly had taken one puff of a cigarette contaminated with Du Pont Teflon and died horribly. Finally, in 1961, when Du Pont introduced its Teflon-coated frying pans, the company sent out hundreds of thousands of pamphlets proving the story was a hoax. Du Pont has also dealt with rumors surrounding alleged miracle products, such as a report in the '70s of a new antiarthritis drug.

Source: Adapted from Roy Rowan, "Where Did That Rumor Come From?", *Fortune*, August 13, 1979, pp. 130–137.

---

isfy basic needs. If a supervisor recognizes this need, perhaps it could be channeled more effectively by developing an atmosphere of open communication within the work environment.

SUMMARY

This chapter has introduced the complicated process of communication. Although each of us communicates daily, often the process is taken for granted. Understanding the elements of the communication process is the first step toward achieving more satisfying personal and professional relationships. The basic parts of the communication process model include the source, or sender of a message; receiver; channel, or means of communication; noise, or interruption of the message between source and receiver; and feedback, or response to the message.

As evident from the above discussion, effective listening skills are a vital part of your chances to achieve success. Ineffective listening errors can cost businesses money and productivity, and lead to a lack of commitment. Reread the short story at the beginning of the chapter. Can you see how a lack of commitment can result from ineffective listening? People may feel that their voices do not count, that management doesn't care about what they have to say. How much commitment or motivation to remain would you feel if management didn't listen to you?

Effective listening can tell you much about how an organization works.

As you can see from the discussion of culture in Chapter 1, you can observe a lot about the workplace culture by listening. Listen to how people greet and speak to each other. Listen to on- and off-task talk, and how superior and subordinates speak to each other. Listening can be a powerful tool!

The grapevine also can be a source of information if listened to with discrimination. Do not minimize the potential power of this source of employee information. The costs and benefits of the grapevine must be weighed carefully.

SKILL BUILDER: LISTENING

For this exercise, think about your own listening behavior. Answer each question honestly, based on your behavior during a typical day.

Yes No 1. Do you easily get bored when listening?
Yes No 2. Do you focus on a speaker's delivery instead of content?
Yes No 3. Do you mentally build arguments *against* a speaker's ideas while you are listening?
Yes No 4. If you answered yes to the above, do you tune out a speaker in an attempt to remember your rebuttal?
Yes No 5. Do you fake attention often when you are listening?
Yes No 6. Do you fidget while a speaker is talking?
Yes No 7. Do you normally quit listening to difficult material?
Yes No 8. Is daydreaming a problem for you?

SKILL BUILDER: THE DANGERS OF THE GRAPEVINE

The purpose of this exercise is to demonstrate how messages can become distorted as transmitted through the grapevine. Divide the class into two or three groups and stand/sit in a straight line. Start a message at the beginning of the line, and pass the message along the line. Each group should report the message as intended at the beginning, and how it was actually received at the end.

- How much distortion was evident?
- Was one group more accurate?
- Why do you suppose the breakdown occurred?

Sample Message   Robert and Thomas have been students at XYZ University for the past three years. One Saturday afternoon they decided to go to the lake but neither knew exactly how to get there. Luckily, Robert's brother knew the way. Robert's brother, Keith, was a freshman at the area high school. Keith wanted to go to the Skate-a-thon Saturday at Leisure World but he had mentioned to Robert that there was a beach party for Keith's friend Allen at the lake. Robert and Thomas thought that they could talk Keith into showing them where the lake is if he was going to the beach party instead of going to Leisure World.

RESOURCES

Burke, Bruce. (1987). *Interpersonal communication skills*. Unpublished manuscript, Michigan State University.

Davis, Keith. (1967). *The dynamics of organizational behavior* (3rd ed.). New York: McGraw-Hill.

Davis, Keith. (1953). "Management communication and the grapevine." *Harvard Business Review, 31*, 43–49.

DeVito, Joseph. (1989). *The interpersonal communication book* (5th ed.). New York: Harper & Row.

Grove, Andy. (1987). *One-on-one with Andy Grove: How to manage your boss, yourself, and your co-workers*. New York: Putman.

Hunt, Gary, and Louis Cusella. (1983). "A field study of listening needs in organizations." *Communication Education, 32*(4), 393–401.

Keefe, William. (1971). *Listen, management*. New York: McGraw-Hill.

Nichols, Ralph. (1957). "Listening is a ten-part skill." *Nation's Business, 45*, 56–57.

Powell, J. T. (1983). "Listen attentively to solve employee problems." *Personnel Journal, 62*, 580–2.

Ratliffe, Sharon, and David Hudson. (1988). *Skills building for interpersonal competence*. New York: Holt, Rinehart and Winston.

Rowan, Roy. (1979, August 13). "Where did that rumor come from?" *Fortune*, 130–137.

Rubin, R. B. (ed.). (1983). *Improving speaking and listening skills*. San Francisco: Jossey-Bass.

Sutton, Harold, and Lyman Porter. (1968). "A study of the grapevine in a governmental organization." *Personnel Psychology, 21*, 223–30.

Chapter 3

Interpersonal Communication in the Workplace

Concepts for Discussion

- Uncertainty reduction theory
- Interpersonal communication competency skills
- Interpersonal communication training

- Internal workplace communication
- Special employee problems that require interpersonal communication competencies

We were standing in line at the Atlanta airport waiting to have our baggage checked. We noticed that some people ahead of us gave the skycap a dollar or two as they asked him to handle their baggage carefully or make sure it got on the right plane. But the man standing just in front of us took a different approach. He didn't offer a tip, but he sternly lectured the skycap about taking special care of his two bags. He swore loudly when one of his bags tipped over accidentally, then angrily stalked off toward his gate.

As we stepped up to take our turn, the skycap's broad grin caught our attention. We asked him how he was able to keep smiling given the sometimes difficult people he had to serve. "What do you mean?" he asked. "That fellow who just swore at you,'' we replied. The skycap smiled again. ''Oh, that dude? People like him are easy. You see, he's heading for L.A., but his bags are going to Detroit.''

A basic principle in human relationships is that people give to get.

Richard Huseman and John D. Hatfield
Managing the Equity Factor Or ''After All I've Done for You . . .''

Many of our daily transactions within the workplace involve communication with people, or what is commonly called interpersonal communication. Though it is a skill often taken for granted, competent interpersonal communication takes thoughtful consideration and practice. Similar to listening, interpersonal skills are ones that we deal with almost every day without realizing the profound effect that competent communicators have on our lives. It is for this reason that we have devoted a chapter to the discussion of interpersonal communication in the workplace.

Chapter 2 was devoted to the introduction of the basic communication process and the fundamentally important skill of listening. In order to have effective interpersonal relationships both on and off the job, one must understand how the process works, and not neglect the powerful role of listening in our lives. With those elements in mind, let us build upon the framework already provided.

In this chapter, we first describe three phenomena that help explain interpersonal communication: uncertainty reduction, communication apprehension, and immediacy. Next, we define ten communication competencies important to those who would be effective interpersonally in the workplace. Following this, we explain approaches to gaining and using interpersonal communication competencies in the workplace: self-disclosure, interpersonal investment, and symbolic congruence. The chapter concludes with practical advice pertaining to a number of special employee problems that require interpersonal communication competencies.

UNCERTAINTY REDUCTION THEORY

According to Dean Barnlund, author of the text *Interpersonal Communication: Surveys and Studies*, interpersonal communication involves ''face-to-face encounters'' where participants ''sustain focused interaction through the reciprocal exchange of verbal and nonverbal cues.'' Stephen Littlejohn, whose text *Theories of Human Communication* is well-known to undergraduate and graduate students in communication, lists five criteria that are included within this definition. These serve as a general guide to understanding interpersonal communication, but are certainly not all-inclusive:

1. There must be two or more people in physical proximity who perceive the presence of one another.
2. One's communicative behavior is the direct consequence of the other's (interdependence).
3. There will be an exchange of messages.
4. Messages are encoded and decoded both verbally and nonverbally.
5. Interpersonal communication is relatively unstructured. Messages are informal and flexible.

Working with others is the nature of most careers. Perhaps that is why we place listening skills and sensitivity so high on our scale of values. Task accomplishment very often depends upon interpersonal trust. We need to be able to communicate to each other and to be able to count on each other. To some extent, we also need to be able to predict each other's behavior. In almost all relationships, we crave to reduce uncertainty.

Uncertainty exists in relationships when we do not have enough information about the other person with whom we are interacting. When we do not have adequate information, we often fill in the blanks with information from our own experience, guessing how we think the person will react in a situation. This tactic can be dangerous. Often the information that we create is inaccurate or stereotypical. Why is this important for you in the workplace? Because inaccuracy in communication is detrimental to professional success.

Charles Berger studied this concept of uncertainty reduction, or what he calls URT (Uncertainty Reduction Theory). In the article "Communicating Under Uncertainty," which appeared in *Interpersonal Processes: New Directions in Communication Research*, he explained that communicating with a stranger can be anxiety-provoking because that person can act in a "number of alternative ways." Therefore, it is hard for us to predict this person's actions.

The U.S. government spends large amounts of tax money to try to reduce its international uncertainties. Thousands of people are employed in intelligence gathering work. People are willing to pay dearly to reduce their uncertainties about the future course of stocks and other investment vehicles. We spend some $100,000,000 a year to obtain investment information (*Wall Street Journal*, 1985).

In addition, consider the substantial sums paid by businesses to economic forecasters and it becomes apparent that uncertainty reduction itself is a major business.

Uncertainty reduction occurs through frequent interaction with the others you work with. While interacting, make sure you are using the effective listening skills that we discussed during Chapter 2. Listen for information, listen for unstated motives, and listen to nurture congenial relationships. Also make the other party feel respected and worthwhile. Wouldn't you like to be treated this way? Think about some of your work and personal relationships that you have held over time. Can you predict the moods, values, and sometimes nonverbal (body language) behaviors of the person at times? Does this make you more comfortable in your relationship with that person? Why?

How we interact with others on the job is related to our own mental and emotional well-being. Our stability and predictability cannot be a matter of will but are a response to the security of our personal base. In order for that base to be secure, we need (1) a bonding with family, (2) an attachment to close friends, and (3) a supporting network in the workplace. When one of these three gets a bit shaky, we usually place more reliance on the other two areas. For example, if you should lose a close friend, then the work network and family ties may become more important. But we are on shaky emotional ground when two out of the three are disrupted, such as loss of a spouse by death or divorce, and simultaneously moving so that we are separated from our close friends. Our stability in our job under such circumstances then may also be affected.

COMMUNICATION APPREHENSION

Some of us are afraid of handling snakes. That fear is reasonable when applied to poisonous snakes but is less reasonable when applied to harmless varieties. Communication apprehension can be reasonable under certain situations. If a superior notifies a subordinate that she or he should come in for an unexpected performance review, anxiety about how that review will go is reasonable. The employee who has left work early without permission, should s/he receive such a message, might be especially apprehensive. That is reasonable. Facing a new audience, knocking on a blind-date's door, and going for a job interview are anxiety-producing events that generate uneasiness for many people. They produce what is known as contextual or audience-based communication apprehension.

Yet another kind of communication apprehension is a general personality trait: anxiety about oral or written sending or receiving messages. Professor James McCroskey is the communication scholar best known for investigation of communication apprehension (CA). He defines CA as "an individual's level of fear or anxiety associated with either real or anticipated communication with another person or persons." He suggests that there are four types of communication apprehension. We have just described these four types:

- Situational, such as being called in for a performance review.
- Audience-based (i.e., an assignment to speak before a certain group).
- Context-based (refers to fear of communication in certain types of settings, such as job interviews, being called on in class, or public speaking).
- Trait, a general fear of oral, written, listening, or singing communication.

Research about communication apprehension in the worksetting by McCroskey and others has largely focused upon the effect it has upon individuals' internally experienced discomfort. How anxious one feels about communication to some degree, but not always, affects one's observable behavior. Those who are apprehensive may be more silent, but all silent people are not internally experiencing discomfort. Those with CA avoid communication and if they cannot avoid it they tend to be nonfluent; subdued in volume; and, in extreme cases, flushed in appearance, with dry lips and a noticeable tremor in voice and body (hands or knees shaking).

Most people experience some of these observable behaviors. All, or nearly all, of us have felt the internal discomfort of communication apprehension in certain situations. We may feel that discomfort, however, and yet it is not observable to others; and that is the case for most public speaking. Almost all students say they experience some anxiety when preparing, practicing, and presenting a speech to an audience, but surprisingly, usually an audience does not notice that discomfort, except in extreme cases.

Those persons who are traitlike communication apprehensive tend to be anxious when communicating with superiors, and are especially anxious when having to explain and justify certain behavior. This simply means those who are communication apprehensive, like most of us, fear talking with or being talked at by a boss and are particularly fearful when put on the spot.

So what can we do about these findings? Knowledge about CA should make those in superior positions more emphatic communicators. Superiors can minimize fear of communication by expressing themselves in a friendly, relaxed, attentive manner rather than in gruff, tense, or aloof ways. They especially should avoid verbal abusiveness: swearing, yelling, and demeaning subordinates' ideas. They should ask questions to learn about how job-related matters are going rather than stating that something is wrong. They should be problem-solvers rather than blame-placers. They should encourage subordinates to brainstorm and think out loud about different ways of doing things rather than squelching them with "That won't work."

Superiors should be especially sensitive when and if they must confront unacceptable employee behavior, such as absenteeism, drug abuse, or dishonesty. They should select a private setting for such confrontations. Information-gathering should come before decisions about what to do. Most organizations have established policies in case of substance abuse and for referrals to the personnel or human resources department. There also are established procedures for disciplinary action that remove the situation from one of boss-employee conflict to a problem-solving, policy-following level.

Subordinates who are apprehensive about communication can do much to manage their anxieties. Taking courses in communication skills is a proactive approach. Rather than avoid communication, we learn by doing. That is what this text is all about. One of your authors is apprehensive about dancing, and he will always be so until he takes enough dancing instruction. That he is doing! Another of your authors is an accomplished musician.

Why? Because she has been trained as a musician and has directed choral groups. Confidence comes from learning the skills appropriate to whatever it is we are assigned or want to do.

The work setting demands interpersonal communication: one-on-one, face-to-face, phone-to-phone, memo-to-memo; seated one-to-group, sometimes standing before an audience. These times will be anxiety producing until one (1) is product knowledgeable, (2) has experience in presentation of information, (3) has knowledge about how best to organize and present messages, and (4) understands the kinds of communication behaviors and channels that are appropriate to a particular corporate culture.

Communication apprehension for those who are particularly reticent may best be approached by individualized or small-group counseling. Professor McCroskey developed muscle relaxing exercises, tapes with soothing mood music, as part of the reconditioning CA training. Others have developed guided instruction employing videotaped feedback to help individuals constructively manage their anxieties in one-on-one, face-to-face stressful work situations and stand-up speaking situations.

One-on-one stressful situations will be less anxiety producing when:

- one phrases her/his disagreements or concerns in "to me" statements,
- one acknowledges the discomfort being experienced,
- one seeks clarification about and solutions to the stressful situation.

For example, if one's superior is piling on too much work, how might a subordinate approach this situation? First, the subordinate needs to explore ways of accomplishing the assignments within the deadlines. Next, should these approaches be inadequate, s/he can request a meeting with the superior to discuss the workload. The subordinate might explain her/his concerns this way: "I've tried to find a way to accomplish what I've been assigned, but I'm coming up short, even when working overtime. I don't want to be a complainer and I feel embarrassed and uneasy because I am failing to meet your expectations." Such a statement puts the cards on the table expressing one's anxiety and lays the groundwork for problem solving. Most superiors will then engage in problem solving about the workload.

Workplace communication apprehension, we have pointed out, is of four kinds: situational, audience-based, context-based, and trait. Interpersonal communicational skills enable organizational members to manage their own internal discomforts constructively in stressful communication situations and to make communication less stressful for others. That is important to the quality of one's work and corporate productivity.

IMMEDIACY

Speech is more immediate than written communication. Speech is live, and a speaker's words, tone, and body language are "read" by her/his auditors. At the same time, instantaneously, an audience sends messages to the speaker, sometimes by yawning and shuffling of feet, other times by applause or intense quietness, yet other times by boos or rolling of the eyes in disbelief.

Some speech is more immediate and therefore more impelling than others. Distance, movement, time, duration, activity, probability, liking, accommodation, and personalness influence how immediate a message is.

Distance Movement toward and closeness capture and hold attention more than a distant presence. Therefore, to emphasize a point, a speaker may approach a listener or "invade" the space of an audience. Contrast and separation in space also place more attention upon the one that is singled out from the many. A speaker will seek a position higher than a crowd. An actor who wants attention will get in the spotlight and will upstage others.

Time   The here and now is more compelling than the then and there. What you are thinking now is more important to listeners than what you thought in the past. Therefore, talk about what you and your audience want, feel, and can do now in comparison to the past and future.

Duration   The length of a message and the number of times of an interaction affect immediacy. A long letter or a long speech conveys more concern about a topic and a relationship than does a short message. Repetition tends to enhance a message's importance; however, it becomes boring and meaningless with too much repetition.

Activity   The energetic and dynamic conveys immediacy. Our language indicates active and passive states. "I am doing" is more immediate than "I have done." However, the boss may be more pleased with "I have done . . ." rather than "I am doing" or "I will do." Jumping into something, putting one's body on the line, and participating actively conveys immediacy, commitment, and caring.

Probability   Certainty versus uncertainty of language conveys immediacy. Saying "I am doing" is more immediate than saying "I might" or "I could do." Therefore, speak as much as possible in terms of tangible and real happenings. People want fact more than uncertainty.

Liking   People are drawn to persons they like, evaluate highly, and prefer. They avoid or move away from things they dislike, evaluate negatively, or do not prefer. Speakers, therefore, generally do their utmost to be friendly, personable, respected, and interesting. Speakers try to avoid language that annoys or insults listeners.

Accommodation   People who want to be liked, respected, and believed adjust and adapt their communication to accommodate the styles of those who are the targets of their communication. When talking with a person who is "laid back," one tends to be similarly relaxed. Friends may cross and uncross their legs in mirrorlike ways while conversing. Casual language begets casual language. Formal begets formal. Empathetic communication calls forth empathetic communication. Not to accommodate to another's messages and situation is to psychologically distance oneself from another.

Personalness   Some words are more personal than others. Some languages, such as French, have both an intimate form and a more formal version of the pronoun "you." One "you" is used among friends, the other with strangers. The personalness of our language is determined in part by the number of personal pronouns: I, me, my, we, ours; you, yours, them, theirs; etc. Also, words that have masculine or feminine gender are more personal than abstract terms. For example, John Jones, father, sister, ice man, and actress are more personal than teacher, doctor, or employee. Direct quotes convey personalness. Direct questions, commands, and requests convey immediacy, such as "Does this sound possible?" or "Imagine the implications" or "Do it." Exclamations, incomplete expressions, and sometimes ungrammatical messages convey immediacy, such as "Wow!" or the ungrammatical "You done good."

INTERPERSONAL COMPETENCE SKILLS

According to the text *The Road Trip: An Interpersonal Adventure*, authored by Rebecca Rubin and Randi Nevins, research has identified ten basic skills that are linked to interpersonal competence. Keep in mind that what is deemed as an "appropriate" or "effective" communication behavior changes with the particular situation and desired outcome.

Self-disclosure   Self-disclosure is the process of sharing a part of yourself with another person. Disclosing requires a certain level of risk. Your level of disclosure typically is based on your feelings of acceptance, self-worth, and trust in a relationship. Rules for appropriate self-disclosure in the workplace are tricky. Some in management say that they want employees to leave their problems at home, and to come to work ready to begin a task without excuses or distractions. Others contend that sharing personal problems and feelings strengthens the bonds of the workers and increases employee commitment. How do you feel? How much disclosure do you think is appropriate in the workplace? Do you bring your personal problems with you on the job? Would you want your workers to talk about their personal lives on company time? Do you think this would increase or decrease productivity in the long run?

Michael Roloff, author of the article "Communication and Reciprocity Within Intimate Relationships," which also appeared in *Interpersonal Processes: New Directions in Communication Research*, stated that there is a norm in our culture to reciprocate self-disclosure if we wish to continue to develop a relationship with an individual. This means that once one is

Box 3-1   **Immediately Interpersonal**

If you want to be more personal, and make your communication more immediate and adaptive:

Verbal Cues to Immediacy
1. Use personal pronouns.

2. Talk about experiences.

3. Ask questions about others' viewpoints.

4. Encourage others to talk.

5. Use humor.

6. Address others by name when appropriate.

7. Encourage others to address you by your first name.

8. Converse socially.

9. Talk in terms of ''we'' and ''our.''

10. Respond, giving supportive feedback.

11. Respond, giving critical feedback as appropriate; tactfully, amiably, and candidly.

12. Ask others' feelings about relevant topics.

13. Invite others to phone you, if you mean it.

14. Praise others work and behavior.

15. Talk about things that matter to you now.

Nonverbal Cues to Immediacy
16. Gesture while talking.

17. Be dynamic and vary voice in rate, pitch, volume, and stress.

18. Make eye contact.

19. Smile.

20. Relax and move.

Adapt to Others' Styles and Situations
21. Adjust your rate, volume, sentence length, and amount of talking to others.

22. Take turns.

23. Be sensitive and empathic.

24. Paraphrase, seek clarification.

25. Be real, avoid affectation and phoniness.

disclosed to, the norm is to disclose back to that person, although that disclosure does not have to be immediate or at the same depth. Therefore, appropriate self-disclosure should be used to develop interpersonal relationships. Of course there is some level of risk involved with disclosure, so it is most appropriate to be gradual in our sharing and to take note of the response of the other party. One also must be aware of the norms of the workplace regarding disclosure depth.

Empathy   Empathy refers to the act of feeling *with* another person, instead of feeling sorry *for* him. When you empathize, you try to put yourself into the other person's shoes, so to speak, and see the situation from his/her viewpoint. Paraphrasing the speaker's responses is a good way to show empathy and to check to see if you are reading the person's thoughts correctly (see Chapter 2). Obviously, in order to be empathetic, you must be a good listener. How can empathetic listening skills help you in the workplace?

Social Relaxation   To be socially relaxed is to be comfortable in a communication interaction. People who seem at ease in interaction tend to be more successful in handling complaints from hostile personnel. Some people are more comfortable in an interpersonal context than in a public speaking situation. This is quite common! There are also some who love the flair of public speaking, but feel awkward in a one-to-one situation. When do you feel most socially relaxed?

Assertiveness   Maurice Lorr and William More found that people communicate more or less assertively depending upon their self-esteem, and that assertiveness breaks down into four kinds of behaviors: directiveness, social assertiveness, defense of rights and interests, and independence. How you answer the following statements will provide clues to how assertive you tend to be:

Directness

- I am usually the one who initiates activities in a group.
- I let others take the lead when I'm on a committee.

Social Assertiveness

- I feel uncomfortable around people I don't know.
- It's easy for me to make "small talk" with people I've just met.

Defense of Rights and Interests

- When someone interrupts me in a serious conversation, I find it hard to ask him/her to wait a minute.
- If I have been "shortchanged," I go back and complain.

Independence

- In discussions, I go along with the group.
- I nearly always argue for my viewpoint if I think I'm right.

In order to become a competent communicator, you must be aware of your actions. After reading the definitions above, decide whether your typical behavior is aggressive, nonassertive, or assertive. Aggressive persons stand up for themselves without considering the rights of others. Aggressive behavior puts down other persons. The aggressive person's goals in a communication situation is to WIN. The other party often LOSES. This is called a WIN-LOSE mode of conflict resolution. Can you think of a situation in the workplace, school, or with friends/family in which you have been aggressive? Did you feel comfortable with that behavior? On the other end of the spectrum is the nonassertive person who fails to stand up for his/her rights, or does so in an ineffective way. The goal of nonassertive persons is to make everyone ELSE happy. This would be a LOSE-WIN conflict resolution. But who is neglected here? When have you been nonassertive? How did you feel about this method of conflict resolution?

There may be situations where the above behavior is appropriate and necessary. However, the most competent behavior is that which is assertive. An assertive person stands up for his/her own rights without violating the rights of others. The goal of assertion is to find a solution that is mutually acceptable to both parties. In other words, it is a WIN-WIN resolution of conflict. If someone at work asked to borrow your brand-new compact disc stereo system for a party, how could you respond assertively, nonassertively, and aggressively? Here is one example:

ASSERTIVE: "I appreciate your need for music for the party, but that system cost too much and is too complicated to set up for me to feel comfortable loaning it out. I have heard about a really inexpensive rental place, though. Let's go look up the number. . . ." Here I stood up for my own rights, but was also courteous to my friend.

NONASSERTIVE: "Sure, go ahead. . . ." Saying yes because I fear my friend would think I was "uncool"—being paranoid or untrusting. Then all night I worry and worry about the state of my system.

AGGRESSIVE: "NO WAY! You have GOT to be kidding. Are you crazy? Do you think that I would lend that to you?" This violates the other person's right for respect.

Interaction Management Interaction management refers to procedural skills. The skills of turntaking (being aware of cues that someone wants a turn and waiting for your turn while not interrupting), turnyielding (letting another person have the floor and not monopolizing the conversation), and playing a role in the development of conversation topics (not putting the burden on the other person). Think about conversations in which you have had a part. Do you monopolize the conversation, or do you not contribute at all? Are you attentive to the nonverbal cues of the other person, such as eye contact, body gestures, or vocal cues such as "uh-huh, yes. . . .?" Interaction management plays an important role in effective business communication and requires attention and practice.

Altercentrism   Altercentric behavior is defined exactly how the word sounds. Alter (other) centrism (centered) describes behavior in which the communicator is concerned about the other party's feelings and input. In order to be effectively altercentric, one must be attentive to what the other person says, but more importantly, must be in tune with what the person is NOT saying. You will understand more of what we mean after you read Chapter 5 on Nonverbal Communication. In any case, we believe that altercentric behavior to some degree is almost always preferable to self-centered behavior. Do you agree?

Expressiveness   Expressive behavior can be communicated both verbally and nonverbally. Nonverbally, one shows expressiveness with facial expressions, eye contact, gestures, vocal variety, and posture. Verbal expressiveness is communicated with clear and interesting word choices. How would you describe a nonexpressive communicator? What verbal and nonverbal behaviors would this person possess?

Supportiveness   Supportive communicators send messages to other communicators that they are there for them when needed and value them as individuals. Although people in business are often in superior/subordinate relationships, this does not necessarily mean that the communication must make one person feel unimportant or unworthy. Communicating equality in "person importance" can be separated from communicating equality in job position if practiced carefully and honestly. Supportive communicators also own their feelings rather than blaming the other person in a situation. Supportive communicators would begin a statement with a phrase such as "I feel that . . ." rather than "You did this. . . ." Can you think of an example in the workplace where you have had an interaction with a supportive and a nonsupportive boss?

Immediacy   We described the characteristics of immediacy earlier in this chapter. Now we mention it more briefly as an interpersonal communicator skill. Immediate behavior means that communicators send the message to others that they are approachable and available for communication. Competent interpersonal communicators convey immediacy with behavior such as direct eye contact, forward posture, and general attentiveness.

We realize that in the workplace it is not always possible for workers to maintain this attitude completely when there are deadlines to meet and projects to complete. But what specifically can we do verbally and nonverbally to show that we do care about the people we work with?

Box 3-2 **Hazards of an Open-door Policy**

In 28 years of management, Everett Suters found an open-door policy to be an indispensable tool. He also found it to be an ongoing challenge. He wrote that, like a surgeon's scalpel, it can work wonders when handled properly and cause untold damage when it is not. On one hand, you want to be responsive to the concerns of all your employees. On the other hand, you can't let a situation develop to the point where you undermine the effectiveness and morale of your managers by letting staff members go over their heads. That, of course, is the greatest risk, but it can be overcome with sensitivity and care.

Some of the benefits of an open-door policy include that by making yourself available to all of your employees, you get an early warning signal when trouble is brewing in the lower ranks. The alarm is sounded early, loud, and clear and is neither muffled nor redirected by going through normal channels. The policy is also a useful reminder to managers that if they are not fair, their people do have recourse. Perhaps the greatest benefit is that people throughout the company feel they have an ally at the top. Even if complaints aren't resolved in their favor, they know they'll be able to have a fair hearing without putting their jobs on the line.

Source: From Everett T. Suters, "Hazards of an open-door policy," *Inc.* (January 1987), pp. 99–102.

Environmental Control   The final communication competence is called environmental control. This competence refers to the ability to handle conflict in a win-win mode (refer to the "assertiveness" section above). People who are competent in this area are good problem solvers, and are willing to cooperate with those in the environment. The person who effectively has control over his or her environment is goal-oriented, and pursues those goals in a way that does not discount the rights of others.

WE MEAN BUSINESS

How do some of the portions of the definition of environmental control overlap with the competencies listed above? Why is this important to you in the workplace?

SPECIAL EMPLOYEE PROBLEMS THAT REQUIRE
INTERPERSONAL COMMUNICATION COMPETENCIES

Much transpires within the work setting that is seen only by the experienced eye. Every workplace seethes with emotion. Employees have strong feelings about the quality of their work and how others are or are not performing their jobs. There are feelings of sexual attraction. There are employees with concerns about discrimination. There are problems of drugs and alcohol. Workers may worry about hazards in the workplace. Superiors must monitor performance, recommend employee assistance, and initiate disciplinary procedures — all this while simultaneously trying to develop a trusting, friendly relationship with subordinates. Being a superior has its own anxieties.

Workplace Romance

Interpersonal communication in the workplace is not without the pleasures and problems that accompany intimacy. A few studies have shown that many people meet their mates in the workplace. Romance does happen within the work setting. The problems of sexually prompted communication in the work setting are potentially explosive. Sexual harassment is illegal and costly. Those who have authority over others should never either verbally or nonverbally send "sexual messages" to subordinates. This means no touching other than a handshake, no teasing, sexual innuendo, or joking, or any remark that may be interpreted as a proposition or invitation to a sexual encounter.

Employees who feel they are being placed in a compromisory position — one in which career advancement depends upon providing sexual favors — should exercise care in the collection of such evidence. They must also be sure that they are all business and make it clear that no such propositions are acceptable. If sexual harassment persists and can be documented, usually by witnesses, an employee victim may seek the counsel of a superior's superior or the personnel department. This should resolve the problem without retaliation. However, if it does not, the victim may seek the aid of the Equal Employment Opportunity Commission (EEOC) and/or a lawyer.

Kaleel Jamison, in *Managing Sexual Attraction in the Workplace*, stated that "Sex in the corporation can wreck careers, damage productivity of the entire company, and even affect profits." The notoriety of the romance of Bendix chief executive officer Bill Agee, and his protégé, Mary Cunningham, is one such example. First, Mary Cunningham, who appeared to have risen too quickly due to Agee's attraction to her, was eased out of Bendix. Not long after, Agee's career with Bendix also ended. The Agee-Cunningham affair, which later culminated in marriage, did not entail any sexual harassment or misconduct. There was no Jim Bakker – Jessica Hahn, boss-taking-advantage-of-a-secretary misconduct. Nevertheless, the Agee-Cunningham romance, however innocent it may have been, proved destructive to two very promising careers in a major corporation.

Discrimination and Sexual Harrassment

Discrimination has been legally defined as any selection or on-the-job practice or communication that has an adverse impact on hiring, promotion, employment, or membership opportunities of members of any race, sex, ethnic group, creed, or age group. Because of underrepresentation, particularly of minorities and women, both the private and public sectors have made special efforts to recruit, train, and promote members of these groups.

The long record of workplace inequities due to discriminatory practices makes it particularly important that communication in the workplace should be sexually, racially, and religiously neutral and nondiscriminatory. This means that written material in corporate newspapers and house organs should avoid racial and sexist language and jokes, and should endeavor to feature employees nondiscriminatorily. Corporate policies and training should help employees know that such language as "niggers," "spics," "dagos," "broads," "dames," "honey," "old man," "old maid," etc., is emotionally hurtful, may be taken as verbal aggression, and is impermissible.

Right To Know

In 1983 the Federal Hazard Communication Standard Act was passed and took effect in 1986. This act mandates worker training in the hazards faced on the job, and a full disclosure of hazardous chemicals used by the company. All industries, except construction, are covered by this legislation. Failure to make disclosures can result in company liability for negligence, and makes possible awards for compensatory damages to an injured party.

Communication is at the heart of this employee health legislation. Employers and all levels of management, therefore, are responsible for identifying and labeling hazardous materials. This also means posting signs and explaining these hazards to employees and the public.

Confidentiality and Privacy

The Civil Rights Act of 1964 limited employers in the type and amount of information they could obtain during the job application or preemployment screening. Personnel departments or managers should not question job candidates pertaining to race, religion, age, height, weight, marital status, national origin, or non-job related mental or physical impairments.

Additional legislation, such as the Michigan Polygraph Protection Act and court interpretations, has repeatedly decided that employers must justify the need for private information. A polygraph test must be necessary to job requirements and should never range into the private topics of sexual practice, labor union activity, political or religious affiliation, or marital relationships.

Drug/alcohol problems or tests and medical records are protected information in most states. Personnel and superiors must protect such information to which they have access from those who have no right to know.

What this means is that interpersonal communication in the workplace should be job-related. Non-job related information should be kept private, and when personal information does become job relevant, it should be held confidentially.

In 1987 the Supreme Court ruled that victims of the contagious disease AIDS (Acquired Immune Deficiency Syndrome) are covered by the same laws that protect the handicapped worker from job bias. Section 504 of the Rehabilitation Act of 1973 prohibits any firm or local government that receives federal funds from discriminating against "otherwise" handicapped persons. This means that a superior may not fire or ban employees from work or force a permanent sick leave if it is discovered they have AIDS.

Here again, personnel departments and superiors must act judiciously in keeping with the law and hold private information in confidence. Knowing when not to communicate is important in the job setting.

Smoking

In 1986 the General Services Administration (GSA) of the United States government issued a proposed regulation that would apply to all GSA-controlled facilities. It would ban smoking in shared work areas, conference rooms, classrooms, restrooms, auditoriums, corridors, lobbies, etc. — all work areas except private offices. Other legislation, such as Michigan's Clean Indoor Air Act of 1986, has sought to reduce involuntary exposure to tobacco smoke. Almost half of the *Fortune* 500 companies have some type of smoking policy. In a few court cases, nonsmokers have obtained unemployment benefits on the grounds that their sensitivity to smoke forced them to quit their jobs. Employers have had to pay compensation benefits for alleged smoke-caused health problems.

Smoking becomes an interpersonal communication issue when nonsmokers object to smoke in the work environment. Personnel cannot ignore such concerns. Superiors dare not ignore these matters. They must be handled respectfully, diplomatically, and in light of corporate policies and state and national laws.

Deteriorating Work

When a superior suspects that a subordinate's performance is affected by an alcohol/drug related problem, she/he should document reasons for this suspicion: days absent, late work, wasted material, rudeness, poor quality work. Whether and when a superior should intervene is a matter of interpersonal communication. How that communication is initiated and conducted requires sensitivity. A supportive relationship will make the employee more receptive to a confrontation. But even then, an employee may deny she/he has a problem. Guidelines for such an intervention are:

1. State the general nature of the concern. Example: "John, I have observed some problems with your work lately."
2. Ask permission to discuss the matter. "Is it okay with you to talk about this now?"
3. The superior should not attempt to serve as a professional counselor in personal problems, but should focus upon the decline in work itself.
4. Inform the employer of existing employee assistance programs if the employee hints that the reason for the lowered performance is personal. Example: "I can't diagnose what a person's problems are or prescribe a solution, but did you know we have Employee Assistance Programs for any number of problems such as family problems, drug, and alcohol problems? Personnel handles referrals to competent professionals in a confidential way."
5. Restate your concern for the employee's performance and general well-being. Example: "We don't want to pry but if, as you say, personal problems may be adversely affecting your work, our staff is there to help if you will make the first move."
6. Restate your need to follow up in monitoring performance. Example: "You know it's my job to know what's happening in production, and I'm held responsible for keeping track of performance."

Most companies have in place some exemptions from standard disciplinary procedures applicable to job performance requirements during the time an employee is being treated in the employee assistance program. This does not, however, exempt the employee from job performance expectations. If performance continues to decline, or fails to improve, the normal disciplinary procedure will apply.

Good Faith and Fair Dealing

Judges have fashioned a "covenant of good faith and fair dealing" in cases where a long-term employee with a good record has been abruptly discharged. What this means is that if a company discharges an employee it had better have a good reason. Just any reason or no reason is not good enough to fire. Some states, such as Montana, Michigan, and California, have been more explicit about what constitutes "good reason." The Montana law (Montana Code Annotated Secs. 39–2–901–914) states that a discharge is wrongful if it is in retaliation for the employer's refusal to violate public policy or for reporting such violation, if it is not for good cause, or if it violates the provisions of the employer's written personnel policies.

Discharge should be for reasonable grounds for dismissal based upon a failure to satisfactorily perform job duties, disruption of the employer's authority, or other legitimate business reasons. What is said about or used as evidence for discharge is a matter of interpersonal communication. Let's look at an example.

Mr. Buck, an insurance broker, was fired by Frank B. Hall and Company.

Box 3-3 **Oral and Interpersonal Communication Skills Rate as More Important than Written in Today's Organizations**

Professors Anita S. Bednar of Central State University and Robert J. Olney of Southwest Texas State, in ''Communication Needs of Recent Graduates,'' report in the December 1987 *Bulletin of the Association for Business Communication* (22 – 23) that recent business school graduates rate verbal communication skills as more important than written:

IMPORTANCE OF SELECTED COMMUNICATION SKILLS IN
TODAY'S ORGANIZATIONS

Skill	Mandatory	Very Important	Moderately Important	Not Important
Interpersonal	69.2%	23.1%	7.7%	—
Oral	64.5%	35.5%	—	—
Written	50.0%	31.3%	15.6%	3.1%

Bednar and Olney indicate that educators ''must continuously update the business communication curriculum'' to meet the real-world skill needs of graduates.

The reason given was that he failed to make his sales goals. Unable to find new employment, he hired a detective to pose as a prospective employer. Thus in disguise, the detective sought information about Buck and was told by Hall, Buck's former employer, that "Buck was a Jekyll and Hyde person, a classic sociopath." Mr. Buck then sued Hall for defamation and was awarded $1,905,000.

This, though a rare and extreme example of how interpersonal communication can be destructive and costly, illustrates reasons for caution in what one says about others within the workplace.

SUMMARY

The major theme of this chapter is interdependence. Interpersonal communication is that which occurs between people. Through this interaction, we get to know ourselves and others better. We need each other to become more competent communicators. The first portion of this chapter describes three phenomena (uncertainty reduction, communication apprehension, and immediacy) that are important to understanding interpersonal communication.

Next we defined the ten most common communication skills linked with effective or competent interpersonal communication. These ten skills are self-disclosure, empathy, social relaxation, assertiveness, interaction management, altercentrism, expressiveness, supportiveness, immediacy, and environmental control. Each skill plays an important role in helping us to become better communicators in the workplace. These skills will also aid in the development and maintenance of satisfying personal relationships.

Next in the chapter, we illustrated how these competencies have been incorporated into management training. Finally, this chapter presents a number of special employee problems that require interpersonal communication competence: workplace romance, discrimination, the right to know, confidentiality, smoking, and deteriorating performance and discharge. Organizations are interdependent networks, networks that entail a repertoire of interpersonal communication competencies. As Gerald Goldhaber aptly wrote, "Communication networks within an organization can be seen as overlapping one another . . . this means that a change in any one part of the system will affect all other parts of the system."

SKILL BUILDER: MESSAGE CHECK EXERCISE

1. Quickly choose a topic, from the list below, with which you genuinely disagree. If you cannot find one with which you disagree, choose one person to argue pro and one con. Designate one person A, the other B.

   • Women are biologically more emotional than men.
   • Children should be spanked when they severely misbehave.
   • Smoking should not be permitted in public places.
   • To succeed, politicians must be dishonest.
   • Schools should not teach morality.
   • A teacher should never say "I give up on you — I can't work with you anymore."
   • Most doctors are grossly overpaid.
   • When a student cannot do what the teacher wants, it's the teacher's fault.

2. On signal, A asks, "Tell me your opinion."
3. B gives her/his opinion on the topic IN NO MORE THAN ONE SENTENCE.
4. A then paraphrases or reflects B's opinion, to B's satisfaction (that is, B must not say "yes" or in some way agree that A understands B's opinion). Then A gives her/his opinion. (If A does not get B's agreement, A must keep trying until successful. If necessary, A can ask B to repeat what has been said.)
5. A gives his/her opinion, in response to B, in no more than one sentence and B paraphrases or reflects as in step 4. Then A and B repeat steps 3 and 4 until five-minute time limit is up.

You cannot state your own opinion until you have convinced your partner you understand his/her opinion. Here is an example:

A: Tell me your opinion.

B: I think grades stink.

A: They're not useful. (Paraphrase)

B: Right.

A: I disagree because. . .

B: So you like grades. (Paraphrase, ineffectively)

A: No, I just think they're necessary.

B: Well, what you're not considering is. . .

Source: From *Attention: The Fundamentals of Classroom Control*, by Carl Rinne. (1984). Charles E. Merrill Publishing Co., Columbus, OH.

SKILL BUILDER: COMMUNICATION APPREHENSION QUESTIONNAIRE

Directions: This questionnaire is composed of 24 statements concerning your feelings about communication with other people. Please indicate in the space provided the degree to which each statement applies to you by marking whether you (1) strongly agree, (2) agree, (3) are undecided, (4) disagree, or (5) strongly disagree with each statement. There are no right or wrong answers. Many of the statements are similar to other statements; do not be concerned about this. Work quickly; record your first impression.

_____ 1. I dislike participating in group discussions.

_____ 2. Generally, I am comfortable while participating in group discussions.

_____ 3. I am tense and nervous while participating in group discussions.

_____ 4. I like to get involved in group discussions.

_____ 5. Engaging in a group discussion with new people makes me tense and nervous.

_____ 6. I am calm and relaxed while participating in group discussions.

_____ 7. Generally, I am nervous when I have to participate in a meeting.

_____ 8. Usually, I am calm and relaxed while participating in meetings.

_____ 9. I am very calm and relaxed when I am called upon to express an opinion at a meeting.

_____ 10. I am afraid to express myself at meetings.

_____ 11. Communicating at meetings usually makes me uncomfortable.

_____ 12. I am very relaxed when answering questions at a meeting.

_____ 13. While participating in a conversation with a new acquaintance, I feel very nervous.

_____ 14. I have no fear of speaking up in conversations.

_____ 15. Ordinarily I am very tense and nervous in conversations.

_____ 16. Ordinarily I am very calm and relaxed in conversations.

_____ 17. While conversing with a new acquaintance, I feel very relaxed.

_____ 18. I'm afraid to speak up in conversations.

_____ 19. I have no fear of giving a speech.

_____ 20. Certain parts of my body feel very tense and rigid while giving a speech.

_____ 21. I feel relaxed while giving a speech.

_____ 22. My thoughts become confused and jumbled when I am giving a speech.

_____ 23. I face the prospect of giving a speech with confidence.

_____ 24. While giving a speech, I get so nervous that I forget.

Source: From Joseph DeVito. _The Interpersonal Communication Book_ (4th ed.). New York: Harper & Row, 1986, pp. 117–118.

RESOURCES

Barnlund, Dean. (1968). _Interpersonal communication: surveys and studies._ Boston: Houghton Mifflin.

Berger, Charles. (1987). "Communicating under uncertainty." In Michael Roloff and Gerald Miller, _Interpersonal processes: New directions in communication research._ Beverly Hills, CA: Sage Publications, 39–63.

Cavanaugh, Gerald. (1984). _American business values._ Englewood Cliffs, NJ: Prentice-Hall.

Durant, Will. (1927). _The story of philosophy._ New York: Garden City.

Friedman, Milton. (1970). "The social responsibility of business is the increase of profits." _New York Times Magazine,_ Sept. 13, 1970, 122–126.

Giles, H., A. Mulac, J. Bradac, and P. Johnson. (1987). "Speech accommodation theory: The first decade and beyond." In M. L. McLaughlin (ed.) _Communication Yearbook 10_ (pp. 13–48). Beverly Hills, CA: Sage Publications.

Goldhaber, Gerald. (1974). _Organizational communication._ Dubuque, IA: Wm. C. Brown Company.

Gorden, William, and John Miller. (1983). _Managing your communication: In and for the organization._ Prospect Heights, IL: Waveland Press.

Frank B. Hall & Co. v Buck, 678 S. W 2d. 612 (Tex. App. 1984) cert. denied, 105 S. Ct. 2704 (1985).

Huseman, Richard C., and John D. Hatfield. (1989). *Managing the equity factor or "After all I've done for you . . ."* Boston: Houghton Mifflin, p. 7.

Jamison, Kaleel. (1983). "Managing sexual attraction in the workplace." *Personnel Administrator*, 45.

Kant, Immanuel. (1959). *Foundations of the Metaphysics of Morals*. New York: Liberal Arts Press.

Littlejohn, Stephen. (1983). *Theories of human communication*, 2nd ed. Belmont, CA: Wadsworth.

Lorr, Maurice, and William W. More. (1980). "Four Dimensions of Assertiveness." *Multivariate Behavioral Research*, 2, 127–138.

McCroskey, James C., Virginia P. Richmond, and Leonard M. Davis. (1986). "Apprehension about communicating with supervisors: A test of a theoretical relationship between types of communication apprehension." *Western Journal of Speech Communication*, 50, 171–182.

Mehrabian, Albert. (1981). *Silent messages: Implicit communication of emotions and attitudes*. Belmont, CA: Wadsworth.

Roloff, Michael. (1987). "Communication and reciprocity within intimate relationships." In Michael Roloff and Gerald Miller, *Interpersonal processes: New directions in communication research*. Belmont, CA. Wadsworth.

Rubin, Rebecca, and Randi Nevins. (1988). *The road trip: An interpersonal adventure*. Prospect Heights, IL: Waveland Press.

Chapter 4

Management Theory, Ethics, and Voice in the Workplace

Concepts for Discussion _____

- Management theories
- Internal communication
- Upward communication
- Downward communication
- Superior-subordinate communication

- Channels
- Business ethics
- Principled reasoning
- Employee voice
- Motivations for voice
- Making Voice Legitimate

_____

On January 28, 1986, the space shuttle Challenger exploded in midair, sending six astronauts and a schoolteacher to their deaths. A presidential commission attributed the cause of the explosion to a burnthrough of the solid rocket booster joint O-Rings — the same O-Rings that had been subject of controversy within the manufacturing company, Morton Thiokol, years before. The press reported that the engineers at Morton Thiokol were angry because they had vigorously opposed the launching of Challenger, and their warning that the cold-weather conditions could adversely affect the rocket seals went unheeded.

    Vehement arguments that a launch at such cold temperatures would be risky were not heard by the top NASA officials, who later declared that if they had received those objections they would not have given the launch the go-ahead.

Adapted from the Rogers Commission.
Presidential Commission on the Space Shuttle Challenger Accident

This tragic example raises communication and ethical issues crucial to the health and safety of employees and the public who use the products and services of corporate America and the government that regulates them.

In this chapter, those issues will be explicated under the following headings: management theories, internal communication, ethics, principled reasoning, and voice.

LESSONS FROM MANAGEMENT THEORIES

Management theories have been designed to explain how organizations work and can be made to work more effectively. A complete description of them is the subject of entire courses in university business departments, but a brief explanation will help you understand some of the practical issues of the workplace. In particular, we will point out how management theories influence communication within the work setting. The theories we will sketch are classical, human relations, and social-cultural systems.

Classical Theory of Organization

Classical theory of organization refers first to how organizations are organized and second to how they can be scientifically organized for more efficient work. Although many individuals helped form classical theory, two names stand out: Max Weber and Frederick Taylor. Max Weber, a German sociologist, developed the principles of ideal bureaucracy. These principles may be seen in most work settings and to some extent are present in every organization. They are:

1. a hierarchy of authority
2. a system of rules, regulations, and procedures
3. their impersonal application without favoritism
4. division of labor into specialized tasks
5. detailed job descriptions
5. rational, logical behavior

Weber wanted organizations to be orderly and efficient, to run smoothly as a good machine should. Expertise and authority took priority over the many ordinary voices within the workplace.

Frederick Taylor, whose work was conducted in factory settings in the early 1900s, took an engineering approach. He is famous for time and motion studies within steelworks. He is notable for on-the-job experiments that resulted in shoveling more iron ore, loading pig iron faster, and inspecting ball bearings faster. Laborers in one steelyard were cut from 600 to 140 by more efficient management and training. Taylor is famous for saying that some workers with an oxlike mentality could be trained to load pig iron. His work, due to his fanatical distaste for laziness and his concern for detail, has been disparaged. The larger picture of his work has been overlooked.

Taylor wanted to raise wages and his techniques for increasing productivity did so. He encouraged employee suggestions. Certainly, he wanted workers to follow the rules set down, but if these rules were wrong, he was willing to let employees help reform them. At one plant, he told the workers that each one who could suggest a better method to do a job would have his name attached to that method. He encouraged employees to discuss any troubles they had and he was impatient with managers who were aloof and noncommunicative. Information and feedback were important to increasing production and quality of product.

Classical management theory, with its emphasis upon authority and assigning jobs to subordinates, emphasizes downward message-sending. *Telling* is the major mode of communication. Feedback from subordinates, for the most part, is expected to be in terms of compliance with orders.

Human Relations

The central contribution of this theory of organization has been its focus upon the worker as human being. The message of a series of management experiments conducted by Elton Mayo and his colleagues at Western Electric's Hawthorne, Illinois, plant was that employees will work harder if given attention. This lesson, however, comes from a flawed interpretation of what happened in those experiments. The story of Hawthorne is that productivity increased no matter what the "treatment" (whether it was raising or lowering the illumination in the work area, increasing or decreasing work breaks, etc.). The shortsighted message of the Hawthorne studies was "Give employees attention and productivity will increase."

The real message of the Hawthorne studies lies deeper. Three other points have been overlooked. One is that the employees worked better when they were provided with immediate feedback about how well they were producing. Two, employees worked harder when the experimenters and managers involved them in planning the experiments. And three, employees worked less well when they were treated as expendable. During the last half of the experiments, after the Great Depression of 1929, many workers were discharged and collaboration in the productivity experiments was replaced by reassertion of authority. Fear of job loss became the motivation for work.

Chester Barnard, who was president of New Jersey Bell Telephone, in his book *The Functions of the Executive*, continued the human relations line of organizational theory. Workers at every level were not machines who behaved predictably, but individuals with wills. To get cooperation, orders must fall within a *zone of indifference;* that is, orders must be received as not conflicting with individual wants and needs, in order to receive unquestioning compliance. The rewards of pay, job benefits, and a pleasant work environment can enlarge that willingness to comply. The foremost responsibility of the executive is to establish and maintain a system of communication, he asserted.

The human relations movement was popularized by Dale Carnegie's bestselling *How to Win Friends and Influence People* and several million people took his courses that provided formulas for good listening, remembering names, gaining self-confidence, and successful public speaking.

The psychologist Abraham Maslow provided the human relations movement with motivation theory that focused upon individual needs — needs that must not be ignored in the workplace: physiological, safety, social, esteem, and self-actualization. (See Chapter 13 for a more complete explanation.)

Human relations theory emphasizes work's social side. Individuals work within departments and work units. A work unit is a subculture that has norms about promptness, how orders are given, what job competencies are needed, amount of conversation, and industriousness. The importance of informal and horizontal coworker communication is an insight derived from the human relations school. Human relations theory, in spite of its overemphasis on attentive supervision, has had a lasting impact favoring employee involvement schemes.

Social Systems Theory

Social systems theory emphasizes the interlocking interdependent nature of sociotechnical systems. Ideas from the sciences of biology, engineering, physics, and psychology combine to explain work organizations as ecocybernetic-psychological systems. The output of a system is seen as more than the sum of its parts. Something transformational occurs when raw materials, finances, human resources, and knowledge infuse an organization.

Canadian biologist Ludwig von Bertalauffy, in *General Systems Theory,* set forth a series of concepts that explain systems, whether biological or socially constructed human inventions. Systems theory conceives of a set of elements bound together interdependently. Collectively these interdependent interactions create a whole that is greater than any of its parts.

Systems are not isolated from other systems. Even purposely closed systems, such as prisons, are not free from outside systems that interact with those within the walls — the law-enforcement arm of government, the legislative branch that appropriates funds, the educational institutions that may fail to provide the necessary skills and values to prevent young people from turning to crime, and even the employees and services from the outside that provide food, fuel, electricity, and sanitation services for those inside.

General systems theory has caused us to see organizations as communicatively interrelated—not just as two-way, but as networks of interested, interdependent communicators. Negative feedback of one subsystem causes another to adjust its actions to a desired behavior. Positive feedback reinforces deviations, rather than causes correction.

Because of general systems theory, communication in the workplace is best understood as having no clear single source, but rather as many interdependent senders and receivers who by their interactions affect and control the whole. Just as the physical world of bacteria, insects, birds, and predators interacts and is interdependent, so are those of us who are part of humanly constructed systems known as cultures, institutions, and organizations.

INTERNAL WORKPLACE COMMUNICATION

Communication is the one skill that is pervasively needed in all organizations regardless of size, hierarchical structure, and function. Communication is unfortunately sometimes the one skill that is taken for granted. Accurate communication is absolutely essential for successful scheduling and meeting timetables. Inaccurate or inadequate communication causes delays, conflict, and dissatisfaction.

Since work cannot be completed without communication, it can be said that communication is the interactive informational process that links one system to other systems. Remember, as we mentioned before, that the purpose of information giving and receiving is to change uncertainty to greater certainty (Uncertainty Reduction Theory).

According to Gerald Goldhaber, author of the classic text *Organizational Communication*, the flow of messages between and among people within an organization is called communication networks. Typically we view communication networks in the workplace in terms of horizontal or vertical flow of communication. In order for tasks to be completed in the workplace, the organization is dependent upon transmission of information in varied configurations: from subordinate to subordinate, superior to superior, superior to subordinate, and subordinate to superior. In simpler terms, communication is both horizontal (message sent to someone of equal status) and vertical (up to superior and down to subordinate).

Upward Communication

Charles Conrad, author of the text *Strategic Organizational Communication: Cultures, Situations and Adaptation*, states that people tend to avoid communicating, or communicate a very small amount with people whose status is greater than theirs. What do you think are some causes for this apprehension? Conrad also says that the effects of these status differences are more likely to be diminished if subordinates are encouraged to interact with their superiors, and if the roles of superior/subordinate are not strictly defined.

Box 4-1   # When Was the Last Time You Hugged Your Boss?

If the boss does something right, nothing is said about it. After all, that's what the boss gets paid to do. However, let the boss make a mistake and people are quick to notice and comment. . . . When you give someone negative feedback, whether it is your boss or anyone else, you take something from that relationship.

Source: From an idea suggested by Dr. Ken Blanchard, author of *The One Minute Manager*.

Status differences are minimized when superiors are frequently on the shop floor. A GE quality control manager told us it is their plant policy that managers should circulate, talking to every employee at least three times a day. In some workplaces all employees carry the title of associate and, like the Japanese, all wear the same uniforms. The Coors Company follows this practice. What kind of benefits do you think come from a minimization of status differences?

Superiors sometimes communicate the attitude that they are too busy, or that the voices of the people in the "lower" chain of command are less important than their own. Under such leadership, subordinates too often feel upward communication is risky and uncomfortable.

In addition to the *amount* of information transmitted upward, another factor to consider is *accuracy*. Empathize with the subordinates for a moment. What would be some reasons why subordinates might distort the information that they send "up"? One reason could be a lack of trust. Another reason could be the subordinates' fear of damaging their chance for a good performance appraisal or for promotion. And as we stated earlier, if the subordinates feel that a large status difference is emphasized, they will be less likely to communicate in much depth. Bad news tends to be sweetened or obscured in upward messages.

Downward Communication

Downward communication generally is screened and carefully chosen. Superiors vary in their feelings about how much information their subordinates should receive. Most agree that job instructions and procedural data should be provided, but even the depth of communication in these two areas varies among organizations. The authors have been involved in workplaces where orientation and procedural messages were informative, supportive, and a natural part of the company's ritual. We have also worked in places where the philosophy was "learn it on your own" or "you don't need to know." Have you had similar experiences?

Distortion can and does certainly occur downward as well. As discussed in Chapter 2, almost never is the message received exactly the same as it started. Downward communication often is distorted in a similar manner. ECCO analysis is a technique developed by the researcher Keith Davis (referenced in Chapter 2 for his work on "the grapevine") to ascertain the speed and direction of messages that were supposed to be sent to subordinates. Davis found that some messages simply do not get delivered. Others are shortened and yet others are misshaped. Other times, a message is glorified or intensified as it travels down the ladder. This is the fuel of which rumors are made!

SUPERIOR-SUBORDINATE COMMUNICATION

The superior-subordinate unit is the basic unit of organizations. In that unit many issues arise. Foremost and most fundamental is authority and the meaning of subordination. A second issue is superior credibility. A third issue pertains to the selection of communication channels and use of language or nonverbal symbols.

Subordination

Subordination means submission to another. The major differentiation of superior from subordinate is authority. In an organization, what is called the Scalar Principle means that from the top to the bottom there is an unbroken chain of command of authority and responsibility. Delegation of power down that chain of command means the right to give orders. Hierarchical scalar authority is the basis for organizational control. Failure to acknowledge the authority of one's superior threatens the whole organizational structure.

Backtalk is taboo. If a subordinate does not like an order, the basic rule of thumb is to follow it and object later. The principle here again adheres to military reasoning. That is, when in battle there is no time for debating or arguing about orders, and when not in battle one follows orders without argument because one is learning the discipline necessary for battle conditions. Where unions have negotiated rules of discharge, the usual agreement is that an employee should follow orders and seek grievance later. Management thus is assured of uninterrupted work flow and labor has won the right to review and arbitration of management's authority—a trade-off to the advantage of both parties.

Management has fought to have the ultimate weapon—to discharge for any reason or without giving a reason. This prerogative is known as the "**at-will doctrine.**" The typical rule states: The refusal to perform or to comply with written or verbal instructions of one's superior or other members of management is cause for discharge. Some handbooks have similar rules for acts of theft, violence, or abusive language.

Are there exceptions to the obey now—grieve later principle? Let's

Box 4-2 **How to Manage the Boss**

Few managers seem to realize how important it is to manage the boss, or worse, believe that it can be done at all. Here are a few do's and don'ts to help "manage your boss" more effectively.

DO'S

The first Do is to go to the boss — at least once a year — and ask, "What do I do and what do my people do that helps you do your job? And what do we do that hampers you and makes life more difficult for you?" This helps you to determine what the boss needs and what gets in the boss's way.

Since each boss is unique, managing the boss also requires thinking through such questions as: Does this individual who is my boss want me to come in once every month — but no more often — and spend 30 minutes presenting the performance, the plans, and the problems of my department? Or does this individual want me to come in every time there is anything to report or to discuss, every time there is the slightest change, every time we make a move? . . .

Another DO is to make sure the boss understands what can be expected of you. The boss must understand what you are up to, must know what to expect and what not to expect. Bosses, after all, are held responsible by their own bosses for the performance of their subordinates.

DON'TS

Be careful not to expose the boss to surprises. Surprises could lead to humiliation. To some degree, bosses need to be protected against surprises. Otherwise they will not trust employees, and with good reason.

It is important that managers accept that managing the boss is the responsibility of the subordinate manager and a key — maybe the most important one — to his or her own effectiveness as an executive.

Source: Adapted from Peter F. Drucker, "How to Manage the Boss," *The Wall Street Journal*, August 1, 1986, p. 1.

consider one example as it actually happened. A contractor for a swimming pool asked an employee to cut back some limbs that were very close to hot electric wires. The employee's usual job had been to excavate ground for pools. He hesitated and told his boss he was afraid to get near the hot wires. The contractor said, "Do it anyway." The employee refused and was fired. Several days later the employee, needing work, returned, apologized, and was rehired.

WE MEAN BUSINESS

In the case above, what could the employee have done?

The only exceptions to obey now – grieve later are when obedience of orders entails *unusually* hazardous, *substantially* injurious, or *abnormally* dangerous activity outside the job description. Some work is usually dangerous, such as mining or building skyscrapers, and such work is part of the job description. But government oversight provides some protection; for example, requiring that workers be informed about dangerous chemicals in the work environment. Such principles or right to know laws, however, provided no protection to our swimming pool excavator who disobeyed orders to trim branches near hot wires. Nor did he have any recourse, because he was not a member of a union. His only alternatives were to persuade his boss that it was a job for the power company, to quit, or to do it anyway. Since this young employee was a high school dropout and could not easily find other work as well-paying as with the pool contractor, he apologized and submitted to following orders, even dangerous orders.

It is not always true that being submissive to requests is the best approach. However, it is important to distinguish between *argument* and *verbal abuse*. Ironically, when argument is encouraged, verbal abuse is less necessary. Why? Argument focuses on supporting and defending ideas. Verbal abuse focuses on damaging another's self-worth. When we meet on the playing field or in a work area, an argument about ideas accords a measure of respect to all parties.

A rare few companies have realized the value of argument. Dana Corporation, for example, encourages employees to "ask dumb questions" and to "talk back to the boss." Such mottoes put one's mind in gear. One cannot easily engage the tongue in argument without engaging the mind and also the emotions. Involved employees are more likely to become committed employees.

Credibility

Respect of superior for subordinate and of subordinate for superior cannot be ordered. It must be earned. How? By being responsible, competent, trustworthy, considerate, and showing concern for the other's welfare. Aristotle defined *ethos* as perceived goodwill, good sense, and good character (see Chapter 11). Both superiors and subordinates need these qualities.

Today's managers need all the help they can get. They seek the direct involvement of subordinates in cutting waste, devising more efficient work sequences, monitoring quality, improving work conditions, and meeting customer desires. Superiors know that effective management minimizes ordering. Rather than styles of telling subordinates what to do, wise superiors join with subordinates in problem solving.

Subordinates are most influential when they praise what is good before they criticize what they dislike. But this does not mean they never voice any displeasure or seek changes. The key is timing and quality of criticism. Constant complainers are rated by superiors as low performers and troublemakers. Subordinates who propose solutions to work problems are rated as **high performers**.

Effective employee voice contains both substance and emotional support. Goodwill is expressed by words and nonverbal demeanor that are friendly, attentive, animated, and energetic. Substance is expressed by a careful observation and detailing of the facts of a situation and systematic reasoning.

Channels

The workplace provides many **channels** for communication. The strategic choice of those channels involves consideration of access, costs, motivation, and interpersonal sensitivity. The channels for workplace communication available to superiors, and to a lesser degree to subordinates, are face-to-face, written (memos, reports, and directives), telephone, and mediated (computer, bulletin boards, house organs and newsletters, video, and facsimilies). Guidelines for channel choice are governed by company policies, practices, and rhetorical good sense.

Employees are wise to learn the policies and practices of their workplace. They must learn if face-to-face communication is sufficient for giving instructions, conveying corporate policy, administering discipline, taking messages, etc. Several rhetorical principles may aid one's choice of channels.

First, consider clarity. Where clarity is especially important, keep messages simple, use repetition and more than one channel (oral plus written), and encourage feedback. Second, where time is essential and distance is a problem, use the telephone if feedback is important. If not, fax will provide a written record. If the message is important, use both phone and a written follow-up.

Third, where personalness is important, use face-to-face contact and/or handwritten notes. Fourth, where discipline is involved, use an oral message in a private setting. Question for clarification before making declarative statements. Follow a progressive discipline schedule in keeping with company policies. Usually serious and repeated offenses will call for written recordkeeping.

Fifth, where special motivation is involved, use personal and exceptional channels such as written notes, personal presentation of awards, and public recognition for exceptional performance. Some employees have never received a formal personal letter, typed on corporate stationery. Formality, when coupled with personalness, enhances recognition.

Sixth, where forewarning is important, trial balloons may be floated by mentioning ideas to subordinates or by general alerting devices, such as "take note," "attention," and numerical signposts — first, second, third — as is done in this list.

Seventh, do not neglect accentuating devices when attention is desired. These include color, size of message, separation by space, underlining, pictures, and unusual wording. For example, some production lines use red, green, and amber signals to alert workers to production problems and success. Many plants post days free from on-the-job accidents, perfect attendance, and product defects. One GE plant has cartoons descriptive of projects on which different quality circles are working.

Eighth, availability and access matter. Superiors should circulate frequently to learn what is happening and to help subordinates obtain the information needed to do their jobs.

Downward communication is more accurate and timely when it is:

- frequent.
- repeated, repeated, repeated.
- accentuated by saying "This is important," "Don't overlook . . . ," "Attention . . . ," and when numbered as First, Second, Third. . . .
- colorful in language and printed signs.
- in both oral and written channels.
- more personal than impersonal.

BUSINESS ETHICS

Ethics in the work setting rests upon what is valued. By ethics, we mean such topics as how power is used, tolerance for criticism and deviation, bribery and coercion, deception and honesty, conflict of interest, overpricing, causing harm, accountability for one's actions and what one says, and even one's silence. In the first chapter, we stressed that quality of product and service was rooted in how people treat people. We said that to make or sell inferior goods or give poor service diminishes both the consumer and the producer's self-worth. The workplace harms itself and those in it when it is inattentive to morality, self-actualization, and democratic rights. In this section we bring these ethical guidelines into focus upon two aspects that are essential to a healthy working environment: trust and responsibility.

Trust

Without trust, control within the workplace is prisonlike. Workers are screened coming in to determine if they have brought onto the property anything that might harm the product. Upon exit, they also are screened and frisked to learn if they have stolen anything. Think of how wary you would be if someone in your family or a roommate had shoplifted. You would always wonder if your pocketbook is safe, even in your own residence. Distrusting is a miserable existence. Wondering if a salesman is lying to us or if our boss is shading the truth is not the way it should be. Truthful communication is fundamental to trust in the work setting.

Responsibility

What does it mean to be responsible? At the very least it means to own what we do and say. Think for a moment about its opposite. To disown or distance myself from what I am doing and saying creates a false picture of what is going on. I don't really take the blame or credit for my action and speech. Several tactics are used by the irresponsible. One is to disclaim responsibility. Those who operated the death camps blamed it on just following Hitler's orders.

Another escape from responsibility is to claim the authority of position: "Do it because I say so" is one of the least satisfactory reasons for insisting upon an action. It is more authentic to say, "Do it because I want you to do it." That is taking ownership for a message. Yet another escape from responsibility is to ask others to do something because of rules. Rules do not consider one's own or others' personal situation.

To behave responsibly is to be aware and thoughtful about one's communication and acts. This means being sensitive to one's own feelings. Behaving responsibly means reflecting upon the implications of one's speech and actions. To behave responsibly is to be professionally and politically accountable. In the work setting, this means paying one's dues to professional organizations and union if there is one or working against one if you are opposed to one. In the society it means paying one's taxes or working to get the tax laws changed.

Responsibility in the workplace, in short, means being accountable for one's actions. It means working to right wrongs, to speak up about misused power, and to strive toward systems that protect employees from harm on the one hand and make the work environment a happy fulfilling place on the other.

The work ethic is not simply working harder. It is not simply behaving honestly. It is being real rather than phony, being trustworthy rather than careless, and being responsible rather than disowning what we say and do.

RUNNING THE BASES OF PRINCIPLED DECISIONS

Answering the question "What is right?" depends upon one's stage of moral development. The lowest stage of development is childlike self-interest. Good or bad and right or wrong are decided in light of imminent pleasant or painful consequences administered by those with the power to make the rules. As time passes, children develop appreciation for the wishes of those who are instrumental in satisfying their needs. Consequently, they try to please and begin to follow the rules of the rulemakers. Socialization leads the young to desire to live up to the expectations of their families, peers, and country. Loyalty develops to these social units and to their norms. Right behavior at this stage grows out of affection for family and/or friends, and then is enlarged to obedience to the laws of the land out of affection for one's country.

The adult stage of moral development moves beyond rule following based upon reward or punishment or norm adherence springing from affection and loyalty. Mature moral development entails a reasoned effort to see a situation in the light of another's perspective. It is a time of searching for principles that enable respect for human dignity, building community, and protecting the environment.

We run the bases first by playing by the rules of those in authority who have made them. As we mature, we play by the rules out of affection for those who have decided the bases of right and wrong. Yet later, we evaluate the rules. We applaud those rules that make the game fair and fun for all the players. And we work to change those rules and circumstances that make the game unfair and frustrating.

In sum we do what is right based upon authority, loyalty, and our weighing of good and bad. The more weighing we do, the more we are making decisions based upon principled reasoning. Ideally that reasoning is logical, consistent, accurate, and responsible. Self-interest is ever present but mature moral development identifies with the interests of society.

What then are the bases of principled reasoning? Three standards are fundamental to principled reasoning: social costs-benefits, justice, and rights. None of us can reach the "home plate" of high-quality decisions until we touch these three bases.

Social Costs

Something is right to the extent that it diminishes social costs and increases social benefits. Social costs-benefits analysis endeavors to weigh the desirable goods for a society (health care, knowledge, and happiness) against its evils (suffering, ignorance, and unhappiness). One asks, "What will produce the greatest good for the greatest number?" Mature principled reasoning reaches beyond self-interest to consideration of communities, regions, and the interdependent peoples. Calculation of social costs and benefits is no simple matter. In short, to get to first base is to seek the most good for the greatest number.

Justice

The second base of principled reasoning examines such factors as need, effort, and fairness. Need is determined by what one confronts when entering the game of life. Some are born into the lifestyle of the rich and famous. Some are blessed with health and good looks. Some are endowed with physical and mental talents. Others are not. Effort is the cost we ask for reward. Those unable or unmotivated to put forth sufficient effort, according to the principle of justice, do not deserve as much as those who do. The component of justice that is fairness, however, does not permit us to decide who should be rewarded or punished upon the criterion of effort alone without taking into consideration the situation. The component of fairness dictates that those born disadvantaged due to physical, economic, or social causes do not have an even chance against those born without disadvantages. The handicapped must be allowed some way to catch up to make the game fair. In golf we allow a handicap. In horse racing we level a handicap. That is the only way to equalize the contest.

Rights

The United Nations shortly after its founding adopted a universal Declaration of Human Rights. That declaration asserted that all human beings should have the right to work; to free choice of employment; to just and favorable conditions of work; to protection against unemployment; to just and favorable remuneration for one's work, and to provide one's family an existence worthy of human dignity; to form and join a union; and to rest and leisure, including reasonable limitation of working hours and periodic holidays with pay.

These are explicit rights. They were a long time in coming to their adoption as a universal standard. They spring from revulsion toward our inhumane history, from long periods of suffering and slavery, from poverty and exploitation. The belief that humans have rights is rooted in the best doctrines of all the great religions and philosophers. Rights are a third base that must be touched if we are to make decisions that flow from principled reasoning.

Running the bases of principled decision-making, like playing any game, gets easier when it becomes a matter of habit. The habit is one of choosing to run the bases of principled decision-making. This means a habit of searching for sufficient data to weigh the social costs and benefits, a habit of carefully evaluating what is just, a habit of preferring the public interest over one's personal interest, and a habit of dialogue and respect for dissent. Good decisions and right decisions are not made in isolation. They hinge upon ethical communication.

Ethical communication rests upon the assumption that decisions that will benefit the most people are possible only when communication is open and uncensored. John Milton in the seventeenth century published the *Areopagitica* in which three fundamental reasons were given for uncensored expression:

- a censored idea may by true and accepted opinion may be in error,
- even truth needs to be tested, and
- there is likely some truth in all opinions.

We are ethical communicators when we are careful to speak the truth and when we are open-minded enough to consider others' opinions. We are ethical communicators when we are careful to weigh the consequences of what we say on the side of the greater good for the society and the environment over self-interest. We are ethical communicators when we strive to improve the quality of products and services and to present honestly their benefits and disadvantages.

Quality in every corporate enterprise must stand the test of principled reason.

RANGE OF EMPLOYEE VOICE

Dissatisfied employees have four alternatives:

1. to keep their mouths shut and remain loyal workers.
2. to neglect their jobs, reduce their efforts, be careless about their performance, be late or absent, be obstructive, and to sabotage and steal from their companies.
3. to exit and possibly in so doing cause their employer to change the dissatisfying behavior.
4. to speak up, to make constructive suggestions, discuss problems with one's superiors; or to bypass immediate superiors to take their concerns higher, to go outside to blow the whistle on wrongdoing, and/or to take one's complaints to union grievance, arbitration, and strikes.

The four alternatives follow the way customers may influence those who manufacture inferior products: loyally continue to purchase those inferior products and there will be no improvement; neglect them by being irregular in buying them; exit by not buying them and turn to other products; or to voice dissatisfactions to those who make and market them. If the manufacturer and marketer listen, accept the criticism, and correct the problems, the dissatisfied customers once again will become loyal.

Employees have a range of communication options for every day of their working careers. These options may be a combination of active or passive, and constructive or destructive. Researchers have found that in work settings in which opportunities for employees to speak up were plentiful, there was less turnover, greater job satisfaction, and more employee commitment. Conversely, in work organizations that had fewer mechanisms for employee suggestions and for registering complaints, there was more absenteeism. In places with a reputation for retaliation for those who were open about their dissatisfaction, employees were reluctant to voice criticism.

Employees whose channels for voicing their concerns are blocked within their work settings will turn elsewhere: They may psychologically withdraw; they may badmouth the company or their coworkers. They may antagonistically fight the company by legitimate means such as a union. Sometimes alienated employees resort to an illegitimate means such as stealing equipment or embezzlement; some go insane, wildly shooting their coworkers. As

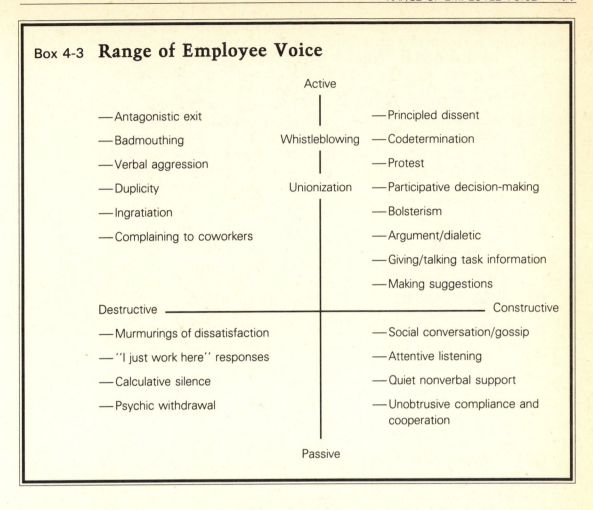

Box 4-3 **Range of Employee Voice**

Active

Whistleblowing

Unionization

Passive

Destructive ———————————————— Constructive

—Antagonistic exit

—Badmouthing

—Verbal aggression

—Duplicity

—Ingratiation

—Complaining to coworkers

—Principled dissent

—Codetermination

—Protest

—Participative decision-making

—Bolsterism

—Argument/dialetic

—Giving/talking task information

—Making suggestions

—Murmurings of dissatisfaction

—"I just work here" responses

—Calculative silence

—Psychic withdrawal

—Social conversation/gossip

—Attentive listening

—Quiet nonverbal support

—Unobtrusive compliance and cooperation

grisly as that may sound, disgruntled employees on too many occasions do go berserk.

WE MEAN BUSINESS

Have you witnessed or experienced any of the above? Describe.

How superiors and subordinates "see" each other matters when it comes to getting the job done. Unless there is mutual affection and respect, the workplace is not a pleasant or a productive place. Subordinates implicitly evaluate their superiors on their competence, support, ability to influence upper management, personableness, and communication skills.

Superiors are required to do performance appraisals of their subordinates. They are trained to be specific rather than general, to collect examples and instances to support the appraisals they place into a subordinate's file. Subordinates are rated on such dimensions as interpersonal skills, knowledge of product, planning, taking direction, knowledge of applications, working with the company, and job completion.

In a study conducted by William Gorden, Dominic Infante, and John Izzo, one group of superiors was interviewed to learn why they rated specific employees as satisfactory. Another set of superiors was each asked to do the same for a subordinate with whom they were dissatisfied, and a third group was interviewed about a subordinate each had rated undecided.

These superiors were asked if and how these specific subordinates voiced disagreement. Those with satisfactory ratings were described as disagreeing constructively and being high in argumentativeness and low in verbal aggression. Their disagreements were expressed at appropriate times and places and interpreted as meant to improve the workplace. Contrarily, subordinates rated dissatisfactorily were often described as apathetic or complaining, as constantly voicing disagreements, as complaining to the wrong people, and in some cases as telling lies. Dissatisfactorily rated subordinates also were low in argumentativeness and high in verbal aggressiveness. This means they disputed less about issues and they attacked others' self-esteem. These findings explain many of the whys of good and bad performance ratings.

Other studies pertaining to subordinate-superior communication by Gorden and Infante lend support to the proposition that when superiors encourage subordinate input and debate about issues in the workplace, verbal abuse is lessened.

It is important to understand the difference between definitions of argumentativeness and verbal aggression:

Argumentativeness — asserting reasons for and/or against policies or practices.

Verbal Aggressiveness — attacking others' competence, motives, and character by sarcasm, innuendo, or insults; denigrating others' self-worth.

Constructive voice, as we have learned in the course of this chapter, is the language with which cooperative work relationships are organized. Constructive voice, as we described above, entails constructive critical voice. Constructive voice is most effective when it is expressed in a friendly, relaxed, and attentive style of communication. That makes cooperation happen.

MOTIVATIONS FOR VOICE

Voice is not simply the tool of organization; it is morally, psychologically, and politically necessary. Employees should voice their ideas because they are human and voice is very much an expression of their nature.

Moral

...ncouraged to voice ideas related to work, you may very well ...ged from your labor. Employers that value only the products and ...voice of those who produce them want slaves or robots rather than ...man employees.

Self-Actualization

Voice is psychologically the path to self-achievement, self-respect, and self-actualization. Sometimes voice is submissive and compliant. Behaving cooperatively promotes harmony and that is self-actualizing. Other times voice is assertive and ego-expansive. Employees' communicative activity should be viewed as motivated by their overarching drive to self-actualize, to be all that they can be, or at least to achieve a sense of self-worth. Another way to describe the self-actualizing motivation for voice in the workplace is to suggest that assertive voice enhances ego and submissive-harmonious voice enhances "Wego."

Democratic Rights

Voice also is an especially natural expectation for employees who work in a democratic society such as ours. They expect the constitutional guarantees of freedom of speech to be contractually theirs because they are citizens. They do not think that it is right to leave their First Amendment rights at the company gate.

WE MEAN BUSINESS

Have you heard or read about any examples of denial to or voicing of employee rights?

MAKING VOICE LEGITIMATE

In simple language, by making voice legitimate we mean corporate openness to employee communication. In this section, therefore, conditions for corporate openness will be discussed. Also, conditions will be described that lead to whistleblowing, and other conditions that make such acts unnecessary.

Critical Involvement

Wanting to improve the job, products/services, and to make the work organization successful and worthy of trust is an employee attitude devoutly desired by corporate management. Most people want to do their jobs well

Box 4-4 ## Critical Involvement Scale

On the following scale respond to each item:

Strongly Disagree	Disagree	Undecided	Agree	Strongly Agree

—I prefer to do my job the way I am told and not try to alter it in any way, even to improve it.*

—I am inclined to voice my opinion if I feel decisions concerning my job are wrong.

—I am inclined to urge my superior to use my ideas for improving the department.

—I am inclined not to question the way this organization is run even if I feel it could be run better.*

Source: These items are taken from a 12-item scale developed by William T. Coombs, in "A conceptualization and exploratory analysis of critical involvement," unpublished master's thesis, Purdue University, Lafayette, IN, 1985.

*Reverse scoring

and to find ways to do what they do better. That attitude and behavior represented in efforts to improve and alter one's job conditions constitutes critical involvement. This usually entails discussing changes with one's superior(s). Employees who are "critically involved" are more satisfied with their jobs and committed to their organizations.

Training

Attitudes that prompt one to do a job better are influenced by job orientation and training. Training that is formal and group-centered tends to produce a role-taking more than a role-making attitude. A more individualistic job orientation, such as learning the job without formal group training, leads to more individualism and sometimes innovation rather than custodial-mindedness.

Employee Rights

Security guards ordered ten employees in the plane landing area, in full view of other employees and passengers, down a guard-lined path to waiting vans. They were taken to a hospital and told to either take a urine test or be fired. The ten tested negative and filed a suit for defamation and invasion of privacy. This illustrates just one of many employee rights issues.

Many employee rights spring from moral and practical reasoning rather than from a legal basis. These include equitable treatment; the right to accurate and timely information and response to questions; freedom to perform one's own job without undue meddling from superiors; the right to reciprocal commitment from superiors to match employees' loyalty; the right to due process; the right to be involved in decision-making that affects employment; and the right to continued employment. These rights are not guaranteed by many employers or by government legislation in this country. Many of these rights have been won by legislation of worklife policies in Scandinavian countries. Such rights as job security are culturally expected in highly unionized industrial European countries and in Japan for the core of its workers. However, in this land of freedom there is growing concern for employee welfare and rights.

When employees believe that their companies attend to employee rights they are more satisfied and committed employees. Some corporations have attended to employee rights much more than others. IBM has been especially progressive in personnel policies protective of employee information and confidentiality of records.

Whistleblowing

Let's first examine some classic situations in which whistleblowers suffered great emotional stress and economic loss because of their efforts to make their employers acknowledge error.

Civilian cost analyst Ernest Fitzgerald blew the whistle on Air Force cost overruns. Because of that, he was fired from his Defense Department job in 1969. After a four-year legal battle that cost him $60,000 in attorney fees (plus $1 million of free legal work), the Pentagon was forced to rehire him, but did so by placing him in a lower-paying, less prestigious job. It was not until 1982 that he was finally reinstated in his original job. He then became a self-appointed in-house ombudsman and he took up cases of others who preferred to leak accounts of wrongdoing rather than risk publicly announcing them. Fitzgerald, in light of his long struggle to be vindicated, understands such hesitancy. He remarked, "No one except the very naive, the masochistic, the slightly deranged, or perhaps the independently wealthy would want to be a whistleblower."

National Aeronautics and Space Administration engineer Bill Bush throughout the 1960s and 1970s received high performance ratings that won him merit pay. Then he learned that he and other older engineers were assigned meaningless jobs and were excluded from promotions. After he filed a grievance with the Civil Service Commission, he was ostracized. Like Fitzgerald, he too has become a supporter of others; and warns those deciding whether to blow the whistle, "understand that you are getting into something that could blast your life. Make sure it's over something worthwhile. Once you've offended the bureaucracy, its not like offending God, who forgives — they'll never forget."

These two examples are included to make it clear that whistleblowing is not a lark or glamorous. Billie Garde was a 26-year-old personnel recruiter for John Hudson in the Muskogee, Oklahoma, office of the U.S. Census Bureau. When she would not sleep with her boss and fix civil service exams at Hudson's request, she became the victim of retaliation and was fired. Eventually the Equal Employment Opportunity Commission in Washington resolved her case, and after a lengthy investigation, Hudson was sentenced to a year in jail.

Far more whistleblowers never get their jobs back and are wrongfully dismissed. David Ewing, who wrote *If You Don't Like It, You're Fired*, estimated that as many as 500,000 people unjustly lose their job this way each year. Richard Hudson (no relation to John Hudson in the above example), a leader of the 1700 Black Workers Alliance at IBM, is one such casualty. His firing — and a legal decision that upheld it — resulted from his distribution of a pay guidelines chart disclosing salaries to the Black Workers Alliance that had been sent to him anonymously. The chart alleged discrimination. IBM charged that he had distributed secret information.

Another example is that of Ray Camps, a Ford safety test engineer who tried for several years to convince management that the Pinto was a bomb on wheels that would explode on impact. He eventually went to the public, but lost his job. Later as a result of wrongful death suits, Ford had to pay millions to the families of individuals who met fiery deaths in several Pinto crashes.

There are many less dramatic cases, such as the Beech-Nut Corporation. The director of research at Beech-Nut sent senior management a memo outlining his suspicion that a supplier was selling ersatz juice as real 100 percent apple juice. His performance ratings then were lowered to "naiveté" and the company's director of operations referred to him as "Chicken Little."

Unethical business practices are not always exposed, but when they are, they are costly. A number of companies have paid a higher price in loss of good reputation than they would have had they corrected rather than concealed wrongdoing. Johns Manville covered up asbestosis and suffered bankruptcy. A. H. Robins was found guilty of deception regarding the Dalkon Shield interuterine device, and paid millions in reparations. Insider trading scandals led to the bankruptcy of Drexel Burnham Lambert. Allegations of bribery, bid rigging, and trafficking in sensitive Pentagon documents have cast a dark shadow upon major defense contractors. The government's Office of Management and Budget, which collates allegations of unethical conduct received by 18 federal agencies, in one six-month period received 12,500 such allegations in the mid-1980s.

Legislation has helped make employee voice legitimate. Several states — California, Connecticut, Maine, Michigan, and New York among them — have passed statutes making reprisal illegal for employees who reported wrongdoing. Courts in half the states have restricted employers' traditional rights to hire and fire at will, ruling that employees cannot be discharged for refusing to violate state laws or revealing violation of those laws.

In 1860 Congress enacted the False Claims Act. The law originally was aimed at crooked Civil War gunpowder suppliers, and allowed workers to sue their companies in the name of the government. The doctrine of that law is known as "qui tam," a Latin phrase for someone who sues for the king as well as for oneself. Some 126 years later Congress added more teeth to that law, allowing whistleblowers to collect up to 30 percent of any proceeds from successful claims. Retaliation against employees who blow the whistle is barred. In 1989 Congress passed and President Bush signed a law intended to protect federal employees who report wrongdoing from unjust discharge and providing up to $250,000 in rewards for whistleblowers against federal contractors. The Justice Department has joined employees in a number of such suits. One of the biggest cases ever brought under the updated False Claims Act is against the Northrop Corporation. Some six employees (five who are no longer with the company) alleged that Northrop overcharged the Pentagon $20 billion in building the B-2 Stealth bomber.

Sissela Bok, in her splendid book *Secrets: On the Ethics of Concealment and Revelation*, suggests that blowing the whistle entails an ethical obligation to consider the seriousness of the wrongdoing. Blowing the whistle breaches the loyalty pledged to one's employer. It points the finger in accusation. Therefore it must not be done before careful investigation, weighing alternatives, and soul-searching about its potential good and possible harm. She said Daniel Ellsberg, in deciding to make public the Pentagon Papers that revealed the government's deceit and manipulation, had to weigh how such revelations would influence the nation's Southeast Asia policies.

Principled reasoning motivates those steps that may progressively lead to blowing the whistle — weighing social costs, what is just, and what is right. First, one must discern if a policy or practice is indeed illegal or can result in imminent and/or long-lasting harm. Dumping drums of radioactive waste or scuttling a radioactive ship off the California coast may not result in immediate damage but will eventually cause long-lasting harm. Second, one must make sure of the facts, because an accusation can do real harm. Third, one ought to seek remedy through existing channels to demonstrate one's loyalty, and only then go public.

Union Voice

Unions are an organized form of employee voice. The 1935 National Labor Relations Act guaranteed labor the right to organize and to bargain. During the late 1800s and the first third of the 1900s, labor received little government support. Its efforts to organize were met with intimidation, dismissal, and violence. Sometimes union themselves employed violence, intimidating plant managers and even their own members who questioned the tactics of union leadership. No small number of unions, through the years, have been found to misuse funds and to be more concerned about the benefits of their officers than their membership. Unions that have become corrupt have become so because their members have allowed those in charge to make the rules and count the votes.

Unions generally are perceived by management as antagonists that threaten work stoppages to get their own way for exorbitant demands. All too rarely are independent unions perceived as working toward the same goals as does management.

During the 1960s and 1970s, U.S. market share and world dominance began a downward slide. This was first realized in such industries as electronics; then steel and shipbuilding; and, in the 1980s, in a wide range of manufacturing, such as automaking, and even in financial institutions. Many U.S. consumers found greater quality in foreign products and that led to a trade imbalance.

Corporate America was forced into a reexamination. What could the United States do to become more competitive? Unprofitable plants were closed. During the 1980s, 42 million workers were handed pink slips. Many of those who found other jobs were forced to take 25 to 50 percent cuts in salary. Despite union objections much work was contracted abroad, and outsourcing became an issue in union negotiations. Unions lost much of their power. Between the late 1950s and the late 1980s, union coverage dropped from 35 percent to represent only about 16 percent of the workforce. And the percentage of the overall workforce that is not union is growing more rapidly than the workforce in general.

At the same time that some industries were shutting down and downsizing, management schemes were being devised to improve employee commitment to quality. Under these conditions, efforts to institute worker teams committed to cutting costs and improving quality have shown less than a genuine concern for employee welfare. General Motors at one point "blew" its effort between union and management to institute quality circles because at the same time wages for unions were being reduced, management was conferring big bonuses on itself.

A history of adversarial strife, of conflict and mistrust, was what brought about government regulations. Now the challenge of plant managers and union leaders is to acknowledge the competing interests of management and labor and to explore creative ways to work together for their common good.

For a quality of worklife program to be successful, information must be shared concerning the company's operation and financial condition. Under the National Labor Relations Act exclusivity doctrine, there is a very limited duty to exchange such information (Section 9a). In reality, management often seeks to paint a very conservative, sometimes pessimistic picture of company finances, while unions, because they have an incomplete picture, overestimate the company's ability to afford pay increases. Experience has shown that employees are more likely to cooperate with cost-cutting measures and worker productivity programs when they have access to relevant information concerning the company's operation and condition.

Corporate Encouragement of Employee Involvement

Government can do much to make employees feel safe to constructively criticize the workplace, but the place where it must happen is in the trenches, on the shop floor, in the offices, at the work stations, and in staff meetings.

Most companies, with both organized and unorganized workforces, have some form of employee involvement and quality of worklife programs. Some companies have set up hotlines for anonymous reports of wrongdoing such as dumping hazardous wastes. General Dynamics, a big defense contractor, logged over 3000 such calls in one year.

WE MEAN BUSINESS

You may want to find out whether employee involvement is part of the culture in the place where you wish to be employed. How can you find out?

Managers want bad news to be sent upward so there are no unwelcome surprises. They have learned the lessons of Johns Manville and Morton Thiokol. They know that if they fire someone who blows the whistle, that can cost them in fines, disastrous publicity, and loss of public goodwill.

Dozens of companies, *Fortune* magazine reported, have set up "ombudsman systems" in which a senior executive operating outside the normal chain of command is permanently available at the end of a hotline to deal with employee grievances on a confidential basis. IBM guarantees the right of any employee to appeal a supervisor's decision without fear of reprisal. Other companies with ombudsmen are Bell Labs, McDonald's, Martin Marietta, General Electric, and McDonnell Douglas. Most complaints tend to be cases of conflicts with supervisors, claims of discrimination, and misunderstandings over benefits or promotions. Some complaints are found to be false alarms, but under an ombudsman system waste, fraud, and abuse have an early warning system.

Major companies are on the partnership train. Worker participation plans are currently in place at AT&T with the Communication Workers of America and the International Brotherhood of Electrical Workers; at Xerox with the Amalgamated Clothing and Textile Workers; and in several steel companies with the United Steel Workers. The concept of collective voice is not dead.

Workplace Codetermination and Profit Sharing

Employee councils for workers in both union and nonunion settings, likely will not become the rule until government legislates workplace democracy as have some European and Scandinavian countries. Such legislation empowers joint management-labor councils to be formed and to monitor policy and practices pertaining to introduction of new technology and human resource allocation.

Joint management-union efforts to create management-labor councils have been made without federal legislation at Boeing, Xerox, Bell Telephone Operating Companies, and Packard Electric.

Another way that employee voice is made legitimate is by Employee Stock Ownership Plans (ESOPs). Employee ownership often has resulted because a company is in or close to bankruptcy, but it also has become a means for major companies to make it more difficult for unfriendly take-overs. At Polaroid an ESOP was used to resist a hostile bid. At about the same time Procter & Gamble Company boosted its employees' stock ownership to 20 percent.

As well as making takeovers more difficult, significant employee stock ownership should increase worker voice in policy. Avis's 12,700 employees bought their company for $1.75 billion. They have active employee participation groups at local, regional, and national levels. Employee stock ownership plans, if and when they are more than a poison pill against takeovers, should lead to restructuring of the working environment. They should elevate employee voice to a vital level, one directly linked to management and productivity. Whether ESOPs will become a major force in American business, however, probably will not be known for some years to come.

SUMMARY

In this chapter, we have described management theories, ethical issues, and principled reasoning, and the vital role of voice in the work setting. An understanding of management theories enables one to see the interdependence of policymakers and doers. There is a logic to organizing. Classical management has emphasized the need for structure and control. Human relations theory made us sensitive to the social side of the workplace, to working conditions, and to internal as well as external motivations of people. The cultural systems theory stressed the interdependence of all members and parts of an organization; also how traditions and history establish the values of a workplace.

The many ethical issues that employees encounter include whether to speak up about alleged fraud, misuse of information, conflict of interests, sexual harassment, inequities, and discrimination. Principled reasoning entails a social cost-benefit analysis, commitment to justice, and concern for rights.

We presented a model of employee range of voice and suggested that constructive active voice is a combination of affirming and argumentative communication patterns. We presented examples of whistleblowing and retaliation. The responsibility of government to protect employees who report wrongdoing from reprisal was explained as necessary.

Companies can do much to make voice legitimate and consequently can prevent socially irresponsible behavior, fines and penalties, and loss of business due to public ill will and mistrust. Speak-up programs, training to prevent excessive conformity, hotlines, and ombudsmen are steps work organizations can take to make voice legitimate.

Collective voice in unions was made legal under the National Labor Relations Act. But that did not ensure labor-management cooperation; often the opposite was the case. When management and union leadership cultivate a climate of trust, they can help meet each other's mutual concerns without rancor. Where adversarial relationships have been replaced by genuine cooperation efforts, both job satisfaction and productivity increase. Labor-management partnerships, employee stock ownership, and profit sharing appear to be the wave of the near future.

SKILL BUILDER: INVESTIGATING ETHICS AND SATISFACTION IN THE WORKPLACE

1. Satisfaction with Superiors. Interview an employee in a low-level position. Examine that individual's reasons for satisfaction or dissatisfaction with her or his superior. How is or is not communication related to that satisfaction or dissatisfaction?
2. Satisfaction with Subordinates. Interview a superior. Ask that individual to describe the performance of:
   a. a subordinate with whom s/he is satisfied.
   b. a subordinate with whom s/he is dissatisfied.
   c. a subordinate with whom s/he is uncertain. How does the assessment of the superior you interview compare with the study reported in this chapter.
3. Handbooks. Examine two policy handbooks to learn the rules of the workplace pertaining to communication. Especially note mention of how to deal with employee dissatisfaction. What is said about subordinates reporting their concerns about:
   a. waste and inferior quality?
   b. wrongdoing?
   c. incompetence?
   d. sexual harassment?
4. Principled Reasoning. Review several businesses featured in current popular magazines. Using the criteria described in this chapter pertaining to social costs, justice, and rights, construct an ethical profile of each business you have selected for review.

RESOURCES

Bok, Sissela (1982). *Secrets: On the ethics of concealment and revelation.* New York: Pantheon Books.

Bowles, Samuel, and Herbert Gintis. (1986). *Democratic capitalism: Property and the contradictions of modern social thought.* New York: Basic Books.

Conrad, Charles. (1985). *Strategic organizational communication.* New York: Holt, Rinehart and Winston.

Gest, Ted (1989, November 20). "Why whistleblowing is getting louder." *U.S. News & World Report,* 64.

Goldfield, Michael (1987). *The decline of organized labor in the U.S.* Chicago: University of Chicago Press.

Goldhaber, Gerald. (1974). *Organizational communication.* Dubuque, IA: Wm. C. Brown Company.

Gorden, William I. (1988). "Range of employee voice." *Employee Responsibilities and Rights Journal,* 1, 283–299.

Gorden, William I., Dominic Infante, and John Izzo. (1988). "Variations in voice pertaining to the dissatisfaction/satisfaction with subordinates." *Management Communication Quarterly,* 2, pp. 6–22.

Kochan, Thomas, H. Katz, and R. McKensie. (1986). *The transformation of American industrial relations.* New York: Basic Books.

Kohlberg, Lawrence, (1976). "Moral Stages and Moralization: The Cognitive-Developmental Approach." In Thomas Lickona (ed.), *Moral development and behavior: Theory and social issues.* New York: Holt, Rinehart and Winston.

Mill, John Stuart, (1975). *On Liberty.* David Spitz (ed.). New York: Norton.

Roe, Emery M. (1989). "The zone of acceptance in organization theory." *Administration & Society,* 21, 234–264.

Schacter, Hindy L. (1989). "Frederick Winslow Taylor and the idea of worker participation." *Administration & Society,* 21, 20–30.

Stieber, Jack (1984). "Most U.S. workers still may be fired." *Monthly Labor Review,* May, 107.

Wallace, Karl R. (1955). "An ethical basis of communication." *The Speech Teacher 4,* 1–9.

Walton, Ronald (March–April 1985). "From control to commitment in the workplace." *Harvard Business Review.*

Whitsett, David A., and Lyle Yorks. (1983). *From management theory to business sense.* New York: AMACOM.

Chapter 5

Nonverbal Communication in the Workplace

Concepts for Discussion

- Origins and importance of nonverbal communication
- Job interviews and nonverbal communication
- Place speaks
- Kinesics
- Facial expressions
- Eye behavior

- Position and posture
- Gestures
- Physical appearance
- Proxemics
- Haptics
- Paralanguage
- Chronemics

Les Nesman, (from the television show "WKRP in Cincinnati") played a radio announcer who complained about sharing space with a receptionist and a salesman. Les drew an invisible line around his desk and would always pretend to open an invisible door before inviting people into his "office." Such an idea illustrates the need we have to mark our territory.

Judee Burgoon, David Buller, and Gail Woodall
Nonverbal Communication: The Unspoken Dialogue

Nonverbal communication forms "an elaborate and secret code that is written nowhere, known to none, and understood by all."

Edward Sapir

Nonverbal communication involves all uses of our body and voice that communicate a message to receivers. Nonverbal communication exists within every human transaction. The nonverbal part of communication is so powerful that it often overshadows the verbal portion of the message. Ray Birdwhistell, a nonverbal scholar, reported that over 60 percent of our daily communication is nonverbal. This is why the study of nonverbal communication is so vital. We are not saying that by the end of this chapter you will know how to "read" all people, or know all about your nonverbal skills. But we are going to introduce you to the general categories of nonverbal communication and illustrate how these areas relate specifically to the workplace. Our goal is to make you aware of the amount of information that is transmitted nonverbally and to increase your sensitivity in sending and receiving nonverbal cues.

Nonverbal communication is the first source of communication used in infancy. Nonverbals serve an incredible range of functions and speak the truth where words do not. In order to better understand the scope of nonverbal communication and its effect on your personal and professional life, we will first define the origins and reasons for the study of nonverbal communication, then discuss the general categories of nonverbal communication. The categories to be studied include: **kinesics** (motion, action behavior, and physical appearance); **proxemics** (space and territory); **haptics** (touching); **paralanguage** (vocals); and **chronemics** (time).

THE ORIGINS AND IMPORTANCE OF NONVERBAL COMMUNICATION

Perhaps the most comprehensive discussion of nonverbal communication is provided by Judee Burgoon, David Buller, and W. Gill Woodall in their text entitled *Nonverbal Communication: The Unspoken Dialogue*. Within the text, they present the following propositions:

- Every communication act carries with it some nonverbal parts.
- Nonverbals may form a universal language system. There exists at least a minimal level of universal understanding in nonverbal communication. Examples include smiling, crying, and caressing touches, which transcend cultural differences.
- Nonverbals can lead to misunderstanding as well as understanding. If we do try to decode nonverbals with universal meanings, then a danger of misinterpretation exists. We cannot draw generalized conclusions without examining all the cues and their context.

- Nonverbal communication is trusted. Usually people, whether intentionally or not, tend to believe nonverbal cues over verbal cues when there is a contradiction in the message sent.
- Nonverbal communication is packaged. When we convey a message, we do not simply "speak" with isolated parts of our body, or merely with words. If we are excited, for example, we tend to convey this theme with several parts of our body — our eyes, eyebrows, mouth, and hands all blend together to send this message.

The principles above give good reason for the study of nonverbal communication. After this introduction to the study of nonverbals, we will examine specific contexts where nonverbal communication affects our interactions in the workplace.

PLACE SPEAKS

The workplace and its environment convey very loud messages. Some workplaces are pastoral, with buildings aptly situated in green landscaped meadows. Yet others are in massive skyscrapers, such as in the canyons of Wall Street or in the glass-mirrored buildings alongside the Dallas freeways. Just as we look with awe upon the Grand Tetons or the Grand Canyon, we are impressed by size and architectural triumphs. Massiveness, since the times of the pyramids, has spoken loudly of power and served as tangible evidence of stability and permanence. That is why government buildings and banks often are constructed of granite and marble, of columns and lintel, of vaulted arches and domes. Hitler, who liked to call himself the master architect, employed size and mass as a spectacle of power. The Nurenburg rally grounds were the size of 15 football fields. The stone viewing stand was backed by a colonnade of 17 stone pillars 60 feet tall, and illuminated by 1,200 spotlights.

Most corporate headquarters are constructed to be read as "signatures of power and permanence." They need not be beautiful and massive to accomplish the managing that goes on within them anymore than are Gothic cathedrals necessary for individual worship or for carrying on the business of a particular religion. But the architecture of a place helps those who see it and use its structures to feel good about that place.

A workplace has both job functional and symbolic purposes. A work setting that contains attractive furnishings and occupies ample space in safe surroundings is a place to which we assign messages of success and power.

Psychologist Abraham Maslow and another colleague conducted an experiment to study the effects of a beautiful versus an ugly work space. They found that college students placed in a beautiful room as opposed to an ugly one were less fatigued while doing a task and "saw" their task more positively. Our work environment does affect our mood as well as our physical health and safety.

Box 5-1 # Can a Pretty Face Persuade Me?

Questions: Will frankly stating our desire to influence enhance or hinder our effectiveness? And will it help if we are attractive? What if we are not attractive to the audience?

Experiment: Opinions of college students on a number of items were gathered some two months in advance of the experiment. The day of the experiment the professor asked the students to answer a similar questionnaire on such topics as "Every college student should receive a broad education" and "Students should not be forced to take courses to make them well-rounded." But before completing the questionnaire he requested that they briefly think about their answers. He suggested to aid this thinking that someone in the class might read his or her answer aloud. A young woman (a confederate in the experiment) volunteered in one case and, in another, feigning reluctance to read her answer, was chosen by the professor. She was attractively groomed on these two occasions. On two other occasions she was unattractively groomed. Her clothing was ill-fitting, her hair was messy, her skin was oily, and a trace of mustache was etched on her upper lip.

Under each of the four conditions the confederate responded to the question: "How much would you like to influence the views of others on this issue?" In the persuade condition (that is, when she had more effect on others' opinions) her response was "Very much." In the nonpersuade condition, her response was "Not at all."

Results: The results are summarized below:

Measures of Favorability to General Education

Four experimental conditions	N	Pretest	Posttest
1. Attractive—"I want to influence."	24	24.3	41.8
2. Attractive—"I do not want to influence at all."	18	23.8	37.0
3. Unattractive—"I want to influence."	26	23.8	31.8
4. Unattractive—"I do not want to influence at all."	29	23.8	37.8

The data demonstrates that an openly stated desire to influence made by the attractive young woman did affect the male audience. But that when she was "unattractive" and stated her desire to influence, it had no apparent effect. A second experiment's results were similar.

Implications: We must always be cautious in generalizing from test-condition experiments. But it is safe to conclude that we are sometimes influenced by appearances; that we may consciously or unconsciously try to please some attractive person of the opposite sex who admits a desire to influence. Such an experiment should alert us to do our own thinking regardless of appearance, providing we do not want to be the puppet of a pretty face or handsome body. It also suggests that we need not hesitate to state frankly our desire to influence, provided that we do not act dogmatically and conceitedly.

Source: From J. Mills and E. Aronson, "Opinions Change as a Function of the Communicator's Attractiveness and Desire to Influence," *Journal of Personality and Social Psychology*, Vol. 1, No. 2 (1965), pp. 173–177.

How work areas are structured also affects coworker relationships. Physical barriers obviously deter interaction. That is the reason, in addition to status, that employees whose work requires concentration want their work space to be separated from others. On the other hand, reducing barriers and distance between workers who must work as a team facilitates communication. Sometimes employees who are seen as troublesome will be assigned to disagreeable work spaces as far as possible from the boss, and they may want such a distant work site because few people will keep tabs on them.

Barriers and various artifacts have other purposes. They are used to convey messages of authority or attentiveness to an organization's public. Barriers prevent and/or limit access. Bank tellers almost always are situated behind waist-high counters and glassed-in work areas. The greater the obstructions to public contact with a worker, the more control and authority that person has over the public.

Notice the various ways customers are controlled by barriers: rails, arrow-marked pathways, counters, partially open windows, desks, protective reception areas. A work area also may house other symbols of authority, such as the national and corporate flags and seals, diplomas, photographs of officers, uniformed security officers, and prohibitive signs.

Attentiveness to customers is shown by concern for their welfare. Doctors' waiting rooms often have toys for children, magazines for all ages, and restroom facilities. Customers "read" corporate attentiveness when there are information booths, snacks available, and ease of access to do their business.

Corporations are especially attentive to their identity. That is why they pay huge sums to create signs and logos. McDonald's golden arches enable easy recognition. Along our highways, we decide what company to patronize by the signs. When a company changes its colors, as did Sohio from blue and red to British Petroleum's green and yellow, often that is accomplished gradually and with lots of hoopla and major expense.

Corporate logos such as the Prudential rock, Texaco star, and Procter and Gamble's man in the moon with 13 stars come to signify tradition. Prudential since 1896 has modified the rock from realistic to surrealistic art through some 14 changes. The company's leaders appear to have wanted to maintain the value of being known for the rock, while from time to time indicating they were willing to change by redesigning the logo. Texaco, since 1903 when it adopted the Lone Star's symbol as its own, has modified it but slightly, changing its colors and form only three times. Procter and Gamble, a company that dates back to pre–Civil War days, has retained its man-in-the-moon-and-13-stars logo through thick and thin. In the mid-1980s, after a four-year battle to muzzle rumormongers who thought P&G's man in the moon was a satanic symbol, P&G decided to drop the infamous logo. However, after the in-league-with-the-devil talk subsided, the company once again sported its logo on the cover of its annual report.

Traditional rituals and symbols define who we are. They combine the oral and visual senses. Churches have known this truth for centuries and by icons and colors that have been assigned special meanings, religious institutions have instilled their doctrines: white is the liturgical symbol of purity; violet the color of penitence; red of martyrdom and sacrifice; green of hope; black of mourning. Nations, too, create and give significance to colors, emblems, and monuments. Assigning meaning to nonverbal symbols is one of the ways humans construct our social and work realities.

It is a law of physics that no two bodies can occupy the same space at the same time. Space, therefore, is very important to any business. People and organizations mark their territories by their possessions, buildings, and signs. These architectural and symbolic ways of marking one's territory are important in defining one's corporate identity. Turning space into "place" is a natural communicative activity.

THE CATEGORIES OF NONVERBAL COMMUNICATION

Kinesics

Kinesics is probably the area one thinks of most when discussing nonverbal communication. This area receives more attention than any other in terms of books and articles. Kinesics is commonly referred to as the study of "body language." Such texts as Gerard Nierenberg and Henry Caleros's *How to Read a Person Like a Book* and John Molloy's *Dress for Success* are examples of how authors have capitalized on the popularity of this category of nonverbal communication. In fact, according to Michael Hanna and Gerald Wilson in their text *Communicating in Business and Professional Settings*, new employees of one of the Big Eight accounting firms receive a copy of *Dress for Success* as part of their orientation material.

The term kinesics, derived from the Greek word for "movement," includes the study of face and eye behavior, posture, position, gestures, and physical appearance. Because of the realm of behaviors included within this code, kinesics is considered the largest category of nonverbal communication.

Facial Expressions

Is your face the YOU that you want to communicate? Many people don't think so. In fact, many of us try to alter our facial expressions and appearance. Facial features affect interpersonal relationships and judgments in impression formation. Although impression formation cues also include clothing, body shape, and personality, most of us first judge others by facial features. In America, it seems that physical attractiveness often influences our impressions and judgments. Look at advertisements, billboards, and movies. Thin, muscular, attractive people are valued very highly.

Since the face is a primary source of nonverbal communication, you must do all that you can to put forward your "best" face. Facial behavior in itself can communicate a message that could cost you a job, a business deal, or an interpersonal relationship. In order to put forward your "best" face, humans use facial management techniques. Although many facial expressions are spontaneous, there are ways that we can control our reactions.

Paul Ekman, Wallace Friesen, and Phoebe Ellsworth, in *Emotion in the Human Face*, describe the four facial management techniques as follows:

Intensifying   Often we are required to exaggerate our facial expressions to meet norms of society. For example, you may intensify your facial expression when given a gift from your boss. We exaggerate our expressions in order to maintain positive social relationships.

Deintensifying   For the same reason listed above, we also deintensify certain emotions. You may feel anger toward your boss, but may also be afraid to risk your job security by showing this emotion. Thus, you may deintensify this feeling of anger with your face.

Neutralize   There are many situations where it is appropriate to completely avoid showing any emotion at all. Loretta Malandro, Larry Barker, and Deborah Ann Barker, in their text *Nonverbal Communication*, describe cultural distinctions in the use of this facial management technique. Men, according to these authors, neutralize because of cultural norms. Within the United States, men are expected to be strong, brave, and independent. Display of emotions such as fear and sadness are considered weak and feminine. Because of these gender stigmas, men often suppress and deny an emotion. Is this good mental health?

Masking   When we seek to cover up one emotion with a facial expression more appropriate for the occasion, we employ the facial management technique called masking. When we mask, we actually try to conceal our real emotion by "putting on a mask" of another emotion. Common emotions that are masked include jealousy and disappointment. Masking is probably the most widely used facial cover-up used within business.

At times, business workers mask their true emotions with a smile or positive emotional expression appropriate for work. This way, they cover up their "personal face" with their "professional face." Although we are in no way advocating deceit, it is common practice for people to try to "put their best face forward" in order to make a good impression. It is not always appropriate in the workplace to show anger, hurt, or grief.

WE MEAN BUSINESS

Think of a situation where you have masked an emotion. Why did you do so? Do you agree with the gender stereotype associated with neutralizing?

Eye Behavior The ancient Greeks believed that the eyes held special powers. They believed that the "evil eye" or fixed stare had the power to cause physical harm or death. In fact, Loretta Malandro reported that a supermarket placed large frowning eyes in the corners of the building. The supermarket had been plagued with shoplifting, but after the eyes were painted, shoplifting was drastically reduced.

The eyes have been called the "mirrors of the soul." Whether or not this fact is supported by research, there is no doubt that we place much emphasis on the eyes for messages of power, status, and relationship. A few general functions of eye behavior are discussed in the following paragraphs.

Establishing and Defining Relationships Establishing eye contact indicates a willingness to initiate and maintain an interaction. This use of eye behavior typically serves a more social function. We can determine if another is attracted to us by their eye contact or avoidance, and length of gaze.

The type of gaze used in an interaction can also define what type of context is expected. Figure 5.1 illustrates the three types of gaze used in business, social, and intimate relationships.

A relationship can be defined by the amount of eye contact given. A well-known business rule holds that people of greater status are required to maintain less eye contact than are those of lower status. You may notice in a job interview that the interviewer looks down or away more frequently than you would dare. Do you feel that you should display much eye contact to show attentiveness?

Direction of Thought or Action Eye contact can show the direction of thought through turn-taking signals. We typically signal with our eyes and face our willingness to listen. Power displays are also largely controlled by eye behavior. Staring is permitted more by someone of greater status.

Reducing Distractions When we need to gather thoughts or concentrate, we sometimes rely on this nonvisual function of eye behavior. Have you ever looked up at nothing in particular while taking a test, or looked off in space or down at the ground while gathering your thoughts in a difficult transaction? These are two examples of reducing distractions with the eyes.

Position and Posture

Position and posture send messages about our sense of self-esteem, competence, gender, and status. This area of study includes all sitting and standing behavior. Your posture in the classroom sends messages of interest and intent or of boredom and lack of sleep. Your posture as you enter an interview or meeting can display your confidence and enthusiasm, or your fear and lack of confidence.

Those in higher status are afforded more relaxed body positions than are those of lower status. At a typical interview, the interviewee will have a

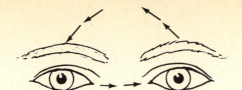

BUSINESS

Eye contact with eyes and forehead

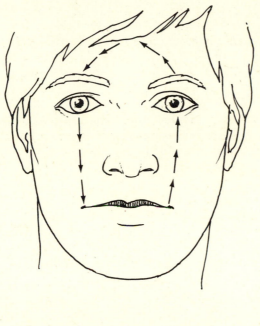

SOCIAL

Eye contact with entire face

INTIMATE

Eye contact with face and
entire upper body

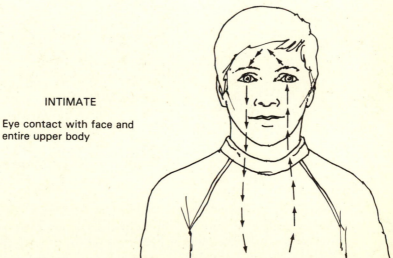

Figure 5.1 Three Types of Eye Gaze in Interpersonal Relations
Source: Adapted from Alan Pease, *Signals: How to Use Body Language for Power* (1981).

tight, closed body position and a slight forward lean. The interviewer, on the other hand, will probably enjoy a much more relaxed posture. S/he may sit with arms down at the side or behind the head, and will probably lean back in the chair.

WE MEAN BUSINESS

Ask permission to sit in on a staff meeting or take notes at business meetings of which you are a part. Do you see differences in posture in relation to status?

In *Body Politics*, Nancy Henley notes there are also some interesting gender differences in posture expectations. See Figure 5.2 for illustrations of stereotypes for posture and power between the sexes.

Gestures

Although some gestures, such as eye opening and closing, are involuntary, most of the symbols that we use to gesture are learned within individual cultures. We need to recognize that attempts to decode gestures universally can be dangerous. Following are different ways in which we use gestures to communicate.

Emblems Emblems are gestures that stand alone, and are substitutes for a verbalization. Examples include holding your hand up next to your ear (I can't hear you), holding up your index finger (wait a minute), and holding your fingers to your nose (what smells?). There must be socially shared meanings for these emblems, or misinterpretations can result. Richard Nixon found this out when visiting Latin America while he was president of the United States. While disembarking from the plane, Nixon flashed what we would interpret as the "A-OK" sign. However, the symbol did not hold this interpretation in the Latin American culture. In fact, literally translated to them, the emblem meant "screw you." So without even saying a word, Nixon insulted the culture.

Illustrators Illustrators are much like emblems, except that they accompany speech. They are used to help describe an event and hold the listener's attention while the speaker "paints a picture" with his words and gestures. Illustrators can help show direction (i.e., "The library is that way") or help describe an event ("The fish I caught was this big.") Illustrators also help to emphasize a word or phrase (i.e., "I am so sick of this") followed by slamming your hand on the table.

Figure 5.2 Body Politics. Expected to be feminine as women and powerful as managers, women play two roles with often-contradictory rules.

Figure 5.2a In an ordinary conversation with men or other women, whether in the workplace or somewhere else, women smile, open their eyes wide, arch their brows, lift and lower their heads, and nod more often than men.

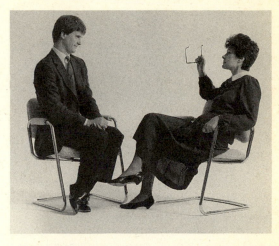

Figure 5.2b Acting out a man's role in a one-on-one conversation, Dr. Janet Mills, professor of Communication and Public Affairs at Boise State University, sits back in her chair, sets her shoulders square, stares directly ahead, keeps her head erect, and gestures forcefully.

Figure 5.2c To pick something up from the floor "femininely," women keep their knees together, their back straight, their arms close to their body, and approach the object from the side.

Figure 5.2d To pick an object up from the floor "masculinely," men generally squat, keep their back flexible, extend their arm from their body, and approach the object from the front.

(continued)

Figure 5.2e Women learn to sit with legs together, crossed at the ankles or knees, toes pointed in the same direction, feet tucked under the chair, as Mills demonstrates. Women also hold their arms close to their bodies, their hands together in their lap.

Figure 5.2f What's wrong with this picture? Volunteer model William D. Coughlan, CAE, executive vice president of the American Physical Therapy Association, Alexandria, Virginia, offers a man's interpretation of how a woman sits.

Figure 5.2g In what Mills calls the "power spread," men sit with their legs in the "broken four"—at a 5 to 15-degree angle and crossed ankle to knee—with their hands behind their head and their elbows away from the body.

Figure 5.2h How would you feel sitting across from this woman at a conference table, over lunch, or in your office? Notice that Mills leans back into the chair in her interpretation of this classic male pose.

Figure 5.2i In a typical office scene, ASAE foundation manager Eric Johnson portrays the dominant man—feet shoulder-width apart, hands in pockets, weight shifting side to side or back and forth, indirect gaze straight ahead.

Figure 5.2j In reverse, it's easy to notice how a man posing as a woman balances his weight on one hip, lowers his shoulders, stands in a "bashful knee bend," with his hands "placed gingerly together."
Source: *Association Management*, April 1987. Photos: The Garfield Studio, Inc.

Regulators   Similar to eye behavior, gestures also hold a turn-taking function. With our gestures, we can show interest or send messages such as "hurry up" or "you are boring me." Typically, we are unaware of this use of gestures.

Adaptors   Adaptors are behaviors used to satisfy physical or psychological needs. Typically these are unconscious behaviors that are habitual. Self-adaptors include behaviors such as scratching your arm, pulling beard or hair, or rubbing your nose. We also use object adaptors, such as playing with a pencil, chalk, or chewing gum to control these needs.

Physical Appearance   Physical appearance cues are especially important in impression formation. When interacting with others, we often make judgments of others based solely on physical appearance cues. As communicators, each of us manipulates these cues.

According to Molloy's *Dress for Success*, men are perceived as more likeable in business when wearing a solid gray or blue suit. The color perceived as most credible is a solid dark blue suit. Within every occupation there exists an informal uniform. That is, people tend to assign certain norms for dress according to job role. For instance, there are both formal and

Box 5-2   # Being Tall Pays

Recently, graduates of the University of Pittsburgh's MBA program were surveyed. The results showed that taller and thinner male executives received higher salaries. Professors Irene Frieze and Josephine Olson surveyed 1,200 graduates and found that tall men earn more than their shorter colleagues, and that men who are at least 20 percent overweight make $4,000 less than their thinner coworkers. These researchers found that the average salary of those surveyed was $43,000, but that a typical 6-foot male professional earned $4,200 more than his 5-foot-5 counterpart. When weight and height were combined, the taller and trimmer man earned about $8,200 more than the shorter and heavier man. Olson explained the survey findings by pointing out that "people imagine a male manager as tall, strong and powerful. And the man who meets that image gets rewarded." The results for women were not conclusive because of the small number of female respondents who were significantly tall or overweight. However, Frieze indicated that being tall and slim are attractive attributes for men, and that "it's more complex for women than men. If a woman is seen as fairly attractive and she is doing these male-dominated jobs...there's a suspicion of how she's gotten there, how much she's used her attractiveness to get there."

Source: From Burgoon, Buller, and Woodall, cited in *Nonverbal Communication: The Unspoken Dialogue*, Harper & Row, 1989.

informal uniforms for doctors, teachers, police officers, and business people. Physical attractiveness can be an asset or a disadvantage. One study found that physical attractiveness can help men who are seeking management positions. Clean-shaven, short-haired men are considered more credible. However, exceptional physical attractiveness can be a liability for women seeking the same jobs. This could be due to the stereotype that "attractive women cannot succeed." Some authors suggest that attractive women minimize their attractiveness when interviewing. Women with long hair could pin their hair up or wear it pulled back. It has even been suggested by some that women wear glasses to appear more credible. One of the author's friends is a stunning blonde. A professor from her college suggested that she pull her hair back and purchase a pair of glasses for law school interviews to minimize her attractiveness. Whether or not that made an impact is unknown, but she did graduate from law school!

Proxemics

Proxemics involves the study of space used to define relationships and power. Each of us has the need for some privacy and distance. We satisfy these needs by establishing territories that are considered our own, and by maintaining comfortable personal space distance zones appropriate to each relationship. How much or how little personal space and territory we are afforded speaks loudly.

The concepts to be discussed in relation to communication at work include personal space zones, territoriality, and arrangement of work space.

Personal Space   Personal space moves with you as you communicate. Personal space is the invisible bubble that surrounds and protects you as you communicate with others. In business, the amount of space one commands communicates power. The CEO may wait alone for the elevator while subordinates stand closely together several paces behind their boss. Anthropologist Edward Hall is known for his categorization of the American personal distance zones (although a caution is in order: Hall's results mainly include white, middle-class North Americans). The distances are defined as follows: Intimate space—0 to 18 inches. Interaction within this distance zone is restricted to private interactions. You are close enough to the other person that you can easily touch and smell, and even feel each other's breath. Most business transactions would not take place within this zone. Personal-casual space—1½ to 4 feet. The close to far ranges within this zone differ in terms of appropriate types of communication. The close end (personal) is used with friends and family, obviously people with whom you are familiar. However, the far phase (casual) restricts the familiarity of the interaction. You are forced to speak louder and cannot touch the other person at the far phase. Less intimate disclosure is likely at this distance, so most interaction is impersonal.

Social-consultive space—4 to 10 feet. This is the distance zone most used in everyday business transactions. Impersonal social conversations could transpire at the social (four feet) distance, but formality increases as distance increases.

Public space—10 feet to the limits of visibility. Public distance communication is typical of the interaction between a public speaker and an audience. The communicator style is usually much more formal, and direct interaction with audience is minimal.

Territoriality   Territory, in contrast to personal space, is a fairly fixed geographic area that you take control of and consider your own. People usually mark a space, feel a certain sense of ownership, and defend against those who invade that space.

Many business people consider their offices a primary or home territory. This means that many feel as though they "own" this territory just as some feel ownership to their kitchen, bedroom, or favorite chair. The business office should be respected by those who enter, just as if they were entering a home.

Territory speaks many powerful messages in business communication. The location of the office, the amount of space provided within the office, and the arrangement of the office space communicate themes of status, power, and invitations for interaction.

According to Michael Korda, author of *Power! How to Get It, How to Use It*, the more windows and space you have in the office, the greater your power. Messages of status are also perceived by the location of the office. Is your office right next to the door where the public enters, or does one have to walk down a long hall, go up the elevator, and past many secretaries to find you? Do you have to share your office with another person?

Arrangement of Work Space

The arrangement of the objects within the office provide cues about the expectations for communication within the environment. Furniture arrangement can encourage or discourage communication. Comfortable chairs and couches invite interactions and ease. Employers who have "power" chairs or sit behind an immense desk when interacting with employees send messages of their desire to keep power on their side of the desk. Placement of objects is an indicator of power. For example, the way the objects are placed can indicate equality or power division. Artifacts, especially gold, marble, brass, and some types of wood, communicate prestige. Careful placement, instead of cluttering, sends a message of order. Review the Skill Builders at the end of the chapter and see how you would arrange your office for "power" communication. Whether an employee has an open or closed door also indicates level of power and willingness to interact. Who do you think is perceived as higher status typically, the person who has an open or closed door? A closed door implies privacy. Since people with higher status are afforded the luxury of privacy, one who has a closed door sends signals of power. However, a manager who desires to send signals of availability for interaction and equality could keep the door open.

Seating Sense

Did you know that approximately 20,000,000 business meetings are held each day in America? According to Bill Lauren, author of *Seating Success*, meetings are that frequent and therefore the chair arrangement is important. The idea of stand-up meetings for work unit announcements makes sense. Standing is not as comfortable as sitting. Therefore saying only what is necessary will be appreciated by a person who is standing. Stand-up meetings are a good way to keep meetings short and to the point. But most meetings are of the sit-down kind.

Donald C. Stone, professor of public service at Carnegie-Mellon University, has studied meeting arrangements. He is a former director of administration for the Marshall Plan and is a consultant to more than a dozen federal agencies including the Tennessee Valley Authority and NASA. His experience leads to these suggestions:

- Chairs should have some padding and armrests. Hard-backed straight chairs are too close to the bone. Overstuffed or reclining chairs are dozers.

- Circular tables, as King Arthur prescribed, make for good communication. Rectangles and T-shapes block lines of sight.
- Larger groups communicate best seated in horseshoe or semicircular shapes.
- Try to estimate the number of chairs needed and then don't provide enough for everybody. Stone says "empty chairs make people wonder where the others are and why they didn't show up." Finding chairs for those who arrive late, of course, is a necessary courtesy. This idea does not apply to a group that meets regularly nor should it be overused lest a leader be considered to have an exclusive inner circle.

APPLICATIONS TO THE WORKPLACE: INTERPERSONAL NONVERBAL UNDERSTANDINGS

Haptics

Every human being needs a certain amount of touch for healthy physical, psychological, and social development. As infants, we crave touch for comfort and protection. Psychologically, touch helps shape our sense of self and helps us to establish bonds socially. Even though the above is true, America has been called "the touch-starved society" by scholar Desmond Morris. America, versus Mediterranean and some European cultures, is essentially seen as a noncontact culture. Americans are raised to be strong and independent. Typical ritualistic greetings include only handshakes, in contrast to some cultures where greetings include hugging or kissing in business.

Handshake Within the norms of business cultures in America, strict rules typically exist about appropriate touching behavior. The only touch permitted is that linked to the ritual of greeting another. Within American culture, this ritual is the handshake.

Each of us has probably given or received at least one type of handshake. The most desirable handshake is one that is firm but not TOO firm, and consists of two and one-half shakes. Be sure to wipe your hands before shaking to remove perspiration! It is advised that a shake that uses excessive pressure may convey negative messages of overaggressiveness. On the other hand, the handshake to avoid is what many refer to as the "dead fish" shake. This shake is soft and limp, and very unappealing.

Each of the above handshakes potentially carries a message of gender and power. Gerard Nierenberg and Henry Caleros, authors of *How to Read a Person Like a Book*, comment about the popularity of the firm typical male handshake. They say that this type of handshake sends messages of "strength," whereas the third type, or a limp handshake, often called the "dead fish," sends negative messages.

WE MEAN BUSINESS

Experiment with the three types of handshakes described above. Do you assign a certain type of handshake to a specific gender? What characteristics are associated with the different handshakes?

Touch and Status   Touch can be used positively to indicate status in business. A general business rule is that superiors control and initiate touching behaviors withing the organization. It would be much more appropriate for the president of a corporation to greet an employee with a pat on the back than the reverse.

Although the rules of "who touches whom" can send signals of power and status, negative messages can also result from touching. Touching that is not associated with functions of the job, such as the ritualistic greeting and necessary touch between doctor/patient, can be interpreted negatively.

The possibility of sexual harassment is an issue that is ever present in the workplace. The Civil Rights Act of 1964, Title VII, as amended by the Equal Opportunity Act of 1972 forbids employer and union discrimination based upon race, color, religion, sex, or national origin. Sexual harassment as defined by EEOC guidelines is defined as:

> Unwelcome sexual advances, requests for sexual favors, and other verbal or physical conduct of a sexual nature . . . when submission to such conduct is made either explicitly or implicitly a term or condition of an individual's employment . . . or the effect of such conduct has the purpose or effect of unreasonably interfering with an individual's work performance or creating an intimidating, hostile, or offensive working environment.

An organization should have a policy that provides for prompt, thorough, and fair investigations of harassment complaints. Policies should be specific with examples of what constitutes sexual harassment:

Physical — unwelcome touching, bodily contact, or proximity.

Visual — suggestive cartoons or posters or "undressing" another with one's eyes.

Verbal — sexual innuendoes, jokes, requests, and language that offends.

Disciplinary action should be reasonably suited to the violation and may include: oral and written warnings, suspension without pay, demotion, and termination. Employers must take care to provide due process and not to unjustly stigmatize either an accused person or a victim.

Another type of touch that is often perceived negatively is self-touch, or the use of self-adaptors, discussed earlier within this chapter. As we dis-

---

Box 5-3 **No More Fanny Pats**

Legislation making it a felony for a boss to pat his secretary on the behind or to coerce her into providing sexual favors has been introduced in the Michigan Legislature.

Bosses convicted under the bill, sponsored by Rep. George Cushingberry, D-Detroit, face up to 15 years in prison.

---

cussed previously, self-adaptors are used to compensate for nervousness. Bosses do not want their executives sending signals of stress to clients and coworkers such as touching face, eyes and hair excessively.

Paralanguage

All behavior that is vocal but nonverbal is included with the nonverbal category labeled paralanguage. Often this voluminous portion of nonverbals is linked with verbal communication. Vocal cues are among the most powerful in the realm of nonverbal language. In fact, paralanguage rivals kinesics in variety and usage. Although we tend to look at kinesics cues most for deception cues, paralingual cues are actually the most accurate place to look for cues of deception. We find it hardest to control our pitch and number of speech hesitations when lying.

According to Mark Hickson and Don Stacks, authors of *Nonverbal Communication: Studies and Applications*, paralanguage includes the study of "all vocal behaviors that complement, accent, emphasize, and contradict" verbal cues. The area includes pitch, inflection, loudness, silence, pauses, laughs, sighs, coughs, sneezes, and disfluencies.

Silence in itself serves several communication functions. Silence can communicate disapproval and concentration. Silence can send messages of power. Those afforded the luxury of silence are those with power. Many people feel uncomfortable with silence, so they fill silence with disfluencies such as "um" and "uh." These sorts of disfluencies can decrease the credibility of a speaker. Words like "um" or "uh" that break the flow of communication tend to signal lack of preparation, confidence, and sometimes competence.

Research shows that we can accurately associate the sex, status, and approximate age of speakers simply from paralanguage. Thus we form impressions about people because of voice types and fluencies.

Vocal pitch is also often a predictor of credibility. Barbara Bates, author of *Communication and the Sexes*, wrote that typically the expectation of the "ideal" female voice type is one that is higher-pitched, soft, and breathy. The expectation for the "ideal" male voice is lower-pitched and louder. However, with the influx of females in executive positions, many women are seeking vocal training to lower their habitual pitch level so that they sound more like the ideal male.

Other research has found that the most credible voice is the **orotund voice**. This voice, according to Hickson and Stacks, is "energetic, pompous, authoritative, proud and humorless." Negative perceptions of credibility in business are associated with the nasal and breathy voice.

Voices that are dynamic typically score high in audience credibility. Dynamism results from variety in pitch, rate, and intensity. Diaphragmatic breathing increases the energy in a speaker's voice. In order to breathe from the diaphragm, you need to picture what is occurring physiologically. When you inhale, the diaphragm muscle tenses and contracts, and moves downward about one inch. This descending motion compresses the stomach, liver, and kidneys, causing a slight bulge of the abdomen. The ribs then expand up and outward. Visualize this motion. Put your hands on your waist and inhale, feeling your ribcage expand up and out. Release your breath with a "hiss" or "ah."

Vocal energy, variety, and confidence are also important to the success of a job interview. Practice answering sample interview questions in an energetic, confident, slow manner. Try to be conscious of breathing from the diaphragm to allow maximum energy flow. When we get nervous, we tend to tighten the stomach and throat, thus making it difficult to speak dynamically. Rehearsal can help improve your voice quality, reduce disfluencies, and increase confidence.

WE MEAN BUSINESS

What characteristics do you associate with a "high-pitched, breathy, soft voice" versus a "low-pitched, louder voice"?

Chronemics

Chronemics is the study of how individuals use time as communication. Some cultures have a very relaxed sense of time, and do not place a great value on promptness or waiting time. However, the United States has been referred to by many as "obsessed with time."

Americans view time as a commodity that is valuable to save and use wisely. Virginia Richmond, James McCroskey, and Steven Payne in *Nonverbal Behavior in Interpersonal Communication* state:

> We have clocks in our desk calendars, in our bathrooms, in our bedrooms, in our kitchens, in our classrooms, in our work place, in our pens and pencils, in our calculators; in our rings, in our necklaces, in our belt buckles, in our earrings, in our money clips, in our computers, in our cards, on our desks, in our radios, TV's, VCR's and even in our exercise equipment. No other culture in the world lets time rule it as we do.

Typically, every culture has in its language many words for something that is important to them. For example, people in Florida or southern cultures probably do not have many words for "snow" because they do not have as much experience with snow. But folks from the North, when asked for different types of snow, can recite many, including "flurries, slush, sleet, and blizzard." The same rule holds true for time communication. Because we Americans use time as such an integral part of our communication, we have many definitions for time in our language. Some phrases include punctuality, on time, and waiting time.

Punctuality Punctuality is a very important concept in business, for lateness implies that you can "waste" the time of another. When interviewing, it is essential that you arrive promptly for the appointment. Lateness carries a negative message.

One example of the power of punctuality comes from Leslie Baxter and Jean Ward, who interviewed secretaries (cited in "Newsline," *Psychology Today*, April 1975). We always warn our students that an interview begins the moment you step out of your car, and that everything you do until you get back into the car is sending nonverbal and verbal messages about yourself. Here is one more instance where this is true; consider the waiting room. Secretaries were questioned about how they perceive people arriving early, late, and on time for appointments. The prompt or punctual people were viewed as the MOST competent and composed. Overly early arrivers ranked low in competence, composure, and sociability, possibly because they communicated messages of apprehension while waiting. This could include self-adaptor behavior, fidgeting, pacing, or smoking—all no-nos!! Late arrivers ranked low in competence, composure, and sociability, but ranked highest in dynamism. Perhaps this occurred because the late people were more flamboyant in their excuse-giving behaviors.

> Time is the ultimate symbol of domination. Those who control other's time have power, and those who have power control others' time.
>
> Robert Levine

On Time and Waiting Time Often, rules of those who wait and those who are not to be kept waiting are important indicators of power and prestige.

Box 5-4   **The King Cannot Be Late**

Playing the waiting game in foreign cultures is tricky. The rules are as divergent as the countries. King Hassan II of Morocco, for example, is a notoriously late arriver. In 1980, when Queen Elizabeth II paid a call, the King kept her waiting for 15 minutes. The Queen was not amused.

On another occasion, Hassan was one of the few influential members of royalty absent from the Charles-Diana nuptials. Because of his eminent position, he had to be asked. But the invitation was qualified by statements alluding to the high value that Anglo-Saxons place on promptness and the hope that His Majesty could manage to be on time for the ceremony. The King responded in due course that certain pressing affairs would, unfortunately, preclude his personal appearance at the wedding. He sent the Crown Prince in his place.

The Moroccans still couldn't understand why the British were so upset by the King's lack of promptness. "The King could never have kept the Queen or anybody else waiting," one of them later said, "because the King cannot be late."

Listen closely and you hear the silent language.

Source: From Robert Levine, "Waiting is a Power Game," *Psychology Today*, April, 1987, pp. 24–33.

Last week, one of the author's students made an appointment with the dean and was kept waiting over an hour outside his office, although there was no one in the office with the dean the entire time. Yet when the dean came to visit this author, a student in her office was asked to wait outside while the dean came to speak to her. Those who can wait, and those who do not. . . .

A famous example of using waiting time to send an intentional message comes from Harry Truman. Not long after becoming president, Truman was visited by a newspaper editor. After a 45-minute wait, the editor asked one of the staff to tell the president that he was becoming annoyed because of the long wait. When told of this Truman replied, "When I was a junior senator from Missouri, that same editor kept me cooling my heels for an hour and a half. As far as I'm concerned, the son of a bitch has 45 minutes to go!"

Rules of "on time" vary from culture to culture. Some cultures, in fact, do not even have a word for "late" in their culture. For example, when American businessmen visit Latin American cultures, they are often insulted when the Latin Americans keep them "waiting" for up to an hour and a half, then do not even apologize when they finally do arrive. Why is this so? Because according to Latin culture, on time is considered "when I get there."

Therefore, the people are not acting rudely, they are simply conforming to their sense of time.

The Job Interview and Nonverbal Communication

Throughout this chapter, references have been made about the impact of nonverbal behavior on the job interview. Examples have been provided about norms of eye contact, posture, physical appearance, handshaking, vocal variety, and punctuality. Reread these examples, as well as the other categories of nonverbal communication, and consider the package you wish to present to a future employer. Interviewing is discussed in depth during Chapter 6.

John L. LaFevre, author of "You Don't Get a Second Chance to Make a First Impression", said:

> Look, talk, act and present yourself as the person holding the job for which you are being interviewed. . . . Your confidence, creativity, appearance, company knowledge, product knowledge, enthusiasm and poise combine to make a clear statement of "who you are."

The job interview will be an important place to put to use the skills mentioned above. The theme of this book is developing communication competence, and sensitizing yourself to nonverbal behavior is an integral part of becoming a competent communicator. Here are a few general tips about nonverbals and interviewing:

- Interviewers typically make decisions to hire during the initial interaction. So, how you enter the work area, your overall posture, presence, and dress will all send signals.
- Interviewers are more likely to notice negative behaviors than positive behaviors. This is especially true when a large number of people apply for a position. Recruiters need to be able to weed people out, and negative impressions are stronger.
- Interviewers often have a stereotype or image or what they feel the "perfect candidate" will look and act like. They often hire in this image.

On-the-job Communicator Style

How employees express themselves nonverbally, we have stressed, may be every bit as telling as their words. This is particularly so in the superior-subordinate situation. Superiors by definition generally are assigned more prominent visibility. Some play their roles with dominance, taking up more space and privileged positions. Subordinates want their superiors to wield influence and to represent them forcefully, but not to come across as pompous.

Superiors who have good relationships with subordinates know that subordinates dislike dominant behaviors. They like to say, "She or he's not stuck up and is like us in spite of being boss." Bosses that come across as warm and friendly are animated in gestures, have a twinkle in their eyes, and warmth in their laughter. Their attitude of body and mind is relaxed, responsive, and energetic. That makes good nonverbal sense.

SUMMARY

This chapter has examined nonverbal communication in the work setting. Nonverbals comprise somewhere between 60 to 90 percent of our total daily communication. Although we are not specifically taught the "rules" of nonverbal communication appropriate to our culture, we learn by observation and imitation. These rules communicate differences in gender, status, and power. As we enter different organizations such as schools, clubs, families, and the workplace, we learn varying standards of appropriateness in each context.

The categories that were discussed in this chapter included the most prominent ones involved in our daily interactions. Kinesics, the largest area of nonverbal communication, includes all motion and action behavior such as posture, position, face, and eye behavior. Some include the study of physical appearance within this category also.

Space behavior or proxemics involves the study of space in relationships and the arrangement of objects within our space as they set the context for communication. We each lay claim to certain territories within our environment.

Another form of nonverbal communication studied was haptics, or touching behavior. Because America is considered a noncontact culture, touching is restrained and status-determined, especially in business environments.

Paralanguage, vocal but nonverbal uses of the voice, is the second largest category in nonverbal communication. Certain voice types are linked to gender and to status.

The final category discussed was chronemics, or the structure and use of time as communication. There are strict cultural rules for time usage. Americans view time like a "jewel" that is very valuable.

Hopefully, you have become a bit more sensitive to your nonverbal behavior and to the differences of those around you. It is very important that you become aware of the nonverbal messages you are sending. As many have said, sometimes actions DO speak louder than words.

SKILL BUILDER: SEATING ARRANGEMENT AND COMMUNICATION

Choose the seat number that corresponds with the following messages. Note your reasoning in justifying communication differences based on seating location.

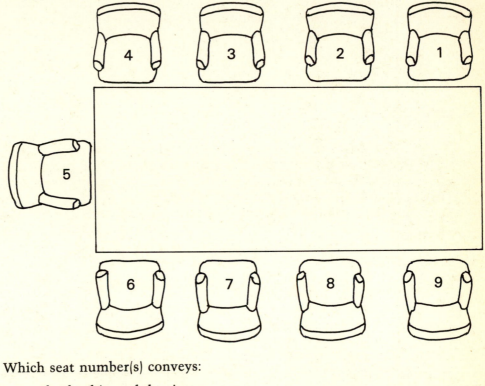

Which seat number(s) conveys:

- leadership and dominance   _____
- nonparticipation   _____
- attraction, involvement   _____

Which seats would normally be used in:

- cooperative task situations   _____
- competitive situations   _____

SKILL BUILDER: OFFICE ARRANGEMENT AND POWER

Place the furniture below in this office. Pretend you are arranging your office to convey a message of power. (*Source:* Adapted from Michael Korda, *Power! How to Get It, How to Use It*, 1975.)

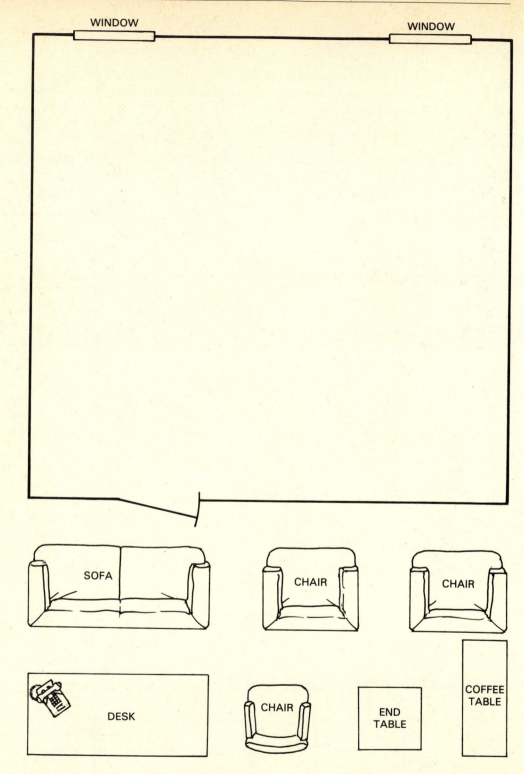

RESOURCES

Bates, Barbara. (1988). *Communication and the sexes.* New York: Harper & Row.

Baxter, Leslie, and Jean Ward. (1975). "Newsline." *Psychology Today,* 8, 28.

Burgoon, Judee K., David B. Buller, and W. Gill Woodall. (1989). *Nonverbal communication: The unspoken dialogue.* New York: Harper & Row.

DeVito, Joseph A. (1989). *Nonverbal communication workbook.* Prospect Heights, IL: Waveland.

Ekman, P., W. V. Friesen, and P. Ellsworth. (1982a). "Conceptual ambiguities." In P. Ekman (ed.), *Emotion in the human face,* 2nd ed. Cambridge, England: Cambridge University Press.

Goodsell, Charles T. (1977). "Bureaucratic manipulation of physical symbols: An empirical study." *American Journal of Political Science,* 21, 79–91.

Henley, Nancy. (1977). *Body politics.* Englewood Cliffs, NJ: Prentice-Hall.

Hickson, Mark I., III, and Don W. Stacks. (1989). *Nonverbal communication: Studies and applications* (2nd ed.). Dubuque, IA: Wm. C. Brown.

Korda, Michael. (1975). *Power! How to get it, how to use it.* New York: Ballantine.

LaFevre, John. (1988). "You don't get a second chance to make a first impression." *College Woman,* 55–57.

Levine, Robert. (1987, April). "Waiting is a power game." *Psychology Today,* 24–33.

Malandro, Loretta A., Larry Barker, and Deborah Ann Barker. (1989). *Nonverbal communication* (2nd ed.). New York: Random House.

Molloy, John. (1975). *Dress for success.* New York: Warner.

Morris, Desmond. (1971). *Intimate behavior.* New York: Random House.

Pease, Alan. (1981). *Signals: How to use body language for power, success and love.* Toronto: Bantam Books.

Remland, Martin S. (1984). "Leadership impressions and nonverbal communication in a superior-subordinate interaction." *Communication Quarterly,* 32, 41–48.

Richmond, Virginia, James McCroskey, and Steven Payne. (1991). *Nonverbal behavior in interpersonal communication.* Englewood Cliffs, NJ: Prentice-Hall.

Chapter 6

Interviewing in and for the Workplace

Concepts for Discussion

- Types and approaches
- The selection interview
- Analyzing the product
- Analyzing the audience

- How to win the job
- The stress interview
- What recruiters are looking for

Interviewing is very much like piano playing—a fair degree of skill can be acquired without the necessity of formal instruction. But there is a world of difference in craftsmanship, in technique, and in finesse between the amateur who plays by ''ear'' and the accomplished concert pianist.

Felix Lopez
Personnel Interviewing: Theory and Practice

In the past 30 years, interviewing has been recognized as a major communication tool of industry, government, health care, and the social sciences. Think of the different types of interviews used by attorneys, social workers, physicians, law enforcement officials, polltakers, journalists, business managers, personnel directors, pastors, teachers, and government. Did you realize that there were so many types of interviews?

The interview is simply a dyadic, or one-to-one, form of communication. In the text *Interviewing: Principles and Practices*, Charles Stewart and William Cash define this form of interpersonal communication as "a process of dyadic communication with a predetermined and serious purpose designed to interchange behavior and usually involving the asking and answering of questions." This mode of communication is relied upon in most economic, political, and social decision making, and certainly deserves attention.

Within this chapter we hope to convince you of the importance of building communication competence in interviewing. You will be introduced to different types of interviews used most often in organizational settings, the general format of an interview, and more specifically the important concerns of the employment selection interview.

TYPES AND APPROACHES OF INTERVIEWS

One large category of interviews involves interaction between an occupational expert and a novice. Some examples of these interactions include doctor and patient, teacher and student, lawyer and client, and manager and employee. The person who conducts the interview is usually the one who assumes the role of interviewer. But because the role of speaker and listener is constantly shifting, it is sometimes difficult to tell which participant is the interviewer. In order to best be able to differentiate the roles of the players and the purpose of the particular interview, it is helpful to discuss the directive and nondirective approaches to interviewing.

The Directive Approach

When involved in a directive interview, the interviewer determines the specific purpose and controls the pace and direction of the actual interview. The interviewer sets certain expectations concerning issues such as time and types of questions asked. Nonverbals of power, such as lack of eye contact and territorial and gesture differences, may be more evident in directive interviews. Information-giving, information-gathering, and employment interviews are all examples of directive interviews. The distinct advantage of the directive approach is that more business can be conducted in a short period of time. Employment interviews, for example, are often scheduled at 20-minute intervals. Recruiters have a set agenda of questions and criteria to fit specifically within this time limit. Directive interviews allow them to manage this time effectively. The major disadvantage of this approach is that it is generally inflexible.

The Nondirective Approach

In extreme contrast, nondirective interviews allow for more flexibility than do directive interviews. Although this type of interview may indeed take more time and may not produce easily quantifiable data, the interviewee feels more in control of this interview. Clinical psychologist Carl Rogers is credited for the development of this approach to interviewing, in which the interviewee initiates and controls the purpose, subject, and pace of the interaction. Interviews that are considered nondirective include problem-solving and psychological counseling interviews. Nondirective interviews generally are more appropriate for therapeutic purposes. The idea underlying a nondirective approach is that the interviewee learns how to solve her/his problems best by taking that responsibility, rather than relying upon the therapist to guide that process. According to *Interviewing: Principles and Practices*, the advantages of the nondirective approach are that it allows the participants to explore in depth a wide range of topics, it allows greater flexibility for the interviewer, and it leaves the door open for the pair to establish an ongoing relationship.

Generally, an interpersonally competent interviewing style will combine both of these approaches. The directive approach in its pure form inhibits genuine disclosure and limits the amount of data received. The nondirective approach may ramble and yet eventually enable the interviewee to get his or her needs met. Of course, there are also dangers of relying solely on the nondirective form of interview. In its pure form, the nondirective interview may focus on personal matters more than business.

TYPES OF INTERVIEWS

Information-giving Interviews

There are three types of interviews that are considered primarily informational. These are the orientation, training, and job-related instructional interviews.

Orientation   Unfortunately much of corporate America ignores the importance of orientation and training interviews. Remember the discussion of corporate culture during Chapter 3? We talked about organizational commitment, a feeling of belonging, and a sense of compliance with the norms of an organization. This process is made easier when one has an orientation interview. Employee identification with his/her organization requires an understanding of expectations for job performance. According to *Managing Your Communication: In and For the Organization*, written by William Gorden and John Miller, without such training companies are inviting the consequences of low organizational commitment: employee turnover, low productivity, poor product quality, and a total decrease in business effectiveness.

Box 6-1 **Types of Interviews**

1. Information-giving
   a. Orientation
   b. Training, instruction, coaching
   c. Job-related instructions
   d. Briefings

2. Information-gathering
   a. Surveys and polls
   b. Exit interviews
   c. Research interviews
   d. Medical: psychological, psychiatric, case worker
   e. Journalistic

3. Selection
   a. Screening and hiring
   b. Determination
   c. Placement (internal)

4. Problems of interviewee's and interviewer's behavior
   a. Appraisal, evaluative, review
   b. Separation, firing
   c. Correction, discipline, reprimand
   d. Counseling
   e. Receiving complaints
   f. Grievances
   g. Receiving suggestions or answering specialized questions

5. Problem-solving
   a. Objective (mutually shared problems)
   b. Receiving suggestions for solutions (especially to problems covering a large group of people)

6. Persuasion
   a. Selling of products
   b. Selling services
   c. Quasi-commercial selling

Source: Adapted from Charles J. Stewart and William B. Cash, *Interviewing: Principles and Practices*.

The purpose of the job orientation interview is to introduce a new employee to this new environment. Typical orientation programs usually include a tour of the organization, an explanation of company policies and procedures, company benefits, and opportunities for advancement. Daily operation procedures should also be discussed to reduce anxiety about performance expectations. We all want to feel that we are competent in our career. Without a proper orientation, how can we know what is expected of us?

WE MEAN BUSINESS

Think of summer, part-time, or full-time jobs that you have held. Did the companies hold job orientation or training? Did the absence or presence of such training influence your level of commitment?

Training   Many companies have formal training periods built into the career path program of new employees. The function of job training is to provide adequate information necessary to an employee's performance while completing tasks during a specified period of time. For example, let's say that you are hired as a management "trainee" at a retail department store. During the six-month training period, you may be required to float between departments, learn as much as you can about merchandising, work the register, provide service to customers and do everything else that is part of the daily operating procedure in that store.

Instruction   Providing instruction about how to do a task is a very important and frequent communicative role for a superior, and sometimes is a task assigned to an employee to explain to a new coworker. Some instructions are simple; others complex. Some pertain to customer courtesies; others to safety. Discourteous service turns away customers. Inattention to safety often results in injuries and lawsuits against businesses. What then are the principles of giving clear instructions and gaining motivations to follow them?

The principles of clarity are proper content, proper sequencing, and redundancy. The principles of motivation entail arousal of the need to know and stress the benefits of doing a task in keeping with work-prescribed standards. Remember that no instruction is a one-way message. Also remember that one individual cannot know if another has understood a message until that individual has heard the response from the message receiver. To ask "Do you understand?" and to hear "Yes," however, is not enough. A yes response does not reveal what another understands. The following steps generally combine principles of clarity and motivation:

1. State the task for instruction.
2. Inquire what is the amount known about the topic.
3. Provide reasons for giving instructions, perhaps instances of where knowhow resulted in doing a job well or where lack of knowhow resulted in injury or loss of a sale.
4. Give an overview of the steps in the process. Perhaps post the steps where they are easily visible.
5. Demonstrate step by step. Use pictures, charts, film/videotapes, and live demonstrations.
6. Ask periodically if there are questions.
7. Now have the trainees do the task.
8. Recognize and acknowledge what is done properly. Redemonstrate if there were mistakes.
9. Leave the trainee on his or her own to do the job and offer support if help is desired. Also say that you will check back to learn how the trainee is faring with the task.
10. Upon checking back, praise that which is done well. Be specific about any errors in the process. Assure the trainee of her or his ability to do the task well and reiterate the value of the task to the business.

These ten steps, of course, should be applied judiciously and with a friendly demeanor. Steps 1, 4, 5, 6, 7, 8, 9, and 10 focus on clarity of instruction. Steps 2, 3, 8, and 9 entail helping the trainee know why her or his good performance is necessary and valued.

Information-gathering Interviews

Information-gathering interviews are conducted primarily to gain information from the interviewee. This group of interviews includes those that involve research such as journalistic, medical, and exit interviews.

The journalist probes to answer the who, what, where, when, and why questions, and to obtain corroborative data from different persons. The medical interviewer, in a similar fashion, asks questions designed to locate and describe symptoms.

When preparing for an exit interview, the interviewer must assemble all material relevant to the employee, such as insurance forms, performance appraisals, vacation time, severance, and pension pay. Confidentiality is imperative in the exit interview. The interviewer wants to make the interviewee relaxed, so that the objective can be met. That objective is to discover the reason why an employee is leaving. The interviewer should prepare a clear list of questions that can be asked in a nonintimidating manner. If the interviewer sets the mood appropriately and listens well to both the verbal and nonverbal messages, chances are greater that the interviewer will gain a fairly accurate message about why the employee is leaving.

Box 6-2   **Smoking Doesn't Pay**

Suspicion of marijuana use is the single biggest disqualifier of otherwise qualified job applicants, according to a survey of top personnel directors among *Fortune* 500 companies.

Source: From the *Akron Beacon-Journal*, January 12, 1988.

Performance Appraisal

One of the most common types of interviews in the job setting is the performance appraisal. The major purposes of such an interview, as noted in Ron Adler's text *Communicating at Work*, are: to let the employee know when he/she is doing good work and areas in which improvement is needed; to improve employee morale and superior/subordinate relationships; to receive information from the employee's point of view; and to identify some goals for the future, including performance standards and promotion opportunities.

The performance appraisal interview usually is an event staged at six-month or 12-month intervals. Many superiors regard it as a necessary unpleasant ritual in which they must emphasize positives and tactfully discuss negatives in a subordinate's performance. A superior must guard against giving too many high ratings, because high ratings are connected to high raises, and these usually are limited. Superiors should avoid too many low ratings lest their subordinates dislike them and be unmotivated.

Superiors should endeavor to keep records of employer performance and utilize these in the interview appraisal. The superior who is credible is one whose day-to-day feedback, both positive and negative, shows up in the formal appraisal interview. An appraisal is a private time to express appreciation and praise. It also is a time for candid discussion of uncertain and/or unsatisfactory performance. Criticism can be presented in "to me" terms. That is to say, "To me, your performance was less than was required . . ." becomes an opportunity for discussing whens and wheres. Also, it is an opportunity for clarifying job expectations, and discussing how performance might be improved.

The subordinate's objectives in the performance interview are to help the superior learn about one's accomplishments, to understand one's problems that prevent optimal job performance, and to negotiate misunderstandings and misexpectations. The performance interview may be an opportunity to discuss one's career path and to solicit help along the way. It may be a time to reassess one's place in the organization and to consider reassignment.

Counseling and Discipline   Other types of interviews that fall under this category are counseling interviews, in which employees can discuss personal problems that are affecting their job productivity; and interviews that reprimand behavior that is not tolerable. Reprimand, or correction, interviews often occur because of poor orientation interviews. When employees are not told proper procedure and expectations, it is more likely that a policy will be violated. While interviewing subordinates, superiors must keep in mind that most employees DO want to behave according to accepted standards and will normally do so when respectfully informed.

Grievances   About 150 grievances went unanswered in an Ohio auto assembly plant that is now closed. Think about issues we have discussed thus far such as listening and commitment. Can you blame these people for their low productivity?

Complaints   Interviewers must also interview customers and employees who have complaints, and must be open to new ideas and suggestions for improvement in product delivery or service.

Problem-solving Interviews

The problem-solving interview occurs quite frequently within the workplace. This type of interview generally does not deal with personal problems, but rather task-related problems that need interaction in order to find the best solution. Problem-solving interviews usually are initiated by either superior or subordinate. Many follow John Dewey's reflective thinking approach to problem solving. According to this model, a problem-solving interview would include defining the problem, analyzing the causes for the problem, establishing criteria for a solution, listing possible solutions, and choosing the best solution.

THE SELECTION INTERVIEW

Getting a job is a personal, persuasive sales campaign. This is what we preach to students who are preparing to start the process of interviewing for careers after graduation. In this case, the product you are building the campaign for is you! Throughout the rest of this chapter we will discuss current research and strategies to help you create the best package possible to present to future employers.

Martin John Yate, in his article "On Trial for Your Life" said:

> At some point between now and graduation day, you'll probably stand on trial for your livelihood. Your ordeal won't take place in a court of law before a distinguished, black-robed judge. Instead, you'll plead your case in an impersonal office building, miles from familiar campus surroundings, with corporate managers. . .

The process begins with you. You are the product designer and sales manager. In order to effectively execute an employment campaign, you must: (1) analyze the product, (2) provide a summary of the product, (3) analyze your audience, and (4) prepare for the presentation.

Analyzing the Product

Interviewing is the time when your communication skills are really put to the test. In order to be effective, an interview must successfully merge skills in written and oral communication. Your total communicator ability must be analyzed and tailored to meet each audience.

The first step in designing the employment campaign is to evaluate yourself. You must know what you are selling before you can effectively sell it! This may seem silly to you, for you may be saying now, "I know myself quite well. I've been with myself now for 21 or so years. . . ." This is of course quite true, but how often have you really thought about what makes you special, or in what areas you shine, or how you would best describe yourself? These are the kinds of things we mean when we say "analyze yourself." When you present yourself to an interviewer, s/he is looking at a total package. This nonverbal, verbal, and written communication packaged–human must speak consistently and with clarity. Therefore, the words you carefully plan in your résumé must be the language you use as a part of your natural description of yourself during the actual interview. Your nonverbals, as discussed earlier in Chapter 5, must also be packaged to display the message you desire.

Since to some degree you can control the sales situation, you must discover as many positive, personality-related qualities as possible about yourself. One way to begin evaluating yourself is to brainstorm. Sit down with a blank sheet of paper in front of you and spend five minutes jotting down whatever comes to mind in response to the phrase "I am. . . ." Then ask friends, roommates, spouses, and family to write down five adjectives that best describe you. Do you see patterns? You should try to create a positive, consistent image of yourself TO YOURSELF, so that you can in turn portray this image to others.

Next, with another sheet of paper, brainstorm all of your activities and accomplishments during college. If applicable, choose outstanding activities from high school years. Ask friends and family for help. Write down everything that comes to mind, and then you can select the information most suitable for your package. (Also, save this information for the activities section of your résumé!) Now you should have three sources of information: family, self, and accomplishments. Hopefully you can see patterns of behavior about your interests, achievements, and capabilities.

Karmen Crowther and Eileen Wilson, authors of the article "How to Research Companies," state that your job satisfaction will depend on how well you understand your own basic values and those of the company. They advocate that you analyze yourself by asking yourself questions in addition to the ones above, such as:

- What lifestyle values are important to me? Small versus large community size? Geographic limitations or flexibility? Cultural/recreational events nearby?
- What are my work values? Independent versus structured responsibility? Small versus large company environment? Norms/values of the corporate culture?

WE MEAN BUSINESS

Take time right now to brainstorm the answer to the question, "I am. . . ." What descriptors come to mind first?

Analyzing the Audience

The next important step in the employment campaign is to analyze your audience. In this case, the immediate audience is a representative from the company where you wish to be employed. Many college graduates become too caught up in the idea that their goal is to get a job as quickly as possible or else be doomed a failure. Thus, they try to present their best self to everyone, in hopes that someone will hire them. We authors do not think that this is a wise approach to the job search.

Rather, we hope that you will think of this period of time as one that involves "selling" from both sides. That is to say that although you are carefully preparing this package to sell to them, the company is at the same time selling itself to you. Most of you probably will be spending an average of 40 years in the workplace. Don't you think that it is worthwhile to shop around and find the place where you feel most compatible? In order to accomplish this, you must learn as much as possible about each company where you wish to interview.

Company recruiters, however, do not appreciate the casual, browsing shopper. They want to talk with prospective employees who are seriously interested in learning about the company they work for.

"Start at the very beginning, a very good place to start. . . ." These lyrics from *The Sound of Music* may sound rudimentary, but the message is important all the same. Here are some steps to guide the process of analyzing your audience.

Occupational Outlook   One of the first considerations you need to face is the outlook for job opportunities in your desired career. Some questions you should research include:

- What kinds of positions are available in my field?
- Is my field overcrowded, or are there many opportunities?

- Are there certain locations where there are more opportunities? Am I willing to consider these locations? Are they too limiting?
- What are the salary opportunities and ranges?

Learn as much as you can about the answers to the questions above BEFORE the interview. You can save yourself disappointment and time, and impress the interviewer with your research and concern for your future.

Research the Company   Take this assignment seriously. Pretend that this is a class term paper assignment worth 100 percent of your grade in college. Evaluating a job interview has some important similarities to selecting a lifelong companion. This appropriate analogy shows the importance of thoroughly researching a company before going into an interview. Ask yourself these questions: Do I want to go out on more than one date with this person? Do I want to see this person daily for at least the next 40 years? Then, since on the average, most employees spend more time at their career than they do with their spouse, shouldn't I want to spend more than five minutes researching the company where I might spent most of my waking hours in the next 40 years?

If you answered no to the above questions, then don't be surprised if you are rejected by most corporate interviewers. Many interviewers say that they are turned off by candidates who haven't researched the company, and do not even know basic facts about the company's product and operations. One interviewer said, "If they haven't prepared any better for the interview, it raises serious questions about how they would perform on the job."

When you research a company, you will want to assume the role of "super sleuth." Using as many sources as possible, investigate the company. Some sources include:

Annual reports

Corporate literature

Moody's Manuals

Moody's News Reports

Business Periodicals Index (H. W. Wilson company)

Standards and Poor's Register of Corporations, Directors, and Executives

Business periodicals (*Business Week, Fortune, Forbes, The Wall Street Journal, INC.*)

Make sure that these sources, especially annual reports and corporate literature, are current. Be sure to find the corporate mission statement. This statement outlines the basic philosophy of the corporation, and will easily help you learn whether your goals and values mesh with those of the organization. In addition, be sure to learn where the corporate headquarters is located, and what product or service the company represents. Do not be-

Box 6-3   # Interviewing the Company: Finding a Place Where Your Goals and the Goals of the Company Mesh

The accounting profession is really changing and Arthur Andersen has realized that with these changes should come new commitments to their employees. They made two renewed commitments. One commitment is to the family and the other is to the professional development of their employees.

Arthur Andersen's commitment to the family has sprung from the change in their employees. When people think of accountants, they often picture older men in suits working on calculators in back rooms. However, today there are more and more women entering the accounting profession. Therefore, Arthur Andersen realized that it must address the needs of these women. Right now over 40 percent of the hires of Arthur Andersen are women. They found the need for a child-care referral service. This service provides information regarding preschools, nanny services, or any kinds of services a mother may need to continue working while providing a safe environment for her children. Arthur Andersen provides these services free of charge.

Another area where Arthur Andersen has committed itself to the employee is in the area of career stability and professional development. Since Arthur Andersen has a sort of pyramid effect, meaning only so many people can go up in the organization, others have to be laid off regularly. That's the accounting profession; there's a lot of turnover.

I experienced the commitment Arthur Andersen makes to the professional development of its employees in my internship with them. They have three training centers around the world and I attended a two-week session in St. Charles, Illinois. They put a lot of commitment into these training centers. Last year they spent over $270 million for the training of their staff. Training centers are run by partners, managers, seniors, and professional teaching staff just for your professional development.

They spent $4,000 per intern for the 100 of us interns that were there when I was. This is a lot for Arthur Andersen to invest on individual recruits they weren't even sure were going to come back to their firm! Arthur Andersen really shows commitment to not only present employees, but also past and future.

Source: Speech presented by Audrey C. Tillis, July 1991. Ms. Tillis, when she presented this speech, was a senior in accounting working towards her CPA. She is a young mother of four children.

come overwhelmed with trying to memorize an abundance of statistics and information about the company. Do try to become comfortable enough with the knowledge you have gained, so that it becomes a natural part of your analysis necessary to perform comfortably in the interview.

If you find outdated reports, call the company. This method will assure that statistics and names are timely, and will show increased initiative on your part. Jeffrey Allen, author of *How to Turn an Interview Into a Job*, suggests that "the fastest, most enjoyable and most effective way to learn about the personality of the employer is by a telephone call." Call the department most suitable to your purpose, whether it be the marketing, sales, public relations, or personnel. Be prepared with questions and to listen. As we discussed in Chapter 3 on organizational culture, listening is a key to learning a lot about the way a place works. Listen to how employees talk about their product and workplace. Listen to paralanguage cues, as described within the nonverbal chapter. Do their voices sound enthusiastic, motivated, and full of pride?

Not only would this phone call add valuable information to your "term paper" about the company, but it could also serve as a contact to help you later. If you effectively build rapport with the person with whom you speak, you may be able to use this person later as a referral. Jeffrey Allen even suggests writing a letter expressing your appreciation to this person for sharing the information during the phone conversation.

Contacts are an invaluable source. Each of you should start building your own personal network of contacts TODAY, whether you are a sophomore, junior, or graduating senior. Gain referrals from parents, relatives, spouses, and friends. Interview informally with any of these people to answer the questions above concerning outlook in your occupation, or to gather specific research about a company. Always be willing to share information about yourself that you gathered through your self-analysis. Don't underestimate the power of a first impression! Sometimes you may meet someone at a party or family gathering who becomes impressed with you, and calls you six months later when there is a job opening within his/her corporation. Here are two examples of how building a personal network of contacts has worked for our students:

Jeremy (a pseudonym) wanted to work within the human resources department of a company on the West Coast. So, he examined the alumni files stored at the university's career placement center, and checked to see if there were any alumni listed who worked in this field on the coast. He found several names, and called the alumni with the opening line, "Hello, my name is Jeremy Peterson and I am a senior at XYZ University majoring in human resource management. I've been doing some research on XYZ company, and I see that you, as one of our alumni, are the vice president of human resource management. . . ." Jeremy's assertiveness paid off. The alumus asked for Jeremy's resume, and a few months later, Jeremy had secured a job with this company in California — Rockwell International.

Melissa also wanted to work within the field of human resource management, but was having trouble getting her foot in the door. Her uncle, who lives in Las Vegas, kept telling her that he would be glad to send her résumé to key people, but Melissa was stubborn. She wanted to get the job HER way. After nine months of pounding the pavement, Melissa decided to use the contact she had. This contact paid off. Melissa's uncle placed her résumé in the hands of key personnel, and now Melissa is a personnel assistant in Las Vegas — at Caesar's Palace.

You Have Won the Interview . . . Now to Win the Job

A job interview is structured much like a speech. Generally, an interview consists of three parts; the opening, body, and closing. Part of preparation for a successful interview involves the understanding of these three stages. As we stated earlier, impression formation begins immediately. Therefore, the first few seconds and minutes may well be the most important portion of the interview. Your behavior, and the behavior of the interviewer during the opening of the interview, often sets the tone for later interaction. If the opening is weak, the interviewer may have already made up his/her mind that the interview is over. Keep in mind that nonverbals "speak," and walk to greet the interviewer with shoulders straight, head high, and responsive face and eye behavior. In order to make this easier, you may want to remember what Jeffrey Allen calls the "Magic four hello." The magic four hello includes the following simultaneous acts: (1) a smile, (2) direct eye contact, (3) the words, "Hi, I'm (first name, last name). It's a pleasure to meet you.", and (4) A firm but gentle handshake.

The opening phase of an interview usually includes the functions of establishing rapport and orienting the interviewee to the purpose of the interview. Many interviewers begin the interaction with some conversation that is intended to relax the interviewee. Charles Stewart and William Cash refer to this process as a means of establishing goodwill and trust between the two parties in the interview. Conversation during this phase could include the greeting, small talk, and nonverbal indications of warmth. Be cautioned that not all interviewers will take the time to establish rapport. We will discuss this a bit later.

Interviewers also typically explain the purpose and time limit of the interview. These orientation behaviors also help to make the interviewee more comfortable, and help give interviewees an indication of whether a directive or nondirective approach will be followed. The opening phase of the interview ends with the interviewer's first job-related question.

The body or development phase of an interview contains the bulk of the interview, for it contains all of the job-related questions. This is the portion of the interview for which we prepare most. Depending on the length of time and amount of interest in a specific candidate, interviewers balance their inquiry with the use of open and closed questions. Closed questions are those that require a yes, no, or very brief answer. Examples of closed questions include: Are you willing to relocate? How many years of experience do you have? When did you receive your college degree? Open questions are the ones that interviewers use to get to really get to know the candidate. Open

Box 6-4 **1977 Endicott Report***
Fifty Questions Asked by Employers During the Interview with College Seniors

1. What are your long range and short range goals and objectives, when and why did you establish these goals and how are you preparing yourself to achieve them?
2. What specific goals, other than those related to your occupation, have you established for yourself for the next ten years?
3. What do you see yourself doing five years from now?
4. What do you *really* want to do in life?
5. What are your long range career objectives?
6. How do you plan to achieve your career goals?
7. What are the most important rewards you expect in your business career?
8. What do you expect to be earning in five years?
9. Why did you choose the career for which you are preparing?
10. Which is more important to you, the money or the type of job?
11. What do you consider to be your greatest strengths and weaknesses?
12. How would you describe yourself?
13. How do you think a friend or professor who knows you well would describe you?
14. What motivates you to put forth your greatest effort?
15. How has your college experience prepared you for a business career?
16. Why should I hire you?
17. What qualifications do you have that make you think that you will be successful in business?
18. How do you determine or evaluate success?
19. What do you think it takes to be successful in a company like ours?
20. In what ways do you think you can make a contribution to our company?
21. What qualities should a successful manager possess?
22. Describe the relationship that should exist between a supervisor and those reporting to him or her.
23. What two or three accomplishments have given you the most satisfaction? Why?
24. Describe your most rewarding college experience.

questions allow interviewers to test verbal skills and gain information such as your ability to organize, think, and be concise; your personality characteristics; and basic philosophies. Examples of open questions include: What was your proudest moment? What extracurricular activities have benefited you the most? Why should we hire you?

Obviously, interviewers can gain more insightful information by asking open questions. But because time is of the essence, interviewers make use of both types to gain as much information as possible within the time allotted.

Because the process is communicative, study of the job interview is a vital topic of investigation. Communication scholar Lois Einhorn, for her doctoral dissertation, studied through content analysis, the rhetoric within

25. If you were hiring a graduate for this position, what qualities would you look for?
26. Why did you select your college or university?
27. What led you to choose your field or major study?
28. What college subjects did you like best? Why?
29. What college subjects did you like least? Why?
30. If you could do so, how would you plan your academic study differently? Why?
31. What changes would you make in your college or university?
32. Do you have plans for continued study? An advanced degree?
33. Do you think that your grades are a good indication of your academic achievement?
34. What have you learned from participation in extracurricular activities?
35. In what kind of a work environment are you most comfortable?
36. How do you work under pressure?
37. In what part-time or summer jobs have you been most interested? Why?
38. How would you describe the ideal job for you following graduation?
39. Why did you decide to seek a position with this company?.
40. What do you know about our company?
41. What two or three things are most important to you in your job?
42. Are you seeking employment in a company of a certain size? Why?
43. What criteria are you using to evaluate the company for which you hope to work?
44. Do you have a geographical preference? Why?
45. Will you relocate? Does relocation bother you?
46. Are you willing to travel?
47. Are you willing to spend at least six months as a trainee?
48. Why do you think you might like to live in the community in which our company is located?
49. What major problem have you encountered and how did you deal with it?
50. What have you learned from your mistakes?

*Northwestern University Endicott Report copyrighted and published by the Placement Center, Northwestern University, Evanston, IL.

videotaped job interviews that were successful and unsuccessful. She analyzed the tapes to check how frequently some 93 rhetorical behaviors were in evidence either verbally or nonverbally. These were clustered under basic principles. Job candidates should: (1) convey positive images of themselves, (2) identify with their interviewers, (3) offer well-supported arguments, (4) organize their thoughts coherently, (5) phrase their ideas in clear and appropriate language, and deliver their messages effectively.

What distinguishes the winners from the losers in the job hunt? Einhorn's research into this question discovered a number of differences in the way those who are hired, compared to those who are not, performed in the job interview. She observed that:

- Those who are successful convey positive images, whereas the unsuccessful do not. That is to say the successful had clearly defined career goals that were realizable with the prospective employer. They wanted careers, not jobs. Those who did not get hired failed to describe a position they wanted and their career goals for the future. Some waffled among many alternatives such as graphics, buying, sales, and going on to graduate school. Employers are not interested in hiring candidates who cannot define what they want.
- Those who are successful identify with the prospective employer and seek a specific job with a certain firm whereas those who fail to get the jobs appear to be shopping around as though they were looking for an attractively packaged job that could be picked from among many on a department store shelf. Shopping around turns the interviewee into screener, a role reversal that does not wear well with personnel. Those who get hired openly express their interest in the firm for which they are interviewing over other possibilities. They show enthusiasm for what they learn about the firm. Those who do not get hired fail to find anything complimentary to say to their prospective employer.
- Those who get hired research the prospective employer. They gather information about the firm from friends, the library, and from the organization's public relations department.
- Those who get hired speak articulately about the qualities they possess that may benefit the prospective employer. They rate themselves positively on such traits as analytical skills, flexibility, initiative, leadership, and organizational skills. The successful make a good argument for their being hired. They are able, modestly, to present testimonials as to their competence and reliability. Those who fail to get jobs discount their assets and sometimes accentuate their faults.
- Those who are hired are better communicators. They ask appropriate questions. They are more certain and have fewer "um hums," "okays," "yeahs," and "nos." They don't need prodding. They take control of their side of the interview. They expand more upon their answers and laugh more than do those who do not get hired. Those who do not get the jobs use more ambiguous and negative language such as "I guess," "pretty good," "awful," "dull," and "difficult." Those who get hired are more assertive and affirmative, using such words as "progress," "improvement," "advantage," "enjoyment," and "success." The successful are able to use the jargon and technical language of the job. They combine their words with clarity, whereas those who don't get hired often speak with jumbled thoughts, and piece their sentences together with many "ands." The successful applicants are active listeners. They look at their interviewers without staring and they nod at what they hear. The difference is significant between those who get hired as compared to those who do not have successful interviews.

Box 6-5   **More on Proving Your Way to a Job Offer**

Listen carefully to all questions during the interview. Relax as much as possible and think in terms of "What is this recruiter asking me to prove?"

1. "Why did you sign up for this interview?" The recruiter is asking you to prove that you are interested in the company and the job.

2. "Have you always lived in the Midwest?" If the job opening is out East, the recruiter is asking you to prove that you will relocate. Most candidates simply say, "Yes, I am open to relocation," and that is simply not enough proof to warrant spending $1,000 for airfare, hotel, and food on a plant trip interview.

3. "What is your greatest strength?" This is the best question you'll ever receive. Here is your opportunity to prove that you have the most important strength required for this particular job. Don't blow it by proving some off-the-wall strength that doesn't have a high priority on this recruiter's checklist.

4. "Why weren't your grades higher than a 2.1?" Be thankful that the recruiter asked this question. If the recruiter is concerned about a liability and doesn't ask about it, he or she has already decided to send you a turndown. In this case, the recruiter is giving you an opportunity to prove that you are technically competent in spite of your average grades.

5. "What is your greatest weakness?" This question is very obvious. The recruiter is simply saying, "Hey, I'm looking for a reason to turn you down. Can you give me a good solid weakness so I can end this interview five minutes early?" Always sidestep the question. Give a recruiter a non-weakness, like "I'm a workaholic" or "I'm overly sensitive to people."

Source: From John L. LaFevre, *How You Really Get Hired*, 3rd ed, Prentice-Hall, 1992.

WE MEAN BUSINESS

Think of one question you have been asked on an interview. Share your question with the rest of the class so you can build a repertoire of interview questions.

Not only must you analyze yourself and your audience so that you can best handle these open questions, but you should also practice impromptu speaking skills. The word impromptu means "speaking off the cuff" or without prior preparation. Effective speakers are ones who can quickly and clearly organize ideas without punctuating them with "um" or "uh." The way to improve impromptu skills is with practice. Within this chapter you will find several boxes that contain sample questions used in interviews. This is a good place to start. Also research other interviewing sources, and use current event topics as subjects of your impromptu mini-speeches. Knowledge of current events can be a definite asset in the interview.

Legal-Illegal Questions

At this point the authors would like to take a moment to recognize the fact that not all questions asked within an interview are appropriate or even legal. Questions are not supposed to be asked if they in any way discriminate on the basis of race, color, sex, religion, age, or national origin, and there are laws that support these restrictions. This is why we discourage you from including personal data within your résumé. You could be allowing discrimination to occur.

Yet this issue is not so cut and dried. When an employer asks a question that is considered illegal (see Box 6-6 for a list of illegal questions), what should we do? This is an ethical issue that only you can decide. We have discussed this issue in our own classrooms, and will share with you a few comments from students. Some students do not consider some questions offensive, and if they really want the job, they will answer without hesitation. Other students remarked that if they did consider the questions offensive, they would either comment that they did not feel that the interviewer had the right to ask the question, or would answer but turn down a job offer from this company. The questions you should ask yourself before you go into an interview are these: "Does it bother me if they ask questions about my ethnic or religious background? Will I answer questions that I consider discriminatory? Do I want to work for a company that uses discriminatory tactics? Are they truly discriminating, or is this simply information they are using to get to know me better? How badly do I want this job?"

For example, one may respond to illegal questions by saying, "Yes, I plan to have children sometime, but now I am career-minded." Or "Like most people, I have a personal life, but I'm determined not to let it interfere with my job." Or simply answer, "You can count on me to be dependable" and ignore an illegal question into your personal life.

When the time limit of your interview is nearing, the interviewer will usually signal that the talk is concluding with some sort of summarization of your discussion and an idea of what you should expect to hear in the future. For example, an interviewer may say, "Well, that is just about all of the time that we have left today. We are interviewing 20 other applicants for these three openings. The last interview is on Friday, and we will contact the finalists by phone Friday afternoon. . . ." This indication that you have reached the closure phase should signal you to get ready for your final responsibility as an interviewee. You should have prepared for the next line, which typically is, "Do you have any questions for me?"

One of the cardinal rules of interviewing is that you should always have questions prepared to ask at the close of an interview. As we mentioned earlier in the chapter, recruiters won't look twice at somebody who hasn't conducted research about the organization where they are interviewing. Recruiters laugh when, after a 20-minute interview they ask, "Do you have any questions?" and the interviewee responds, "No, you have told me everything that I need to know." In fact, Mark Satterfield, a former human resource director at Kraft, Inc., reported that nothing "kills" an interview faster than when a candidate either has no questions to ask at the end of an interview, or asks pointless questions. Box 6-7 provides a sample list of questions that could be asked at the end of the first interview. Write a list of several questions and bring these questions with you so that you remember them. Be sure to include many questions on your list, as much of the information may be covered during the interview.

The closing of an interview mirrors the opening in that the nonverbal behavior expectations are similar. You are expected to rise with poise, thank the interviewer for his/her time, and indicate that you look forward to hearing from them. You then should shake hands, and walk with head high out the door. Do not show any signs of nervousness, relief, anger, etc., until you are safely in your car.

The Stress Interview

> The recruiter lounged in her chair, Marissa's résumé in hand, studying it indifferently. The recruiter tossed the résumé carelessly across the desk, looked up, and shrugged. "So, Marissa Edwards, I'm Paige Bailey from the Data Corporation. Go ahead and start."
>
> Adapted from Sandra Davis
> *How to Handle the Stress Interview*

The excerpt above illustrates a type of interview many of us do not prepare for — the stress interview. Many reports from students and recruiters indicate that stress interviewing techniques are being used more and more frequently. Why? Because classes such as the one in which you are enrolled now and books such as this teach students interview preparation. Stress interviews are a way to elicit unrehearsed responses and see how candidates react under pressure.

Stress techniques can play an important part in extracting information that only spontaneous answers and actions can provide. A recruiter may tell the applicant to "prove they are worth" being hired by their company. When this question is posed, the interviewer could want the applicant to prove why he or she should be one of the top 5 percent asked back for a final interview. Other questions that are sometimes included in a stress interview are:

Box 6-6   **Interviewing and Your Legal Rights**

Federal law restricts employment interview questions to areas clearly related to job requirements. The following are questions that are generally considered legitimate and those that are not.

Questions an Employer Can Ask
1. Asking applicant to submit proof of age by supplying birth certificate or baptismal record if required to support alcoholic beverage minimum age requirements.

2. Asking applicant if he or she is a citizen of the United States.

3. Asking applicant to indicate what foreign languages can be spoken, written, or read fluently.

4. Asking applicant about past work experience.

5. Requesting applicant to provide names of family or relatives who work in unit or in company.

6. Telling applicants they must observe prescribed standards to obtain a position in your unit (for example, to get a haircut).

7. Asking applicant if he or she has reliable transportation to work. (Do not ask what type.)

8. Asking if applicant has ever been under the care of a psychologist or psychiatrist. (In some states you cannot ask this.)

9. Asking an applicant to "trial" perform the job prior to hiring if physical height, weight, or other personal stamina conditions are in question.

10. Asking an applicant how he or she can be reached if he or she has no phone.

11. Asking an applicant if he or she is a veteran and to state type of military work.

12. Asking an applicant for the names of references.

Questions an Employer Cannot Ask*
1. Asking if applicant has ever worked under another name.

2. Asking applicant to name birthplace.

3. Asking for birthplace of applicant's parents, spouse, or other close relatives.

4. Asking applicant to submit proof of age by supplying birth certificate or baptismal record (that is, asking an obviously older person to state his or her age).

5. Asking applicant for religious affiliation, name of church, parish, or religious holidays observed.

6. Asking an applicant if he or she is a naturalized citizen.

7. Asking an applicant for the date citizenship was acquired.

8. Asking an applicant if he or she was ever arrested for any crime and to indicate when and where.

9. Asking a veteran what type of military discharge was received.

10. Asking the applicant how he or she acquired the ability to read, write, or speak a foreign language.

11. Requesting an applicant to provide names of three relatives other than father, husband or wife, or minor-age dependent children.

12. Asking an applicant for his or her weight and height.

13. Asking an applicant if he or she is married, single, divorced, separated, or engaged.

14. Asking a female applicant for her maiden name.

15. Asking an applicant for mother's maiden name. .

16. Asking a woman if she has children and if she has babysitting problems.

17. Asking for the names of brothers and sisters.

18. Asking if membership is held in any clubs, societies, and lodges and to name them.

19. Asking that a photograph be included with application for employment.

20. Asking for addresses of relatives such as cousins, uncles, aunts, nephews, and grandparents who can be contacted for reference.

21. Asking an applicant to specify the type of transportation available to work.

22. Telling a female applicant that the job is a "man's job."

23. Refusing to hire a qualified female applicant because she is three months pregnant.

24. Advertising for "hostess only" position. (This would be considered an unlawful practice.)

25. Not interviewing or considering an older person for a position because he or she does not fit the image of the position.

26. Asking an applicant if he or she lives with anyone or if he or she sees his or her ex-spouse.

27. Asking applicant if he or she owns or rents or if he or she lives in an apartment or a house.

Source: From Ronald Adler, *Communicating at Work*.

*Questions cannot be asked if they in any way discriminate on the basis of race, color, religion, sex, national origin, or age. Questions like these can only be asked if they are clearly job related.

Box 6-7   **Appropriate Questions to Ask at the End of the Initial Job Interview**

Remember to select questions that may directly influence you.

1. What could I expect as a typical first assignment?

2. Which of your locations have the type of opportunities I am looking for?

3. What type of orientation would I have?

4. What type of training program do you have? How long is the training period?

5. What career path can I expect in your organization?

6. How often would my performance be reviewed? What is the procedure for review?

7. Do you have any recent graduates from (your university) working for you?

8. What percentage of supervisory positions are filled from within the company?

9. How frequently do you relocate professional employees? Is relocation voluntary or expected?

10. How much travel is normally expected?

11. Are there any immediate plans for expansion in your organization, either in new offices, new market areas, or new fields? Are there possibilities for new employees to become involved in these ventures?

12. How would you describe the atmosphere of the organization? In your opinion, why is this a good place to work?

- What makes you think we ought to pay attention to you?
- Why do you think you are of high enough caliber for us?
- We have tried to hire business majors before, and they never seemed to work out right. What makes you different?
- See this pen I'm holding? Sell it to me.
- Pretend I'm your boss and I just told you that the presentation that you made this morning was terrible.

Impromptu skills are tested with each of the above questions. This is why practice is so important! Although you cannot anticipate the exact questions asked, by perfecting the art of organization and delivery you will score higher in the game. Dr. Sandra Davis, an industrial psychologist and author of *How to Handle the Stress Interview*, says that the content of your answer is often not as important as how you field the question.

Dr. Davis also wrote about nonverbal games played during this type of interview. Within the nonverbal chapter we discussed nonverbals and power. You remember that nonverbals such as lack of eye contact, and general kinesic cues that display disinterest are linked with power. The "stress" interviewer will most likely send these cues. Another nonverbal cue he or she uses to increase stress is silence. Silence creates awkwardness for most of us. You need to learn to use silence to your advantage. Try to keep in mind that these manipulations of nonverbal cues are just that, and don't take it personally.

Consider the three stages of interviewing: the opening, body, and closing; and what the responsibilities typically are of the interviewer. If the interviewer does not fulfill these responsibilities, as was illustrated at the beginning of this section, the interviewee should take it upon him/herself to handle these functions. If an interviewer says "Go ahead and start," he or she probably wants to see how you can take control of an awkward situation. So, begin with the functions of rapport and orientation!

Typically stress interviews do not occur during the first round of interviews, and will almost never occur at the campus interview. This style of interviewing is used to weed out candidates, see how you would handle stress and challenge on the job, and observe your impromptu and nonverbal skills. This technique is used to learn more about you, the interviewee. Preparation for every answer is impossible, and these interviewers just want to see you as "yourself." If you are subject to this type of interview, relax, take a deep breath, and accept the challenge!

What Recruiters Are Looking For

The sections above have outlined many responsibilities and expectations of an employment interview. Let us add a few final notes. The nonverbal chapter mentioned "dressing for success," and we would like to emphasize the importance of dressing appropriately. The best colors are conservatives such as dark blue and gray, and for women maroon is also acceptable. Do be sure to wear a suit, not just slacks and a blazer. Also be aware of what accessories you select. Mark Satterfield once interviewed a 22-year-old college student who wore a gold Rolex to the interview. Throughout the interview Mr. Satterfield kept wondering, "How could a 22-year-old afford such an expensive timepiece? Did he really need the job he was interviewing for? Would he, and could he financially, quit work the first time the going got tough?" Satterfield couldn't remember a word that the young man said during the interview. But he did remember that watch! The moral: Do not wear accessories that will draw attention away from you.

Time is another nonverbal factor worth mentioning again. Remember the study mentioned within Chapter 5 about the secretaries who were asked to judge competence based on arrival time? Jeffrey Allen, in his book *How to Turn an Interview Into a Job*, echoes these ideas. Many students are taught to arrive early, but as the study of secretaries and Jeffrey Allen prove, this can be a deadly mistake. Arriving early does not mean that you should rush

Box 6-8   **Ten Surefire Ways to Improve Your Chances of Getting a Turndown**

1. Be shy and reticent, with a lack of self-confidence.

2. Indicate that you are a ''window shopper,'' a candidate who already knows where he or she will probably work, but who just wants to check around in the job market.

3. Indicate that you aren't sure what you want to do.

4. Ask for counseling in the interview.

5. Bring a copy of you senior class project for ''show and tell.''

6. Have a nervous mannerism such as drumming your fingers on the desk or ending each statement with ''. . . you know?''

7. Don't ask any challenging questions. Instead, say things like, ''Boy, it sounds great. I can't think of any questions.''

8. Apologize because you didn't have time to read the company's literature in the placement office.

9. Knock on the door to get the interviewer to hurry up with the evaluation he or she is trying to complete on the last candidate.

10. Answer a question with that age-old statement, ''I really like working with people.''

Source: *CPC Annual, 32nd Edition,* 1988–1989, 40.

in to wait in the reception area for half an hour. It does mean that you arrive about 20 to 30 minutes early and stay outside the building where you can review your notes and get your bearings. On the other hand, lateness conveys messages that you are neither time-conscious nor considerate. Both messages could lead to rejection.

Finally, practice your oral communication skills, including greeting behavior and impromptu communication. The article ''On Trial for Your Life'' included rankings of the seven categories chosen by recruiters surveyed as the top areas of evaluation. Notice how each one of these involves demonstration of oral, written, or nonverbal communication skills. These seven areas in rank order are:

1. Personal impression—neatness, presence, business maturity, confidence, attitude, sociability, tact
2. Communication skills—logic, written and oral skills, conciseness, articulateness
3. Enthusiasm—interest, sincerity

4. Leadership — leadership potential, leadership indicators
5. Competence — knowledge in field, expertise, work experience, grades
6. Vocational maturity — clearly defined goals, knowledge of strengths and weaknesses, realistic self-concept
7. Interest — knowledge of company, interview preparation

A colleague of one of the authors sent a letter he had received from a personnel specialist. The last paragraph of the letter read, "By the way, in my experience the one trait that most frequently eliminates new graduates from obtaining a given position is weak oral communication skills. Perhaps in your advisory capacity you can stress this to students."

SUMMARY

Interviewing is a form of dyadic communication in which the roles of the speaker and listener are constantly changing. Most interviews involve interaction between people of differing status. The interviewer typically determines whether the interview will follow a directive or nondirective approach.

Although as college students we are most familiar with the selection interview, there are many other important forms of interviews with which we will be involved once in the workplace. Some of these include information-giving and -gathering, problems of employee behavior, problem-solving, and persuasive interviews. It is important to be aware of these types of interviews from the perspective of both superior and subordinate.

The majority of the chapter focused on preparation for the selection or employment interview. In order to have a successful interview, it is essential to recognize the responsibilities of both the interviewee and the interviewer. Awareness of the procedure involved in the opening, body, and closing of an interview will help guide the interview more smoothly. Understanding these stages also will help if the tables are turned on the candidate, as is the case with the stress interview.

Perhaps the most important message of this chapter is to acknowledge the pervasiveness of one-on-one communication, and the need to refine our communication skills for the interview. With careful analysis of ourselves as our product, we can put our best self forward. Interviews are often won or lost within the first few minutes, for reasons intangible to some. Some interviewers get a feeling that this person will fit easily into the company's culture; some like the ease and energy of the person's presence. Each interviewer will be different, and we need not get discouraged if indeed we are not the best "package" for a particular recruiter. The real test of an interview is to learn enough to make a wise decision, wise both for the organization and for the job candidate. The interviewer should seek to provide realistic expectations for the candidate. The candidate should seek a realistic picture of what the job entails. Remember, you are trying to choose a company that is right for you, and if you can obtain enough information, you will probably know when it "feels" right for you. The company must do the same in its decision process.

Writing skills, so necessary to getting and keeping a good job, will be discussed in the next chapter.

SKILL BUILDER: STRESS INTERVIEW

Divide the class into groups of three, including one interviewee, interviewer, and observer. The interviewees will leave the room while the interviewers are told the type of interview tactics to use. Half of the interviewers will perform stress interviews, and the others will use regular interviewing tactics. Observers should fill in the following information about the interviewee.

Each member of the group should be given the opportunity to play each role.

Determine whether the interviewee did or did not demonstrate the desired nonverbal behaviors listed in the right column. Check "yes" or "no" in the left column to indicate your judgment.

Demonstrated Behaviors	Desired Behaviors	Yes	No
1. Eyes	Eye contact—Maintained consistent eye contact without gazing or staring.	————	————
2. Face and head	Facial expression—Punctuated interaction with occasional eyebrow lift and head nods. Mouth—Punctuated interaction with occasional smiles.	————	————
3. Facing client	Body orientation and posture—Faced the other person, slight lean forward (from waist up), body appeared relaxed.	————	————
4. Leaning forward		————	————
5. Relaxed body		————	————
6. Completed sentences	Paralanguage—Completed sentences without "uhs" or hesitations in delivery, asked one question at a time, did not ramble.	————	————
7. Smooth delivery— no speech errors		————	————
8. Distance	Distance—Seats of counselor and client were between 3 feet and 5 apart.	————	————

SKILL BUILDER: INTERVIEW GAME

Directions Four to eight persons may play. Players should be seated on opposite sides of a conference table or in chairs without a table; three or four members on each side. One side plays the role of employers; the other candidates and sides may be selected by choice or by the flip of a coin. The employers should assume a need for each candidate. The candidates should assume that each of them is applying for a real position in his field or probable vocation.

Employers take turns in each stage directing questions to candidates or the first employer may read a general statement to the candidates as the cards so designate. If the game is played by individuals already employed in their chosen occupations, it may be played without advance preparation. Students ought to be allowed to prepare for one hour to one week. A careful examination of the questions in each stage is permissible and advisable. The lasting value of the Interview Game is COMMUNICATION of vocational training, and therefore serious preparation is recommended when played as part of a course of study. The length of the game depends upon the number of players. If four candidates are playing and each candidate is expected to answer all four questions, that stage may last 80 minutes. In the shortened version each candidate answers a different question, thus a stage lasts 20 minutes. There is no hurry or pressure in time inherent in the game. More than ample time is allowed to answer questions. The game may last for several periods.

The goal of the game is to be offered a job and to be the most wanted candidate among the four applicants. For maximum value as a class exercise, the employers and candidates should reverse roles after completing the five stages for the first group of candidates.

Goal — A favorable impression

Attitude — A fair, yet modest description of one's probable worth as an employee

Stage 1: Conversational Ability

Read by the first employer: Each of you has just arrived for your interview. The secretary says that the regional office is on long distance and therefore the interviews will not begin for 15 minutes. She offers coffee and suggests that you candidates get acquainted with each other.

The employers' scores for this first stage are based on each candidate's conversational ability. (See score sheet.)

Stage 2: Knowledge of Field

First employer: "Tell me a little about your training." (Allows up to five minutes for the first candidate to answer if playing the short version. All candidates answer in turn each of the questions if playing the long version.)

Employer two: "What are some of the exciting things happening in your field?" (Same directions as above questions.)

Employer three: Have you formulated some ideas about the kind of place you'd like to work?"

Employer four: "Do you have any questions you'd like to ask me?" (The employer does not answer these questions, but rather evaluates the candidates' ability to ask questions. In the long version of the game each candidate is invited to answer all four of the above questions.)

At the close of this stage all employers rate the candidates in stage two on score sheet.

Stage 3: Personality and Humor Quotient

Read by employer two: "The setting for this exercise is a cocktail party for the candidates. Fifteen minutes is scheduled for this. Short stories, jokes, and incidents appropriate to the candidates' occupation or to other topics that arise indicate the candidates' ability to mix. The employers do not sit back and watch in this stage. Rather, they join the party."

Employer two calls time and all employers score each candidate on the score card.

Stage 4: Bargaining

Employer one: "Now perhaps we're at the stage where we can talk business. We would be interested in hearing from you what kind of financial arrangements we might make that would be attractive to you. Do you have such a figure in mind?" (In long version, each candidate is permitted an answer.)

Employer two: "What are your goals for the next few years?"

Employer three: "How do you feel about unions and collective bargaining?"

Employer four: "Are there any fringe benefits or secretarial help you feel is important to you?"

After each candidate is allowed up to five minutes to answer all questions in the long version or just one in the short, the employers rate each candidate on the score card in stage four.

Stage 5: Creativity

Employer one: "We've had some problems here. In short, we're all interested in improving our output and cutting costs. We know you can't analyze our situation, and we're not bringing you in as an efficiency expert, but we would appreciate getting your ideas and impressions. So would you brainstorm with us for a few minutes?"

Employer two: "Occasionally we have some problems with our employees. If you were supervisor, how would you handle a problem of tardiness and excessively long coffee breaks?"

Employer three: "Do you have any suggestions for encouraging leadership or improving administrative communication with our employees?"

Employee four: "What would you suggest to improve morale in our organization?" Alternate question: "In light of the technological revolution, what future do you see for your vocation?"

Each employer now rates each candidate in the stage five section of the score card. Tabulate scores for each but do not disclose them until sides are reversed and the second group of candidates have completed all five stages.

INTERVIEW SCORE SHEET

Candidate's Name	Stages					Total
	1	2	3	4	5	

Scores entered under each stage:
1 = weak   2 = fair   3 = adequate   4 = good   5 = excellent

Total of all five stages:
0–7 = weak   8–12 = fair   13–17 = adequate   18–22 = good   23–25 = excellent

RESOURCES

Adler, Ronald B. (1986). *Communicating at work* (2nd ed.). New York: Random House.

Allen, Jeffrey G. (1983). *How to turn an interview into a job.* New York: Simon and Schuster.

Davis, Sandra L. (1987). "How to handle the stress interview." *Business Week's Guide to Careers*, 26–29.

Drake, John D. (1982). *Interviewing for managers.* New York: AMACOM.

Einhorn, Lois. (1979). "The rhetorical dimensions of employment interviews: An investigation of communication behaviors contributing to applicant success." (Doctoral dissertation, Indiana University.)

Goodall, H. Lloyd, Gerald L. Wilson, and Christopher L. Waagen. (1986). "The performance appraisal interview reassessment." *Quarterly Journal of Speech*, 72, 74–87.

Gorden, William I., and John R. Miller. (1983). *Managing your communication: In and for the organization.* Prospect Heights, IL: Waveland.

LaFevre, John L. (1988–1989). "Interviewing: The inside story from a college recruiter." *CPC Annual*, 32, 37–40.

McCombs, K. B., and Fred M. Jablin. (1984). "Verbal correlates of interviewer empathic listening and employment interview outcomes." *Communication Monographs*, 51, 353–371.

Satterfield, Mark. (1989). "Why you weren't hired." *Managing Your Career: The College Edition of the National Employment Weekly*, 24–26.

Stewart, Charles J. (1976). *Teaching interviewing for career preparation.* Falls Church, VA: Speech Communication Association.

Stewart, Charles J., and William B. Cash, Jr. (1988). *Interviewing: Principles and practices*, (5th ed.). Dubuque, IA: Wm. C. Brown.

Tengler, Craig D., and Fred M. Jablin. (1983). "Effects of question type, orientation, and sequencing in employment interviews." *Communication Monographs*, 50, 245–263.

Yate, Martin John. (1987). "On trial for your life." *Managing Your Career: The College Edition of the National Employment Weekly*, 35.

Chapter 7

Written Communication in the Workplace

Concepts for discussion

- Résumés
- Application letters
- Follow-up letters
- Rejection letters
- Acceptance letters
- Inquiry letters

- Memos
- Resignation letters
- Recommendations and evaluations
- Invitations

James H. Boren, founder of the International Association of Professional Bureaucrats, noted in one of the organization's newsletters that he had learned that universities had "the ability to answer letters without first reading them."

As part of a study of academic search committees, he said he applied for several deanships. One typical application letter contained such candid information as this: "I have been giving some thought to implementing a program of partial retirement. More specifically, a position that would involve very little work while carrying with it a nice title that would enhance one's social position in the community. It appears that the position of Dean, College of Business Administration, might offer the combination I seek." He said he knew nothing about the field, but promised ''I never question policies enunciated from above no matter how stupid they may be.''

A reply from the search committee said, ''We are very pleased to have your application and to have the opportunity to consider you for the position.''

Reader's Digest
February 1989, p. 138

Effective communication involves more than just proper nonverbals and a great sales pitch. The written communication channel communicates powerful messages of competence, and too often of incompetence.

Written communication in the workplace serves many functions, both before and after you become employed. The ability to write a letter of application effectively and persuasively can make the difference between rejection and landing the job. After you have found a suitable job, written communication is vital for success and advancement in the workplace.

Writing for business applications requires many of the same steps as most other writing tasks. First, you must determine your purpose and the reader's needs, then develop an outline. Next, prepare a rough draft and proofread it, preferably leaving it for a period of time so you'll be more objective in rereading. Revise the rough draft, making sure all grammar, spelling, and punctuation are correct. Also check to be sure you are saying what you mean in a clear, concise fashion. The style you use should be appropriate for the person receiving the letter—you write differently to a good friend than you would when writing to a stranger. In business, there is also a variety of appropriate styles, depending on the purpose and recipient of your letter.

In this chapter, we will first discuss the written communication that takes place while you are still outside of the workplace. We'll give you the ''how to's'' of writing résumés, cover letters, follow-up letters, and inquiry letters.

After we've gotten you the job you want, we will examine the kinds of writing you will have to master in your job. You'll learn how to write memos, minutes of meetings, and how to handle resignation letters. Also, we present guidelines for measuring readability and channel choice.

The purpose of this chapter is to demonstrate the importance of and variety in writing skills that will help you get the job you want, and once in, will allow you to communicate effectively both inside and outside of the organization. This way, when you write, people will know that you mean business!

WRITING FROM OUTSIDE THE ORGANIZATION

"If a good résumé is a work of art, a bad résumé can be a masterpiece of self-destruction."

David Hizer and Arthur Rosenberg
The Résumé Handbook

Résumés

A résumé is a key element in the job hunt. It is often the résumé, along with a cover letter, that provides the employer's first impression of an applicant. The résumé's primary purpose is to convince the recruiter to grant you an interview. This is accomplished by highlighting your qualifications for the position in a visually attractive format. Résumés also serve other functions, such as helping you in self-assessment while preparing for interviews (See Chapter 6 to review details), reminding the recruiter of you after the interview, and aiding employers in making their final decision about applicants.

Most college students would do well to prepare a résumé. You never know when opportunity will knock, and if your résumé is ready, you won't miss the chance. Also, preparing your résumé will help put past experiences into perspective and give you a clearer view of your abilities and career goals.

In preparing to write your résumé, the first rule to remember is that there are no rules. There is no one right way to write a résumé. We will provide suggestions based on our experience and research, but the information you include and the format you use should be determined by you and your background, and the job for which you are applying. You will need to decide what about you would most impress an employer, and then determine how best to highlight those facts in a very brief format.

Content of the Résumé

The first step in writing your résumé is to collect the information you will need. You should write down a complete history of your education, employment, and activities. Use the technique of brainstorming at this stage; think of every skill, interest, or past achievement that could possibly interest an employer. Once you have all your past experiences on paper, then begin prioritizing the lists and eliminating those items of least importance.

When you become serious about job searching, you may wish to prepare a different version of the résumé for each interview situation, and you may prioritize your lists uniquely for each. Each ranking will be determined by what is most applicable to the job for which you are applying.

Now that you have a prioritized list of the most important of your experiences, you are ready to place them into a résumé format.

WE MEAN BUSINESS

Write down all activities and experiences of your college years that come to mind. Prioritize these in the order you think would be most effective for a résumé for the career in which you are interested.

Elements of the Résumé

While there is much variability in what you include in your résumé, most experts agree that a résumé should contain these basic sections:

- Identifying Information—The essential information is your name, address, and telephone number, and this should be placed at the top of the résumé (where it is easily identifiable). If you have different current and permanent addresses, include both. Be sure to include a phone number where you can easily be reached.
- Education—List any degrees attained, major, minor, and the college or colleges you attended. Also include any academic honors you earned, and grade point average if you feel it will impress a recruiter. The dates of your schooling should be included as well. You may wish to also include significant coursework that would help target a specific position.
- Employment History—In this section, list the jobs you have held, beginning with the most recent. Include job title, name of employer, and date of employment. Provide a short description of specific duties or responsibilities that are relevant to the job you are seeking. Also specify any promotions, special honors, or outstanding achievements that occurred on each job. Again, what you include in this section should be determined by its relevance to the prospective employer and the position for which you are applying. Be sure to use action words that highlight skills used. Also be certain that all material is consistent in tense.
- Activities—A wide variety of information can be listed in this section. Membership in service or professional organizations is commonly noted here. Other entries could be special skills or hobbies you have developed, leadership positions you have held outside of a work setting, or awards you have received. Remember that employers will be looking for people with whom they can get along, so if they see a common interest, you have an edge on others trying for the job.

This category encompasses many things, so be selective in what you include. Recruiters are increasingly looking at this section for evidence of leadership, teamwork, time management, and community responsibility.

Box 7-1 **Your Résumé "Speaks" About You**

A résumé ''speaks'' to a prospective employer. Here are some qualities that can be revealed within a carefully crafted résumé:

1. Industriousness and ambition. Activities, employment, and achievements illustrate this.

2. Cooperative attitude. Participation in activities, clubs, and sports speak to this.

3. Interest in the work and enthusiasm for the employer's product or service. Any courses, employment, and activities that reflect that interest should be highlighted on the résumé.

Source: Adapted from John L Munschauer, ''The Résumé: How to Speak to Employers' Needs,'' *CPC Annual*, 1988, pp. 20–32.

- References — Most experts recommend that names of references not be provided on the résumé itself. This saves space, and a phrase such as "References furnished upon request" is probably sufficient. Some go further, and suggest devoting any space to references is unnecessary, but if your résumé is particularly short or you have secured a prominent person as a reference, you may want to include that information on your résumé. Giving the names of your references also makes it easier for the recruiter to contact them. If you decide to include your references, you should list their names, titles, addresses, and phone numbers.

    Regardless of whether you use your references on the résumé, be sure to have their phone numbers and addresses available for an interviewer. Of course, always secure permission from your references before listing their names.

In addition to these most basic elements of a résumé, there are other sections that you can include at your discretion. It is especially important to tailor these to the individual situation for which you are preparing your résumé.

- Employment Objective — The objective should be a simple, brief statement usually including the kind of job you are seeking, as well as any long-term goals for your career. Most experts advise including this on the résumé if you have room to do so. Remember, the employer will check to see if you have experience that backs up what you claim is your employment objective. The employment objective serves the same function as a thesis statement in a presentation (see

Chapter 11). Everything in your résumé should support this claim. Here are a few examples of possible employment objectives:

— Desire to work with a team of professionals to further expand my experience, knowledge, and skills in the fields of interpersonal communication and human resource management.

— Desire an entry-level position in information systems field that utilizes my analytical, communication, and programming skills productively. Aspire to be a systems analyst.

— Desire challenging entry-level position that will utilize my skills and provide more experience in sales, marketing, and advertising. Aspire to advance to position of greater responsibility within upper management.

• Personal Information—This category may include facts such as height, weight, date of birth, health status, or other similar facts about yourself. This information was standard on résumés until recent years, but most résumés today do not include it. One reason is that federal legislation now prohibits employers from asking for information such as age, religion, height, or weight. Even though some employers may expect to see personal information on the résumé, providing it may give them a reason to discriminate against you. Also, including personal facts often does not increase your chance of being hired, because it is usually irrelevant to job performance. So, the decision to include personal information on your résumé should be made carefully. Only include facts that will enhance your chance of getting hired, and that have a direct bearing on the job you want.

Organization of the Résumé

Two patterns of organization are most commonly used for résumés: functional and chronological. For the most part, both patterns will include the same information with differing organization and emphasis. You should choose a format for your résumé based on what you want to stress to the prospective employer.

A chronological résumé is the traditional form and the easiest, because you simply list what you have done in the past in reverse chronological order. This type of résumé is often used by those without a lot of work experience.

In a functional résumé, the candidate lists abilities and past accomplishments in order of their importance, rather than the order they happened. This format emphasizes qualifications and skills, especially those you feel apply to the job for which the résumé is written. You will have to think of a few particular skills or abilities you have acquired that qualify you for this position. Functional résumés are often used when the applicant has significant gaps in his or her work history due to unemployment or illness.

See Box 7-2 for some advantages and disadvantages of both types.

Box 7-2   **Résumé Formats**

Advantages of a chronological résumé

1. Employers are familiar with this traditional format.

2. Traces your past and tells the reader what you have done.

3. Easy to compose.

Disadvantages of a chronological résumé
1. Readers must decide from your past what you are capable of in the future.

2. Your experience may not support your job objective.

3. May look like all the other résumés.

Advantages of a functional résumé
1. Tells the employer what you think your greatest strengths and weaknesses are.

2. Relates specific skills to the job objective.

3. Allows you to combine educational, work, and unpaid experience in one section.

4. May catch readers' attention because it isn't the standard form.

Disadvantages of a functional résumé
1. If job objective and skills are not adequately specified, résumé will be ineffective.

2. More difficult to write than the chronological resume.

Source: Adapted from Lois Johnson Rew, *Introduction to Technical Writing: Process and Practice.*

Appearance of the Résumé

While the appearance of your résumé may not ultimately get you the interview, it can certainly guarantee that you *won't* get the interview. Employers often believe the résumé reflects the personality and level of professionalism of the applicant. Thus, if your résumé looks sloppy or unprofessional, the employer will form a negative impression of you, and you will very possibly never be given the opportunity to counteract that impression in an interview.

Statistics show that most employers only spend about 20 seconds looking at your résumé before deciding whether it deserves further study or the rejection pile. Because 20 seconds is not enough time to read the entire résumé, you must organize the information to highlight your best features. You need to find a way to make your résumé stand out from all the others the recruiter is looking through, and you cannot give the person an excuse to reject you before he or she even reads the résumé.

Writing the Résumé

Now that you have gathered all the pertinent data you need and have decided on the best pattern of organization for that information, you are ready to actually put it down on paper. Having put all that effort into compiling and organizing an effective résumé, it makes good sense to show off your work as attractively as possible.

First, you need to find the paper that will best display this information. Generally, you should use good quality, heavy bond paper, either white or an off-white such as eggshell or tan. Certain fields such as arts or advertising might find other colors acceptable, but for most professions, a more conservative look is preferable. Also, the size of the paper should be the standard 8½″ × 11″. While legal-size paper will grab attention, it may not be appreciated by meticulous employers.

Next, there are some basic principles to follow in organizing the material on the page. These help the résumé look appealing and make it easy to read. The organization should draw the reader's eyes to the main points you want to emphasize. Distribute the information on the page evenly, avoiding big white spaces or large blocks of print. Try to make the material appear somewhat symmetrical, and be sure to leave at least a one-inch margin on all four sides of the paper.

Résumés of people seeking entry-level positions should be kept to one page when possible. Often, anything beyond that will be ignored anyway. Your résumé should be long enough to state all the pertinent information, but not so long that it will bore a reader. To help keep the résumé concise, remember to avoid first-person pronouns and to start sentences with action verbs: "Supervised 20 employees," not "I supervised. . . .'

Of course, your résumé must be completely free of any errors in grammar usage, spelling, or typing. There should be no smudges or erase marks on the paper. Always have several people proofread the résumé and give you comments on style, punctuation, and organization.

Once you have the final draft ready to be printed, leave your work for a few days. This will allow you to be more objective when you look over the résumé once more before printing the final copy.

Printing the Résumé

Opinions vary on the relative merits of professional printing, word processing, or simply typing. One important fact to keep in mind is that the absence of mistakes is much more important than a very attractive printing job. Michael Markel, in his book *Technical Writing: Situations and Strategies*, says that most employers agree that a neatly typed or word-processed résumé photocopied on good-quality paper is just as effective as a professionally printed résumé.

While professional printing is not a must, ensuring good quality is. If you decide to forgo professional printing, be sure that you are using a high-quality printer or copier to produce each copy of the résumé. Charles Bird and Dawn Puglisi found that people asked to judge candidates for a job could not ignore the fact that the résumé of an otherwise superior candidate was a poor-quality photocopy. Always avoid using dot-matrix or old ink typewriter ribbons, as these cannot produce high enough quality print.

An important consideration in this decision is that people who either type or word-process their own résumés are more likely to revise them to fit various jobs, which is a good strategy. Those who submit their résumé for professional printing often use the same résumé for all applications. This severely hampers the process we mentioned earlier of adapting your résumé to a particular job. Also, printing your own résumés will make the process of eliminating any mistakes that escaped your proofreaders much easier.

Box 7-3 provides an example of a letter of application and a résumé. Boxes 7-4 and 7-5 provide examples of a job announcement and a letter of application.

Writing Letters to a Business

Business letters are a form of communication that you will use many times in your career, so it's crucial that you master the techniques for writing them now. Why are letters so important in business? Because of their many advantages over face-to-face communication or a telephone call. Letters do not interrupt their receiver, but rather allow him or her to respond when it is convenient; the phone or a visitor demands immediate attention. Letters can serve as a reminder of the message to the receiver, and provide a written, more permanent record. Also, writers have more time than do speakers to choose carefully the words they want to use. This aids in presenting facts logically and completely.

There are some disadvantages to writing a letter that must be weighed against the advantages we have just examined in deciding if a letter will be the most effective form of communication. Letters will not receive instant feedback, nor do they obligate the receiver to answer at all. Also, letters are usually more work than a phone call, more time-consuming, and therefore, more costly. If these disadvantages do not outweigh the advantages, and you decide a letter will be the communication of choice, what are the "rules" of business letters?

Letters will follow the basic steps for business communication outlined at the beginning of this chapter. The exact form a letter takes is often determined by the company.

Elements of Business Letters

Heading   The heading contains the writer's full address (street, city, state, and ZIP code) and the date. Company letterhead stationery will already have the address printed, so the date is all that needs to be added.

Box 7-3 **Résumé**

Tina Stein   Current Address
Permanent Address   415 N. Mulanix
808 Chicago St.   Kirksville, MO 63501
Audubon, IA 50025   (999) 999-9999
(999) 999-9999

EDUCATION:
   Northeast Missouri State University (NMSU) Kirksville, MO
   Bachelor of Arts in Interpersonal Communication
   Emphasis in Organizational Leadership
   May 1988
                     Financed 100% of my college education

JOB EXPERIENCE:
   Office Assistant for Instructor of Communication (Aug. 19---May 19--)
   • Responsible for office efficiency
   • Maintained academic advisee records
   • Typed memos and assignments and graded tests
   • Gained experience with personal computer

   Practicum, Communication: Division of Language & Literature (Spring 19--)
   • Assisted in coordination of Fall '-- Freshman Orientation Conference
   • Attended all organizational meetings
   • Handled correspondence with faculty
   • Worked with peer advisors

Inside Address   The inside address contains the reader's name, title (if appropriate), organization, and full business address. This should be placed on the left margin, between one and five lines below the heading, depending on the length of the letter. This address should be the same as the address on the envelope.

Salutation   The salutation is placed two lines below the inside address. Address the person as "Dear" and end with a colon. In most letters, the salutation should contain the courtesy title (such as Mr., Ms., Dr., etc.). If you do not know the name of the reader, address the letter to a specific position, such as "Dear Personnel Director." Often a phone call to the organization you are writing will enable you to obtain the name of the person and its exact spelling, and the complete address of the person you are writing. When addressing a group of people, use a salutation such as "Ladies

Admissions Representative for the Division of Language & Literature
- Selected to speak at prospective student visitation days
- Wrote follow-up letters to the visiting students

Office Assistant for Instructor of Physical Education (Aug. 19-- – May 19--)
- Responsible for office efficiency
- Typed memos
- Answered phone and scheduled appointments

Waitress (Summers May 19-- – Aug. 19--) Various establishments
- West 83, Perkins, Mustards, and Travelers Restaurant
- Satisfied customers' needs and dealt with complaints
- Balanced the register and handled cash transactions

ACTIVITIES:
Delta Zeta (social sorority).
- Recording Secretary
- Coordinator for Missouri State Day. Organized workshops, speakers, ordered food for approximately 350 women.
- Rush Party Chairman. Organized a party for approximately 150 women.
University Usher — Served as usher to the public for cultural events at NMSU.
Purple Packer — Supported basketball team and acted as hostess to the public.
IPC Club (sophomore year)
Wrestling Cheerleader (sophomore year)

REFERENCES:
Available upon request at The Career Planning and Placement Center

and Gentlemen," but not "Dear Sir" or "Dear Gentlemen." These once standard phrases have become inappropriate.

Body   Of course, the body is the main part of the letter, and should begin two lines below the salutation. Generally, business letters should be kept to one or two pages, and are single-spaced with double spaces between paragraphs. In cases where the letter is very short, you may double-space throughout to give the letter a "fuller" appearance. In such instances, indicate paragraphs by indenting five spaces.

Complimentary Close   The close begins two lines below the last line of the body of the letter. The traditional closings are "Sincerely," "Sincerely yours," or "Yours truly." These are acceptable in almost every case. If you know the reader well, you may choose a more informal close such as "Cor-

Box 7-4   **Employment Advertisement**

S O F T W A R E   P R O F E S S I O N A L S

Join the people breaking new ground in systems software.

Pansophic Systems, Incorporated, one of the largest independent software companies in the world, has set new standards in systems software through ground-breaking developments like TELON, PANVALET, EASYTRIEVE PLUS, PM/38, and more. Our software professionals, who are among the industry's best, are dedicated to taking software in new directions. And we see to it that they have the technology, creative freedom, and resources necessary to keep us at the forefront of systems software innovation.

If you're serious about software—there's no better place to be than with us at our new corporate headquarters in Lisle. Consider the following growth-generated opportunities:

- **Senior Systems Developers**—with mainframe ASSEMBLER or Pascal programming experience and compiler theory background; for development of EASYTRIEVE PLUS.

- **System 36/38 and AS/400 Developers**—with RPG III experience

- **TELON Developers**—experience with COBOL. IMS/DB-DC, DB2, or CICS

---

dially.'' Type your name and business title four lines under the complimentary close, and sign the letter in this space.

Other Information   Some letters will require additional steps after the close. This information is placed in the lower left-hand corner of the letter.

If someone else typed the letter, they and you are identified by initials on the REFERENCE LINE. The form to follow is writer's capitalized initials first, followed by typist's initials in lowercase type. The two are separated by either a slash or colon.

If the letter contains an enclosure, such as an application letter with a résumé, this is noted on the ENCLOSURE LINE. Simply type the word ''ENCLOSURE'' in all capital letters. If you choose, it is acceptable to describe the enclosure by following ''ENCLOSURE'' with a colon and a one or two-word description.

If you want to let the reader know that others are receiving a copy of the letter, use the symbol cc followed by the names of the other recipients.

Keep these points in mind when reading the following descriptions of the various types of letters you may be called upon to write in your business career.

- VTAM Product Support Specialists—experience with session managers and/or systems programming

- MVS/DB2 Systems Programmers

- Customer Support Specialists—with mainframe programming experience

- Bulletin Board System Specialist—to set up and maintain a PC network system

- Systems Quality Assurance Specialists—programming experience in COBOL, ASSEMBLER, IMS, DB2, and CICS

- Technical Writers

We also offer opportunities with non-standard workday hours for technical product support. Background should include experience in the areas mentioned above.

We offer highly competitive salaries and superb benefits. Please send your résumé, indicating the position(s) in which you are interested. We are an equal opportunity employer, M/F/V/H.

PANSOPHIC

A Systems Software Company You Can't Outgrow

The letter of application (Box 7-5) is written in response to this ad. Note how the writer incorporated part of the corporate message within his letter.

WE MEAN BUSINESS

Analyze a business letter that you received recently in the mail or at work. Does the letter follow the criteria established? How could it be improved?

Application Letters

Every résumé sent should be accompanied by an application letter targeted to the specific job opening. In fact, any letter that you write to a prospective employer must consider the person who will read the letter. In this letter, you need to answer the things that the reader is going to want to know: Who is this person? What does he or she want? How can I or this organization benefit from this person?

Before your letter can answer these questions, it must catch the reader's attention. You can accomplish this by saying something the reader wants to hear, especially in relation to his or her business or department. Also keep in mind that the reader does not have unlimited time, so come right to the point and deliver your message. Simply, letters should be brief.

Certainly these guidelines apply to writing an application or cover letter. This type of correspondence is appropriate when you are writing in reference to a specific position that has been advertised or that you've heard about through a contact, or if you feel very strongly about a company and hope your qualifications will meet their needs. Because most of us don't take the time to write a completely new résumé for each application, the application letter accompanying your résumé should target the position and employer very specifically. Judith Rogala and Laura Liswood quoted one executive who said: "Make me feel like I'm your first choice, not one among fifty. The cover letter should be directed toward my company and its needs. Don't make it a fill-in-the-blank exercise."

This letter is crucial to the application process because it is often the first thing a recruiter sees, and thus creates that all-important first impression.

Content of the Application Letter

The application letter should accomplish three objectives: make a favorable first impression, convince the reader that you are qualified for the position, and request an interview. Because you have to convey these three messages in only one page, you cannot waste time with unnecessary information.

There are many ways you can use content to form a favorable impression in the mind of the reader. You could state why you want this position or refer to a common interest. Demonstrating your qualifications will also make a favorable impression. The information in the application letter should not simply be an expanded version of your résumé. Rather, include in your letter only the two or three facts from your résumé that will most interest the reader.

Most application letters will contain some standard sections:

Greeting   If responding to an advertisement or other job posting, address your letter to the person and department indicated in the ad. If the announcement doesn't list the specific person to whom to address the letter, try calling the company to find the name of the specific manager for whom you would be working. Avoid sending the letter to a department (unless the ad instructs you to) because no one may feel responsible for dealing with your application. Your letter may meet the same fate as mail addressed to "Occupant."

Opening Paragraph   The opening of your letter will be absolutely crucial to gaining the attention of the reader. One way not to accomplish that objective is to be too general. Rather, state the position you are applying for and how you came to know about the opportunity. If a person in the company suggested you apply, be sure to name that person as your source. This tells the reader that an employee of the company believes you are qualified for the position.

If you are applying for a position that has not yet been announced as open, obviously you cannot state what position you are applying for. In this case, let the reader know that you believe you are qualified for a position in the company, and then support this claim in the remainder of the letter.

The last sentence(s) of the opening should give an idea of what the rest of the letter will contain. Summarize the main points of the letter and present them very briefly.

Body Paragraphs   Now that you have caught the attention of the reader, your goal is to convince this person that you are qualified for the position that is open. Expand on the qualifications that you touched on in the opening paragraph, and state any other applicable education or experience. Most of this information will already be summarized in your résumé, but here you should emphasize those factors which make you particularly qualified for this job in this company. If you read about this job in an advertisement that listed the job's qualifications, your job is to match those as closely as you can without stretching the truth. For college students seeking their first job, educational history will usually be stronger than work experience. Thus, the paragraph on education should be emphasized by appearing first.

As with the rest of your correspondence, let the job for which you are applying be your guide in writing the paragraph about your education. Include any specific coursework which relates to the job, but choose carefully. Most courses shown should be advanced courses. Evidence of participation in extracurricular activities can be a big plus, especially when they show leadership, organization, or related experience. Remember, your education paragraph should have a focus, rather than a list of unrelated, possibly irrelevant facts. Show that your time in school has prepared you for this job.

Your application letter should also contain a section on your employment history. Highlight any related experience listed on your résumé that is especially relevant to the job that you are applying for. Again, focus on a single idea — that your experience has prepared you for this job. Define the specific duties of your past positions to give the reader a clear idea of what you can do and what you have learned.

Conclusion   The concluding paragraph of the application letter should stimulate some action, usually an offer of an interview. You should request an interview directly and make it easy for the reader to get in touch with you. Give your phone number and times when you are available.

Keep this paragraph brief and to the point. Be polite but confident and use assumptive language in your request for the interview.

WE MEAN BUSINESS

Write three alternate tactics you could use in an application letter to capture the attention of a reader.

Printing the Application Letter

Usually the application letter should fill up most of one page. A full page will provide adequate space for most students to summarize their credentials, while not being so long that the reader loses interest.

As with the résumé, your application letter should be single-spaced on good-quality paper, using adequate margins. Once your letter is typed, it must be proofread to ensure there are no misspellings, grammar mistakes, smudges, or other errors. Don't just proofread it yourself, have at least two others look over the letter as well.

Because this letter will target an individual job, you won't be able to use copies of an original. So, you must go through the steps of this process for each application letter you write.

Follow-up Letters

The follow-up letter is the last step in the job search process and can accomplish the most with the least effort, because not all applicants take the time to send follow-ups. Sending one shows the interviewer that you are interested enough in this position to put forth a little extra effort.

The follow-up letter serves to keep you in the interviewer's mind after the interview is over. Either reinforce the positive impression you made during the interview, or try to turn around the results of a negative interview.

Writing the letter in response to a negative interview is obviously more of a challenge than writing to reinforce a positive interview. If your interview was weak, you must not have sufficiently communicated the fact that you are "perfect" for the job, so you need to take this last opportunity to change the interviewer's first impression.

Begin the letter by thanking the interviewer for his or her time. Mention that after learning about the company during the interview, you definitely want to work there. Within the letter, make your sales pitch, highlighting your qualifications that show that the job and you were made for each other.

If you had a positive interview, you should still write a follow-up. In this case, thank the interviewer, give your reactions to the company and some points of the interview, and remind the interviewer of one or two of your most impressive qualifications.

Keep this letter especially brief, and get it in the mail only a few days after the interview. If you think you'll forget the key points of the interview in that time, jot down those points right after the interview so you will have them for the letter.

This letter will have to be adapted depending on whether the interview took place at the plant or office of the interviewing company. Boxes 7-6 and 7-7 give examples of both varieties of follow-up letters.

Box 7-5   **Letter of Application**

May 1, 19 ___

(Name)
Pansophic Systems, Inc.
2400 Cabot Drive
Lisle, Illinois 60532

Dear _____:

I read **Pansophic**'s ad in the April 23rd Chicago Tribune with much eagerness. The openings in technical writing appeal to me most, and my experience and education put me in a unique position to fill this employment niche.

My experience is in computers; my degree is in English. I feel these two backgrounds come together in me to form an excellent candidate for a position in technical writing. I have, for two years, given support to nonexperienced computer users, demonstrating that I can take technical data and present it to individuals lacking specific knowledge. My superior grades on papers and essays prove the quality of my writing. I have had several papers singled out as exemplary and used as teaching tools, and one chosen for publication.

The information within this letter and the enclosed résumé should validate my qualifications to become a technical writer for **Pansophic**. I would like to meet with you to discuss my potential to help **Pansophic** take software in new directions. I look forward to hearing from you in the near future. If otherwise, I will contact your office to stay abreast of the developing situation. Thank you for your time and consideration.

Sincerely,

Richard H. Watson

enclosure: résumé

Box 7-6 **Follow-up Letter After Interview**

May 11, 19 ___

Elena Raymond
Corporate Recruiter
Electronic Data Systems Corporation
One Forest Plaza
12200 Park Central Drive, Suite 200
Dallas, Texas 75251

Dear Ms. Raymond:

Thank you very much for taking the time to interview with me for a position at EDS. The information about EDS that I gained from our meeting was beneficial. Your honesty about my gregariousness was very refreshing and appreciated. I will take your recommendations to heart and try to maintain my responses at a brief and direct level.

Once again, thank you for meeting with me and recommending enhancements for my interview skills. I look forward to meeting with you in Kansas City sometime in June.

Sincerely,

Richard H. Watson

Job Rejection Letters

If all these steps have worked successfully and you have been offered a job that you find you can't accept, you will need to write a rejection letter. The form is standard for business letters but you must be very careful about the letter's tone. You can never be sure that you won't want to reopen your connections with this company in the future, so don't offend or be abrupt. Thank the company for their consideration of you—remember, they have spent their time and money to learn about you.

Box 7-7   **Confirmation for Future Plant/Office Visit**

THANK YOU FOR PLANT/OFFICE VISIT

Your Address

Inside Address
(If possible, use individual's name.)

Dear _____:

    Thank you for your letter of _____(date)_____ suggesting a plant/office visit at _____(time)_____ on the following dates: _____(list/dates)_____.

    The most convenient date for me would be _____(date)_____. I will arrive at your office at _____(time)_____.

    Enclosed is a copy of my résumé, along with the application for employment. (If necessary.)

    I appreciate the opportunity to visit your plant/office. I am very interested and eager to learn more about possible employment opportunities with _____(organization name)_____.

                Sincerely,

                (Written signature)

                Your name typed

Source: From the *CPC Annual*, 1988.

Box 7-8 **Letter of Rejection**

Your Address

Inside Address
(If possible, use individual's name.)

Dear _____:

    After considerable thought, I have decided not to accept your offer of employment as outlined in your ____(date)____ letter. This has been a very difficult decision for me. However, I feel I have made the correct one for this point in my career.
    Thank you for your time, effort, and consideration. Your confidence in me is sincerely appreciated.

                        Sincerely,

                        (Written signature)

                        Your name typed

Source: From the *CPC Annual,* 1988.

Job Acceptance Letters

When you do finally find the right job and write the job acceptance letter, be enthusiastic! Phillip Lewis says, in *Organizational Communication: The Essence of Effective Management,* that you should begin your letter with the fact that you are accepting the position, and state what position that is. Next, Lewis suggests that you tell the company when you will be ready to work, and the details about your moving, if necessary. Conclude with an indication that you are excited about working for the company.

Inquiry Letters

Not all letters that you write to businesses will be pursuing a job opening. Inquiry letters are written requesting an infinite variety of information from

---

Box 7-9 **Letter of Acceptance**

Your Address

Inside Address
(If possible, use individual's name.)

Dear _____:

    I am very pleased to accept your offer _____(state offer)_____ as outlined in your letter of _____(date)_____. (Include all details of offer—location, starting salary, starting date.)

    (Mention enclosures—application, résumé, employee forms, or other information—and any related commentary.)

    I look forward to meeting the challenges of the job and I shall make every attempt to fulfill your expectations.

                Sincerely,

                (Written signature)

                Your name typed

Source: From the *CPC Annual*, 1988.

---

a company. Many college students write inquiry letters when they need information for papers or projects.

Some inquiries will be in response to an advertisement inviting interested readers to write for more information. These letters are very straightforward; simply ask for the information that was offered. In most cases you can expect a quick and enthusiastic reply, especially in those cases where the business is trying to sell the product that you asked about.

There will be times where the writer will take the initiative in sending an inquiry letter. These letters are not quite as easy to write, because your reader may not benefit from answering you but instead may simply be doing you a favor. Thus, you will have to convince the person that they want to do you this kindness; that it will benefit them somehow.

In the first paragraph of the letter, state why you chose to direct your inquiry to this specific organization and person. Michael Markel, in *Technical Writing: Situations and Strategies*, suggests trying subtle flattery at this point, such as, "I was hoping that as the leader in solid-state electronics, you might be able to furnish some information about. . . ." Explain next why you want this information: "I plan to use this information to write my term paper in my business management class." Also, if you need the information by a certain time, let the reader know.

The next section of the inquiry letter is where you list the specific questions that you need answered. Keep this section concise and also as specific as you can. Simply asking for "all the information available" on a topic is not a good strategy for getting a response to your letter. Since you will be intruding on this person's time, ask as few questions as possible. Because of this limitation, you will want to be sure you are asking the questions you really need answered.

In most cases, the only thing you can offer this person in return for his or her time and energy is a copy of your work. State in the letter that you'll be happy to send a copy when it is completed. To wrap up the inquiry letter, give a quick statement of your appreciation.

To be courteous, you should enclose a self-addressed, stamped envelope for your answers to be returned in. And, if your letter is answered, send a brief thank-you note to the person who supplied the answers.

See Box 7-10 for a sample of an inquiry letter written with the writer's initiative.

WE MEAN BUSINESS

Write a sample inquiry letter requesting information from a company. Whether for a speech of tribute or interview, it is always a good idea to get your "foot in the door".

WRITING WITHIN THE ORGANIZATION

The process involved in writing within business is very similar to that for writing from the outside, which we've already discussed in this chapter. Again, the key is to adapt your tone, style, form, and content to the receiver.

Box 7-10 **Letter of Inquiry**

14 Hawthorne Avenue
Bellview, TX 75234
November 2, 19——

Dr. Andrew Shakir
Director of Techical Services
Orion Corporation
721 West Douglas Avenue
Maryville, TN 31409

Dear Dr. Shakir:

I am writing to you because of Orion's reputation as a leader in the manufacture of adjustable X-ray tables. I am a graduate student in biomedical engineering at the University of Texas working on an analysis of diagnostic equipment. Would you be able to answer a few questions about your Microspot 311?

1. Can the Microspot 311 be used with lead-oxide cassettes, or does it accept only lead-free cassettes?
2. Are standard generators compatible with the Microspot 311?
3. What would you say is the greatest advantage, for the operator, in using the Microspot 311? For the patient?

My project is due January 15. I would greatly appreciate your assistance in answering these questions. Of course, I would be happy to send you a copy of my report when it is completed.

Yours very truly,

Albert K. Stern

Source: Walter Oliu, Charles Brusaw, and Gerald Alred, *Writing that Works: How to Write Effectively on the Job.*

Memorandums

Memorandums, or memos, are the most common form of written communication among members of the same organization. They form a written record of many of the communications and decisions in the organization.

Memos are written to inform, ask, or persuade, but beyond those basic categories they have a wide variety of uses. Walter Oliu, Charles Brusaw, and Gerald Alred give the following partial list of memo applications in their text, *Writing that Works: How to Write Effectively on the Job*:

Announce policies	Request information
Confirm conversations	Transmit documents
Exchange information	Instruct employees
Delegate responsibilities	Report results

Oliu, Brusaw, and Alred say that memos also play a role in management because memos are used to keep employees informed about company goals, to motivate employees to achieve these goals, and to build employee morale.

Writing Memos

Memos are designed to provide quick, efficient communication within an organization. This is an important fact to keep in mind when you write a memo, and is reflected in the memo's basic form. The formalities found in a business letter such as inside address, salutation, complimentary close, and standard signature may often be omitted to save time when writing a memo. Courtesy titles may also be omitted in some cases, though if one uses a courtesy title in speaking to the addressee, it should be included in the memo.

Memos usually begin with four items: date, reader's name(s), writer's name, and subject of the memo. Include the full date for later reference. Use either first and last names, or first initial and last name, and include job titles if this memo will become part of a permanent record. In most other cases, the writer's formal title may be omitted, unless you think the reader is unaware of your title. Start the body of memo with your main idea, including background information if your reader is not familiar with the topic of the memo. Even if the receiver is acquainted with your subject, it is still a good practice to remind him or her. For example, you might begin with a phrase such as "As we decided at the faculty meeting this morning. . . ." Oliu, Brusaw, and Alred suggest the only times you should not state your main point early in the memo is when the reader will not agree, or when you are disagreeing with someone "higher up" than yourself. In these cases, you should first state the problem and specific support for your plan of action. After proving that a problem exists and that you can solve it, come to the main point — your solution.

The use of specificity is often important when writing memos. In cases where the writer is suggesting new policies or practices for the organization, these must be spelled out explicitly. When stating specific points in a memo, the use of lists can add emphasis. Headings can also be effective in strengthening main points. For example, instead of "Our office mail system must be changed," write:

1. Office mail should be delivered by 9:00 a.m.
2. Office mail must be delivered by the day after it is sent.
3. Office mail is to be delivered directly to the addressee instead of the office where he or she works.

The final step is to sign or initial the memo, which signifies the writer's endorsement of its contents. This can either be performed next to the typewritten name of the writer at the beginning, or at the end of the memo.

As we mentioned above, memos can be written to inform or persuade. Each requires slightly different writing techniques.

Informational Memos   These are the most common and easiest-to-compose items of internal communication in business. When the memo is simply conveying information about the operation of the organization, a straightforward statement of the facts is best. If the memo will involve personnel and their emotions, you must be more careful to plan the memo in terms of the reader's reactions. Tact is of the utmost importance if the memo has an unpleasant message. Remember, you will have to work with this person in the future.

Persuasive Memos   Persuasion in a memo is accomplished more through careful, logical presentation of information than through emotional pleas such as one sees in advertising. This is a case where one needs to delay presenting the main point until the idea has been supported.

In preparing to write memos, keep these points in mind:

- Plan your letter before you begin to write.
- Prepare a comprehensive subject line.
- Keep in mind that the message should stand by itself and should not rely on the subject line for thought.
- If you have several items that lend themselves to tabulation (numbering), do so.
- As you write, remember you are writing to communicate for the good of the organization and not to impress the reader.

Memo Format

The format of memos is determined by the organization, so this will be decided for you. Box 7-11 gives some sample memos.

Box 7-11 **Memo Headings**

July 1, 19——

To:

From:

Subject:
_____

Interoffice Memo   Coventry Brass, Inc.

To: Date:

From: File #:
_____

Belitz Communications, Inc.   Memorandum

Memo To:

From:

Date:

Subject:

Sending Memos

The people who receive a memo, and the order in which they receive it, can affect the organizational culture of the office. You need to be aware of the proper etiquette within your organization relating to who should receive the memo you've just written, and in which order. Carla Butenhoff quotes an

---

Box 7-12 **Too Many Memos!**

The average executive spends 11 weeks a year writing or reading memos. The average executive says 39 percent of all memos are unnecessary. So, assuming both of those observations are true, the average executive blows a month of his or her valuable time every year just dealing with worthless memos.

Source: Bob Dyer, "The Workplace," *The Akron Beacon-Journal*, June 22, 1987.

---

employee in her article "Bad Writing Can Be Good Business" who illustrates the import such decisions can carry.

> If I put my supervisor's AND the vice-president's name on the top, it says I report to both equally. If the supervisor's name is on the top and I send a copy to the vice-president, it means that, though I report to the supervisor, I have direct access to the VP.

Writing too many memos will be detrimental to the quality of communication in an organization because they can begin to clutter the communication channels with unnecessary messages. Memos are meant to be quick and efficient communication, so it follows that employees should strive to avoid memo clutter.

WE MEAN BUSINESS

What decisions should be made before sending a memo?

Resignation Letters

Almost all of you will decide to change jobs at some point, many of you in the first few years of your career. This will necessitate writing a letter of resignation, which must be handled with tact and courtesy.

Remember, in almost any job you will have benefited, not only by receiving a salary, but also through learning. Therefore, your resignation letter should be appreciative and pleasant. Make positive comments about the organization, and express regret at leaving. Generally it is wise not to write a letter of resignation unless and until you have a firm offer of another job and you have spoken with your superior about your intentions to leave. Include your reason for resigning and the effective resignation date. Conclude with a well-wishing closing.

Always give ample time for your employer to find a replacement. You want to stay in the good graces of the people that you may need to recommend you for future employment. Remember this old adage: "Be kind, courteous, and considerate to people you pass on the way up the ladder of success; you will likely meet them on your way back down."

Recommendations and Evaluations

Managers frequently are expected to evaluate employees' performance. Anytime appraisals are made they are subjective judgments. But subjective judgments should not be made without careful documentation, particularly if that judgment is negative. Ethical and legal challenges place an individual whose evaluation or recommendation cannot be verified at risk. That risk can mean being sued for defamation and/or losing one's credibility with one's organization. For example, to say an employee has a drinking problem is dangerous unless one can back that up with arrests for driving while intoxicated, coming to work while drunk, being seen drinking on the job, etc.

The risk of lawsuits is so great that some corporations have a policy of never disclosing to another prospective employer why an employee was discharged. Internal corporate evaluations should be descriptive more than evaluative. Such terms as "unreliable" are evaluative. It is better to present the evidence, such as: John reported late to work five times in the last six months and was absent 12 days. Also, his reports contained factual errors and were late on three occasions.

Federal law entitles employees to see their personnel files. They also may read letters of recommendation unless they waive that right. Usually those requesting recommendations do waive that right because they realize that recommendations without waivers may carry less weight. Erroneous information that prevents employment or promotion can be cause for legal action. Those who write always should be accurate, prudent, and discreet in both oral and written evaluations of others. Another's well-being and career are at stake. Letters of recommendation should therefore be balanced and fair.

Invitations

The proper degree of formality dictates the style of invitations. Special occasions call for printed invitations, such as a 75th anniversary celebration of the company. Less formal events such as an invitation to participate in a panel discussing corporate efforts to measure and monitor quality should describe the purpose of the event, the role for which individuals should prepare, the time and place, and the deadlines for acceptance of invitations.

Response to invitations should be brief with regrets or acceptance. Handwritten replies will personalize one's correspondence. A one-sentence response is adequate, such as:

Ms. Wanda Smith regrets that she is unable to accept your invitation to participate on the panel on quality.

or

Mr. William Smith is pleased to accept your invitation to attend the reception for President Chalmers on July 7.

CHANNEL CHOICE

Whether one selects oral or written channels for organizational communication depends upon a number of variables: time, cost, legitimacy, permanence, memorableness, relationship, need for secrecy, and sequence.

Time

Messages that must be transmitted quickly should be delivered face-to-face or by telephone when possible. Radio or television should be used to reach a large audience.

Cost

Personally delivered messages to many people usually are more costly than written forms. Fax is convenient, but as yet somewhat expensive. Many organizations use computer networks that cut costs of communication, but are expensive to install.

Legitimacy

Messages that need official authorization usually employ written directives in order that they not be misunderstood or forgotten.

Permanence

Messages that need to be part of a record, of course, must be put into written form.

Memorableness

Messages that must be accurate and easily retrieved should be written. If accompanied by oral emphasis, before and after they are transmitted, they will be more easily remembered. Two channels are more effective than one.

Memorableness also depends upon uniqueness. Therefore, the style of both written and oral messages affects their memorableness. That's why special occasions are sometimes celebrated by sending singing telegrams, balloons, or flowers.

Redundancy increases memorableness, up to a certain point. But excessive repetition, repetition, repetition bores!

Relationship

Friends and business associates want to be communicated with via personal messages. Usually oral messages are preferred. Business protocol often calls for follow-up written confirmation of oral understanding. Of course, one cannot always telephone those in high positions; therefore written messages, in such cases, can pave the way for oral communication.

Sequence and Channel Choice

Organizations employ oral and written channels according to the purpose of the message. Disagreeable news is usually best transmitted face-to-face before it is put into writing. That's why reprimands are usually given orally before they are written.

Oral channels enable give-and-take response. Inaccuracies and misunderstandings can be prevented and corrected more easily in oral transactions. When records are essential, written communication should accompany oral.

WE MEAN BUSINESS

List the many oral and written channels available to you as a student. How do these differ from those available to employees and management in the workplace?

SUMMARY

Written communication will undoubtedly play a role in your daily routine before and once you have landed a job in the workplace. This medium is just as crucial in providing impressions about you and your communication competence as is oral communication. Yet, we sometimes take for granted the power of this channel.

Conducting the job hunt correctly takes a lot of time and energy. It also takes a commitment to present your best self. Thus, we detailed the steps to help you organize an effective and uniquely tailored résumé and application letter. Allow ample time to write, rewrite, proofread, and organize the layout of these two important forms of written communication. The résumé and application letter are the first messages of "you" that you send to a potential employer—don't make them your last.

We also highlighted proper procedures to follow when it is to your advantage to write a follow-up, job acceptance, job rejection, or inquiry letter. Each of these letters is an important part of proper business etiquette expectations.

Written communication within the organization can help save time, increase productivity, and provide records of transactions for future reference. One type of communication used frequently is the memorandum. Use memos when they can serve one of the functions listed above. Do not overuse them. People who receive too many memos will either scan them or not read them at all.

Another form of written communication discussed was the resignation letter. Although this may seem like a letter you will not need to write for awhile, such may not be the case. Most Americans change jobs four to five times in their careers. In fact, many of our recent graduates have changed jobs within a year after graduation.

Recommendations and evaluations are other examples of writing within an organization that you will need to master. In all probability, you will be called upon to evaluate another person's performance, and it is imperative that you handle that task with tact and honesty.

Another written task to handle with tact is the writing and answering of invitations. Perhaps not as crucial as some other writing we discussed, these can still ruffle many feathers if not done properly.

SKILL BUILDER: SMOG CLEARANCE FORMULA

Apply the following smog formulas.

Readability

One way to measure readability is to count the number of words per sentence. Incomplete sentences or sentence fragments should be counted as sentences also.

Here is how you may interpret your results:

Description of Style	Typical Magazine	Average Sentence Length
Very easy	Comics	8
Easy	Pulp fiction	11
Fairly easy	Slick fiction	14
Standard	Digests, *Time*, mass-market non-fiction	17
Fairly difficult	*Harper's, Atlantic*	21
Difficult	Academic, scholarly	25
Very difficult	Scientific, professional	29

Limitations of the Instrument

Short sentences can be filled with difficult words just as long sentences can be filled with simple, monosyllabic words. Either combination can be hard to read, to listen to, and to understand.

Another way to measure readability is to count in each sentence the number of syllables above one per word. This is called the easy listening formula (ELF). For example, take these two sentences: (1) He was a magnanimous supervisor; and (2) He was a generous boss. The first sentence has an ELF score of 6 and the second sentence has an ELF score of 2.

Here is how you may interpret your results.

Writing source	Average ELF Score for Each Sentence
New York Times	17.4
CBS-TV News	9.8

No highly rated television news writer had an ELF score above 12. Television network news writers averaged 10.4; newspapers averaged 15.0.

Limitations of the Instrument

ELF measures clarity. A sentence that scores 20 may be perfectly clear and may be the best way to deliver a fact. A series of parallelisms, delivered rhythmically, may be perfectly comprehensible, yet it lengthens the sentence and increases the ELF score. Despite these limitations, the ELF is much easier to use than Flesch's Reading Ease Formula and takes into consideration the same two variables as Flesch does: average sentence length and average number of syllables per 100 words.

Human Interest

Human interest is measured by the average number of personal words and the average number of personal sentences.

Personal Words are:

a. All first-, second-, and third-person pronouns except the neuter pronouns *it, its, itself,* and the pronouns *they, them, their, theirs, themselves,* if referring to things rather than people. For example, count the word *them* in the sentence "When I saw her parents, I hardly recognized them," but not in the sentence "I looked for the books but couldn't find them." However, always count *he, him, his* and *she, her, hers* even where these words refer to animals or inanimate objects.

b. All words that have masculine or feminine natural gender, e.g., John Jones, Mary, father, sister, iceman, actress. Do not count common gender words like teacher, doctor, employee, assistant, spouse, and chairperson, even though the gender may be clear from the context. Count a phrase like President Jimmy Carter as one "personal word" only. (Only the word Jimmy has a natural masculine gender.) Mrs. Gorden contains one "personal word" with natural gender, namely Mrs. Ms. Gay Gorden contains two, namely Ms. and Gay.

c. The group words *people* (with the plural verb) and *folks*.

Personal Sentences are:

a. Spoken sentences (direct quotes). But do not count quoted phrases such as, the senator accused Moore of being "a hypocrite." Count all sentences included in a long quotation, as part b (below).

b. Questions, commands, requests, and other sentences directly addressed to the reader as: "Does this sound possible?" or "Imagine the implications." Do not count sentences that only vaguely address the reader, like: "*This is typical* of our national character."

c. Exclamations.

d. Grammatically incomplete sentences as "Handsome, though." If a sentence fits under two of these classifications count it *only once*.

There are two ways to compute *Human Interest Score:* mathematically or visually.

Mathematically

Multiply the number of personal words per 100 words by 3.635

_____

Multiply the number of personal sentences per 100 sentences by .314

_____

Add the products of the previous two lines for *Human Interest Score*

_____

Visually

Use the chart below: How do you interpret the *Human Interest Score?* Human Interest Score will put the writing on a scale between 0 (no human interest) and 100 (full of human interest).

Human Interest Score	Description of Style	Typical Magazine	Percentage of Personal Words	Percentage of Personal Sentences
60 to 100	Dramatic	Fiction	17	58
40 to 60	Highly interesting	*New Yorker*	10	43
20 to 40	Interesting	Digests, *Time*	7	15
10 to 20	Mildly interesting	Trade	4	5
0 to 10	Dull	Scientific, professional	2	0

Realism

Realism or the lack of abstraction may be measured in this way:

1. Count the number of finite verbs per 200 words. Count all verbs of any tense that are in the first, second, or third person and that have subjects, either expressed or understood. Do not count nonfinite verb forms or verbals. In verb forms with auxiliary words, count the auxiliary rather than the main verb. Do not count any form of the verb "to be" (is, are, were, will be, have been, etc.) when used only as a copula to link the subject with a predicate complement.

2. Count the number of definite articles and their nouns per 200 words. Count both the article *the* and the noun it modifies, but only if that noun is a single word not otherwise modified, either by an intervening adjective or by a clause or phrase following the noun. Do not count *the* when modifying adjectives or noun-adjectives, as in *the best*, *the Irish*.

3. Count the number of nouns of abstraction per 200 words. Count all nouns ending in the suffixes *-ness*, *-ment*, *-dom*, *-nce*, *-ion*, and *-y*, including the plurals of such nouns. Count nouns ending in *-y* even when they are the end of a longer suffix like *-ity* or *-ology* but not when they are used as a diminutive (tiny).

4. Add the numbers found in Steps 1 and 2 and add 36 to this sum.

5. From the total found in Step 4, subtract the result of Step 5. The result of this subtraction is the abstraction score.

How Are the Scores to Be Interpreted?	What Scores Do Different Sources Get?	
0–18 Very abstract	*True Confessions*	68
19–30 Abstract	*Reader's Digest*	51
31–42 Fairly abstract	*Atlantic Monthly*	41
43–54 Standard	A college philosophy test	31
55–66 Fairly concrete		
67–78 Concrete		
79–90 Very concrete		

Read about these formulas in the following:

Rudolf Flesch, *How to Write, Speak, and Think More Effectively* (New York: Harper and Row, 1960), 303–307.

Irving Fang, "A Computer-Based Analysis of T.V. Newswriting Style for Listening Comprehension," Unpublished Ph.D. dissertation, University of California (Los Angeles), 1966, 136–137.

Paul J. Gillie, "A Simplified Formula for Measuring Abstraction in Writing," *Journal of Applied Psychology*, 41 no. 4, (1957), 315–320. This formula was validated against the Flesch abstraction formula. It cannot be any more valid than Flesch's, but it is easier to apply.

SKILL BUILDER: FOG CLEARANCE

Calculate the fog index for a sample from the opening paragraphs of IBM's *Marketing and Services News*:

> IBM has launched a bold campaign to make the corporation's performance second to none in the world of quality. To introduce this aggressive drive to reach world-class quality standards within Marketing and Services, we are including a special edition of IBM Horizons on market-driven quality, published by IBM United States. Look, too, on page 7 of Marketing and Services News for related stories.
>
> The *Horizons* issue reports on the strategy, objectives, methodology, and timetable of IBM's effort to achieve quality leadership. You'll also find reports on several market-driven quality accomplishments that have won high honors.
>
> Terry Lauterbach, IBM senior vice-president and IBM US general manager, stresses that the campaign builds on IBM *tradition*. "Our quality efforts," he says, "really go back to basic beliefs. We are trying to return to our heritage."

Answer

Steps:

1. Count 100 words to end of sentence.   110 words
2. Divide number of words by number of sentences.
   $$110/6 = 18.33$$
3. Calculate number of difficult words and their percent of the sample. (Difficult words counted are words with three syllables or more. Do not count those that are capitalized, those that are made up of short, easy words like "bookkeeping" or verbs that are formed by adding *es* or *ed*. Titles in italics are excluded.)
   $$21/110 = .1909 \times 100 = 19.1\%$$
4. Add average sentence length and percent of difficult words and multiply by .4.
   $$18.33 + 19.1 = 37.43 \times .4 = 14.97 \text{ or college sophomore level}$$

We have provided one example of how a "fog" index could be calculated. Now, select a paragraph and try to apply this formula. (Source: Gunning's Fog Index, New Guide 9-11.)

RESOURCES

Bottom line: Basic skills in the workplace. (1988). Washington, DC: U.S. Department of Education and Labor.

Butenhoff, Carla. (1977, June). "Bad writing can be good business." *The ABCA Bulletin*, 12–13.

Gunning, Robert. (1968). *The techniques of clear writing.* New York: McGraw-Hill.

Hanna, Michael S., and Gerald L. Wilson. (1988). *Communicating in business and professional settings* (2nd ed.). New York: Random House.

Landers, Ann. (1988, May 22). "Real life offers the best laughs." *The Akron Beacon-Journal*, B9.

Lewis, Phillip V. (1980). Organizational communication: *The essence of effective management*. Columbus, OH: Grid.

Markel, Michael H. (1988). *Technical writing: Situation and strategies* (2nd ed.). New York: St. Martin's Press.

Munschauer, John L. (1988). "The résumé: How to speak to employers' needs." *CPC Annual*, 32, 20–32.

Noble, John H. (1989, spring). "Résumés that make sense." *Managing Your Career: The College Edition of the National Business Employment Weekly*, 27, 31.

Oliu, Walter E., Charles T. Brusaw, and Gerald J. Alred. (1988). *Writing that works: How to write effectively on the job* (3rd ed.). New York: St. Martin's Press.

Rew, Lois Johnson. (1989). *Introduction to technical writing: Process and practice*. New York: St. Martin's Press.

Rogala, Judith, and Laura Liswood. (1980, July 29). "The briefcase." *San Jose Mercury*.

Weaver, Richard L., II. (1985). *Understanding business communication*. Englewood Cliffs, NJ: Prentice-Hall.

"Xerox chief gives schools failing grades." (1987, October 27). *The Akron Beacon-Journal*, A3.

Chapter 8

Group Communication in the Workplace

Concepts for Discussion

- Types of groups
- Interpersonal needs within groups
- Norms within groups
- Cohesiveness within groups
- Conformity and groupthink
- Leadership in groups
- Phases of group decision making

In a boat at sea one of the men began to bore a hole in the bottom of the boat. On being remonstrated with, he answered, "I am only boring under my own seat." "Yes," said his companions, "but when the sea rushes in we shall all be drowned with you."

Talmud

Every one of us is a member of some type of group. Whether that group is comprised of those who go out together Saturday nights, members of the Business Administration Club, fellow churchgoers, or the corporation where we work, we all have some ties. There are certain needs that can only be fulfilled by interaction with others. When groups operate optimally, the product of a well-coordinated group often will be superior to that created by any one member. None of us is as smart as all of us.

Within organizations, people function both as individuals and as members of various work groups, departments, and divisions. A manager often acts as a leader, and is the representative who speaks for his unit to upper administration. At the production level, employees must interact cooperatively, or else time, material, and energy are wasted. Advancement and job satisfaction will depend upon how effectively we are able to work in groups and how effectively our group functions within our larger organization.

In this chapter, we will examine the dynamics of groups within organizational settings. In order to best understand the components of effective groups, we will first define what a group is. Next, we will explain several types of groups and the interpersonal components of group communication, including needs, norms, and cohesiveness. Leadership emergence and types will then be discussed. Finally, we will introduce phases through which groups progress when making decisions and a common method of problem solving.

DEFINITIONS AND TYPES OF GROUPS

What is a group? A group is not merely a collection of people. It is a collection of people who frequently interact over time, in the hopes of achieving interdependently what they cannot achieve singly. These people define themselves as members, and are defined as members by people outside the group. Groups fulfill our need to belong and our need for interaction. Typically, members of an effective group take on a group personality and think in terms of those who are *in*, and those who are *not in* our group.

Almost all of us were born into families and spent our early years as members of this primary group. We were taken to community gatherings, to church or synagogue, to school. We aspired to belong to and be like people who belonged to other groups. When we belong to teams, clubs, gangs, fraternities, sororities, and the like we are in the in-group. Occasionally we declare that others not in our group are not one of us and refer to them as the out-group. Most communities have certain circles that are the "in" group for the upper class, and other organizations of subcultures that are considered by the rich to be "out" groups. Can you identify with any of the above?

From the simplest tribe to the most complex civilization, our lives are dependent upon the commitment of people to invest energy in collective efforts. We want to work together toward fulfillment of our goals. Ours is not a nation of individuals, but of interpersonal, interdependent relationships, of committees, organizations, and institutions. This is part of the reason that groups and organizations have such a strong hold on us, as we mentioned in Chapter 1.

Groups form for many purposes or functions in society. Some serve a social function, such as dormitory parties, family reunions, and that Friday night gang that gathers to "paint the town red." This function helps to fulfill the essential interpersonal needs mentioned earlier such as belonging, being with other people, interacting, and receiving feedback. Interpersonally supportive groups are usually a bit more formal than purely social groups. The goal of interpersonally supportive groups is sharing and growth. Examples of these types of groups include Weight Watchers, Alcoholics Anonymous, and Mothers Against Drunk Driving.

The department's bowling and softball teams serve the social function. Coworkers golf together and chat over coffee. Being sociable is an expected part of working life.

Other groups come together for the purpose of accomplishing goals or solving existing problems. These groups serve task functions, such as practicing for a symphony concert, deciding company policies, and designing school curricula. Task groups are called decision-making and work groups. Of course, groups can serve both task and social functions. The workplace entails much decision making about task performance.

A final type of group to be discussed is the learning group. Each of you is probably a part of between two and six learning groups each semester. Learning groups are not limited only to the classroom, however. A learning group is that which focuses its task on the function of increasing knowledge. Young Democrats and College Republicans invite political speakers and sponsor campus awareness events to increase learning.

The workplace invests billions of dollars in training employees regarding safety, product knowledge, skill performance, and management practices. The learning group is an active part of the workplace.

The goal of a group, whether social or task, should be to reach consensus. Each member should want to work toward building a sense of collectiveness and toward reaching approved group decisions. Whether the decision is to achieve a polished performance, decide what to do Saturday night, or to complete a corporate project, the end result should reflect group input, agreement, satisfaction, and commitment to the final project.

But how does this collectiveness and "teamness" develop in groups? How does a group become cohesive? Collectiveness and cohesiveness within a group emerge as a result of effective interpersonal interactions.

INTERPERSONAL NEEDS WITHIN WORKGROUPS

Working with people cannot always be pleasant. In volunteer groups, such as church boards or civic organizations, morale is low when attendance is poor. In such cases, a leader often runs *from* rather than *for* office! Business also has its difficulties with employees who are irregular in attendance, who don't do their share, and who are disagreeable.

Box 8-1 **If You Were in Combat . . .**

A psychologist came to speak to the Dallas Cowboys in an effort to help the players understand their motivations and attitudes. The psychologist said, "If you were in combat as a squad leader, and were ordered to take an enemy hill, what seven teammates would you want to go with you? Pick anyone you want, but choose quickly. Just give your first thoughts."

Football great Don Meredith was surprised by the names that first came to his mind. People he would rely on in a life and death situation turned out *not* necessarily to be close friends or even people he knew well at all. In fact, some men that Don chose were people he didn't even like. Don realized that he had selected men who he felt had a lot of courage, a trait he found necessary in a survival situation.

Source: Adapted from David Mahoney, "How not to Evaluate People." *Management Digest.*

Suppose for a moment that you were able to pick an ideal group. Who would you choose, and why? Obviously, you would first select people with abilities and skills to get the job done. You would want people in your group who would pull their own weight. Next, you might select people you like and get along with well, although this may not be a primary consideration. Studies have shown that when groups can choose their own members, the morale of the group and the productivity is higher than when individuals are assigned to groups.

Groups form and develop by interacting and working together. Social psychologist William C. Schutz reasoned that the developmental process of groups entails individual fulfillment of three fundamental interpersonal needs: inclusion, control, and affection. A balance of these needs is necessary to build satisfaction, commitment, and a sense of collectiveness in the group.

Inclusion

Inclusion involves the desire to belong. As stated earlier, this need is strong within many of us. We feel a certain sense of confidence and competence when we are recognized by others as worthy, and as a part of their group. The in-group feeling is a powerful one.

Control

Control can exist in various degrees within a group. Control means that we have a desire to have influence over others and their decisions or outcomes. Some members of a group will have a stronger need for control than others. We may even have varying degrees in the type of control that we desire.

Box 8-2   **Strategies and Tactics in Interpersonal Conflict**

Following are five tactics often used to resolve interpersonal conflict. The styles used by group members certainly affect the norms and cohesiveness of the group.

Strategy of Manipulation — Be especially sweet, charming, helpful, and pleasant before bringing up the subject of conflict. Act so nice that he/she later cannot refuse when I ask him/her for my own way. Make this person believe that he/she is doing me a favor by giving in.

Strategy of Nonnegotiation — Refuse to discuss or even to listen to the subject unless he/she gives in. Keep repeating my point of view until he/she gives in. Argue until this person changes his/her mind.

Strategy of Emotional Appeal — Appeal to this person's love and affection for me. Promise to be more loving in the future. Get angry and demand that he/she give in.

Strategy of Personal Rejection — Withhold affection and act cold until he/she gives in. Ignore him/her. Make the other person jealous by pretending to lose interest in him/her.

Strategy of Empathic Understanding — Discuss what would happen if we each accepted the other's point of view. Talk about why we do not agree. Hold mutual talks without argument.

Source: From Raymond Ross, *Small groups in organizational settings*, (New Jersey: Prentice-Hall, 1989). Ross cites M. Fitzpatrick and J. Winke, "You always hurt the one you love: Strategies and tactics in interpersonal conflict," *Communication Quarterly*, *27* (1), 1979, p. 7.

Some feel the need just to have control over themselves and their daily lives. Yet others, many who seek leadership positions, have a strong inner drive to control others. They want to lead more than to be led.

Affection

We all need to be liked. Our need for affection in groups means that we desire friendship, warmth, and concern from members of certain groups. Although we cannot always achieve fulfillment of this need within all of our task groups, a certain recognition for our humanness is necessary. How much a part of a group do you feel if you get the "vibes" that no one in the group likes you?

Within the group as a whole, affection is the stage where cohesiveness emerges. If there is affection in the group, people likely will work together cooperatively and will be more likely to feel committed to achieving their goals and continuing their interaction with the group. An important characteristic of this stage is trust. Trust elicits a feeling of confidence about the group.

NORMS WITHIN WORKGROUPS

The first step toward improving communication in groups is to promote desirable norms. Norms are rules or standards that determine appropriate versus inappropriate behavior. These unwritten rules establish expectations of how group members should behave and are determined very early. Classroom norms, for example, are defined within the first few days. You learn how you are expected to greet the instructor, whether you need to raise your hand to speak out, the rules about tardiness, and grading expectations. Knowing what to expect, when to report to work, how much time is allowed for lunch, and who does what and how saves time; and, therefore, normal job expectations are often explicitly stated in work rules. Some norms, however, are more subtle. One student told how she went to a group meeting dressed in a sweatsuit and with her hair in a ponytail. All other members of the group were still dressed as they came from work, in suits. She felt uncomfortable and excluded because of her different apparel, and dressed accordingly the next time the group met. She felt much more accepted once she adapted to this norm.

Norms that develop within groups help to reduce uncertainty that occurs with any type of interaction. Our speaking style, the clothes we wear, and our timing (late, early) are all determined by group norms. Group norms shape member relationships. They set standards for appropriateness in social interaction. Although most norms are unspoken, many group members can identify certain standards of behavior that their group considers acceptable. One way to identify norms is to observe any behavior that is repeated over time.

WE MEAN BUSINESS

Write down the norms of one social, learning, or decision-making group of which you have been a part. How many of these norms were unwritten? Was there any punishment for disobeying these norms?

COHESIVENESS WITHIN WORKGROUPS

Cohesiveness refers to the degree of attraction that members feel toward one another and the group as a whole. It is an overall feeling of loyalty and "groupness." Members of a highly cohesive group value their membership and work hard to maintain positive relationships with other group members. There is a sense of pride and commitment to the tasks of the group. As a result, members tend to conform to the norms of the group. Thus, cohesiveness results from the interaction of a number of variables including interpersonal attraction, shared experiences, length of membership, feedback, commitment, and conformity.

Interpersonal attraction refers to the notion that you feel good about yourself and the other members in your group. Attraction does not necessarily imply that your feelings have to be romantic, however! You do not need to feel that "She's a babe" or "He's a hunk" in order to get along with your group. Interpersonal attraction means that you feel positive about working with these other people, a feeling that things "click."

If there is constant friction between group members, a group's productivity will probably suffer. Have you ever been a member of a group where you really disliked some of the members? Did you look forward to meeting with that group? Did you ever skip group meetings?

The second factor that influences cohesiveness is shared successes and failures. In order to feel good about the group's productivity, most groups need to share more successes than failures. When a group consistently fails, morale and productivity often suffer. Groups that share successes tend to feel more pride and identification with the group. However, there are some exceptions. Some groups are drawn closer by their failures, and their determination to turn the group around. The film "Major League" detailed the experiences of a "losing" baseball team that worked together to overcome its poor self-image and failings. As that togetherness grew, they began to share successes and then won the pennant. Another group that has remained cohesive over time, in spite of failure, is the Vietnam veterans. Suffering, shared trauma and defeat, and lack of heroic recognition has bound them together.

Length and regularity of membership also affects cohesiveness. The most basic measure of workgroup loyalty is regular attendance. Many of you can recall groups of which you have been a part where one member of the group was consistently late or absent. In fact, both of the authors have had their classes keep journals of group activity and participation in a class research assignment. There was high dissatisfaction from the groups in which some attended irregularly. They reported frustration in their journals when one or more members either did not appear for group meetings, or were very late. Liking for no-shows and latecomers diminishes.

Doing one's share is an essential part of creating a productive atmosphere. it is not enough for a person merely to attend group meetings regularly if he/she does not participate in completion of the tasks. Membership in groups can be frustrating when you feel as if some people within the group are just riding on your coattails. Before judging someone, however, be sure to ask for participation with nudges, such as "Kim, what do you think we should do?" or "Would you like to add anything, Kerry?" Interaction and feedback are necessary for fulfillment of the basic interpersonal needs described above, and as a group member you want to make sure that everyone has a chance to voice his/her ideas.

Cohesiveness and commitment to a task are closely linked. Chapter 1 discussed organizational commitment in detail. Remember the definition of commitment that we provided in that chapter? Recall that commitment involves (1) a feeling of shared beliefs in the goals and values of the group, (2) a willingness to devote considerable effort, and (3) the desire to remain within the group. Think about the groups to which you currently belong. Can you answer yes to all three parts of the definition for any of these groups? You probably know that when you feel committed to a certain task or group, you are much more likely to be concerned with the group outcome.

A final element that influences cohesiveness is conformity. Conformity refers to the level of members' acceptance of group norms. That is, how much each is willing to agree with and adapt to the group's standards of appropriate behavior. When group members deviate or violate norms of the group, they are generally penalized. Groups have a powerful way of letting members know of their disapproval.

Being accepted within a group sometimes causes us to sacrifice our own beliefs. This is an ethical issue that you must consider when involved in a group. How much is membership in this group worth to you?

CONFORMITY AND GROUPTHINK

You may very well be thinking that conforming to group norms sounds like the sensible way to gain collectiveness and cohesiveness in a group. A group that is cohesive will be more productive, but too much cohesiveness can be too much of a good thing. When the group centers more on interpersonal socializing instead of accomplishing a task, interpersonal attraction can be detrimental. Cohesiveness is not positive if it results in sacrifice of a group member's individuality or critical thinking.

There is a real danger in too much cohesiveness. When individual members are discouraged to say or act in any way that will detract from the group's cohesiveness, or when members lose their ability to critically evaluate the quality of their decisions, a group has become a victim of groupthink.

Social scientists discovered a similar tendency in the small group to go along with the judgments of most others. Muzafer Sherif, in his study called *The Psychology of Social Norms*, demonstrated that a person's estimates of the distance of two lights in the dark was influenced by the distance estimated by other subjects. Since lights in a dark room are difficult to judge, individuals relied on the estimates of those with them. When uncertainty is high, we tend to rely on the judgment of others. From this research and other similar studies, evidence indicates that in the face of the majority, it is difficult for some of us to stick to our opinions. Hopefully, by becoming aware of this common tendency to bow to social pressure, it should forewarn us and help us not to compromise our convictions. But this is often easier said than done.

A group that works well together can get a feeling that it can do no wrong. Irving Janis, in his classic investigation of fiascoes that resulted from decisions made by government leaders, defined the core principle of groupthink as follows:

> The more amiability and esprit de corps there is among the members of a policy-making in-group, the greater the danger that independent critical thinking will be replaced by groupthink, which is likely to result in irrational and dehumanizing actions directed against out-groups.

Groupthink can be very dangerous both for the in and out groups. To some degree, groupthink exists within any group that refers to itself as "better than all the rest" and tells its members "not to rock the boat," or else to "get off the boat" if they question norms. Any group that does not explore alternatives or question the validity of its solution is showing signals of groupthink. But large-scale groupthink actions have already had detrimental effects on our nation and world.

Each of us has heard over and over about the horrors of World War II. Germany's economy was depressed. Germany had lost World War I and had been charged high reparations. Adolf Hitler rose to power at a time when the German people needed a boost, a sense of belonging and esteem. Hitler fulfilled these needs, and promised the people that their nation would rise above the rest. And so the people followed. Those who questioned were not only ostracized, but often were killed. Groupthink escalated to a frenzy as power and hunger for glory ran through Hitler's veins. The one voice and one will preached by him permitted the atrocities of the concentration camps and gas chambers.

The film "Mississippi Burning" illustrates anther example of dangerous and destructive groupthink. The KKK "decided," much as Hitler did, that there was a superior race. In this case, the in-group were the white people, and the out-group were the blacks. Senseless killing of these innocent people and even mass suicides such as the Jonestown cult's can be explained in terms of groups that were isolated from both external and internal debate. No leader, however charismatic, should be followed if she or he does not encourage critical examination. We must never forget these powerful examples in history during which conformist communication distorted our image of right and wrong.

WE MEAN BUSINESS

Can you think of an example of groupthink that occurred in a group of which you have been a member? Describe your experience. Were you in the "in" group or the "out" group?

What does this have to do with the workplace? Plenty. Groupthink can and does happen on both a large and small scale. Each time members are not given time to offer feedback, suggest specific criteria for solutions, test their solutions for validity, and question the value of the solutions, they risk groupthink. Here are some suggestions by Irving Janis and others of ways you can safeguard from groupthink occurring.

- The leader should request that the group be critical of his/her ideas and play the devil's advocate. Leaders should adopt an impartial stance and probe many possibilities.
- Outside experts may be invited to examine plans of action and to sit in on meetings.
- Occasionally the group might be split into two groups to examine a proposal critically.
- Scenarios of how out-groups might respond should be written. "Second chance" meetings should be conducted to provide opportunities to reconsider decisions, when time permits.
- Avoid averaging, coin tossing, majority vote, bargaining, and such conflict-reducing techniques. Do not feel that if one person loses, he or she must later be rewarded.

Differences are natural. Seek them out and try to involve everyone in the decision process. Conflict can be extremely positive and profitable. Workgroups in which difference of opinion is encouraged are more involving. Conflict that permits reasoned argument can enhance the cohesiveness of a group. In a wide range of alternatives, there is a greater chance for an optimal solution.

What we have stressed in this discussion of groupthink is that there are dangers in groups in spite of the general superiority of group decisions over individual ones. The dangers include conforming to the assumed correctness of the majority; taking risks and doing what our cooler, more rational selves would not; and "groupness" causing us to isolate our leaders from negative criticism and causing us to censure our doubts.

LEADERSHIP IN WORKGROUPS

What effect does leadership have on group behavior? Probably the most influential figure in a group is the leader. His/her style of leadership and procedures employed greatly affect the quality of solution and the group's morale. Often leaders do not realize the impact their communication skills and actions have on the entire group interaction.

One's style of leadership has a direct correlation to subordinates' task and interpersonal satisfaction. The three different styles of leadership are laissez-faire, autocratic, and democratic in groups performing tasks.

Laissez-faire means "let it go." This style of leadership is extremely permissive. The leader does little to lead task completion or provide direction. There is minimal control over members of the group, deviation from standard group norms, or over the delegation of duties. Although students at first may think this would be a "fun" way for a class to be taught, the novelty of this approach tends to wear thin quickly. When there is little structure or direction, interpersonal satisfaction is usually low. Under laissez-faire leadership, task completion tends to be low.

At the other end of the spectrum is autocratic leadership. The autocratic leader is assertive and takes almost complete control of the group. This person typically directs tasks with an iron hand, and allows little participation from group members. Thus, task completion tends to be high under dominant supervision. Although this is true, the greatest danger of autocratic leadership is member overdependence upon the leader, and the probability of groupthink is greater. When group members are given minimal freedom of choice, they are sacrificing individualism or creativity, and their satisfaction is usually low. When decisions are controlled by someone else, we become frustrated.

The balance between these two extremes is democratic leadership. Democratic leaders maintain responsibility for task completion, but invite participation from all task members. These leaders seek to discover the will of the group and through joint deliberation produce quality decisions. Since group members have a stake in decision making and implementation, interpersonal satisfaction is highest under this type of leadership. It is also true in most cases that task completion will also be high, since there is control and direction. When people feel commitment toward completion of a task, they tend to be more productive and feel more pride in reaching the final result.

From the above examples, it is clear that groups need both task and interpersonal leadership. The effectiveness of leadership depends upon many factors. Some group leaders only fulfill either a task or interpersonal function. If one of these functions is shortchanged, typically another member of the group will emerge as the secondary leader to fill this gap. Obviously, the optimal group leader would be aware and competent in meeting the task and interpersonal needs of the group. As a task leader, you should show competence in the subject content, be articulate, and be able to present well the group's concerns to superiors and outsiders. As an interpersonal leader, you must earn the confidence of the group, achieve your own job satisfaction in seeing others succeed, and be concerned about promoting positive interpersonal relationships among the others.

J. Kevin Barge and Randy Y. Hirokawa, authors of the article "Toward a

Box 8-3 **Learning to Inspire**

How corporate chiefs can go beyond managing and learning to inspire.

1. Trust your subordinates. You can't expect them to go all-out for you if they think you don't believe in them.

2. Develop a vision. Some executives' suspicions to the contrary, planning for the long term pays off. And people want to follow someone who knows where he or she is going.

3. Keep your cool. The best leaders show their mettle under fire.

4. Encourage risk. Nothing demoralizes the troops like knowing that the slightest failure could jeopardize their entire career.

5. Be an expert. From boardroom to mail room, everyone had better understand that you know what you're talking about.

6. Invite dissent. Your people aren't giving you their best or learning how to lead if they are afraid to speak up.

7. Simplify. You need to see the big picture in order to set a course, communicate it, and maintain it. Keep the details at bay.

Source: From Kenneth Labich, "The Seven Keys to Business Leadership," *Fortune*, October 24, 1988, pp. 58–66.

Communication Competency Model of Group Leadership," studied leadership based on increasing communication competencies. They proposed that performance of these competencies in the leadership process will allow the group to perform better and manage their problems more effectively. Their approach to the study of leadership included the idea that leadership occurs through the process of interaction and communication.

Barge and Hirokawa expanded the definitions of task and relational competencies of group members: Task competencies include the ability to establish operating procedures, analyze problems, generate criteria for good solutions, apply criteria to solutions, and select solutions. Failure to be competent in these areas will probably result in frustration in group members, for communication incompetence makes task completion difficult.

Relational competencies allow members of the group to maintain and manage productive relationships. The four relational competencies cited were already discussed in Chapter 3. Let us briefly restate them in context of workgroup relational communication. The first is *interaction management*, or the ability to manage conversational turn-taking and turn-yielding functions appropriately. The second competency is *expressiveness*, which is a nonverbal characteristic. Expressiveness refers to vocal variety, body movement, and facial animation while communicating. *Altercentrism*, or other-orientation, is the third relational competency noted. Altercentrism means one has concern for the other people who are communicating. As a group member or leader, you would show concern, attentiveness, and interest for the other person's feelings and emotions. The final relational competency discussed in this study is *social relaxation*. This refers to the level of anxiety that the speaker shows. In order to feel socially relaxed, one must feel comfortable in the environment.

Extensive research has led to the conclusion that good managers are characterized by three factors: interpersonal competence, motivation, and participatory management, which combine in a style that balances production and people. Group members want leaders who both help *create structure* and *show consideration* to all concerned. Study Box 8-4 to learn more about task and relational competencies.

In addition to the views of Barge and Hirokawa, there are several other leadership theories. One such theory is that of Likert. Rensis Likert's theory of leadership revolves around the notion that organizations typically function in two characteristic ways — authoritative and participative. He then places four leadership styles on a continuum along these two characteristics.

Organizational Leadership Continuum

Authoritative	Participative
A — Exploitive Authoritative	C — Consultative
B — Benevolent Authoritative	D — Participative Group

Some of his research focused on finding out how the attitude of the employee toward his/her work and employer affected productivity. The results of one study indicated that seven out of ten of the supervisors who had employees within the high-producing group were "employee-centered." Similarly, seven out of ten supervisors within the lower-producing groups were reported as "job-centered."

Evidence from their work indicates that effective managers provide a work climate where employees are provided with clear tasks, objectives, and directions. Yet these employees are also given sufficient latitude to feel they can accomplish the tasks with some sense of ownership. Supervisors who were in charge of low-producing groups were found to spend much time with their employees, closely monitoring the work accomplished. As Raymond Ross said in his text, *Small Groups in Organizational Settings*, "better supervisors apparently know when to ignore mistakes, letting experience be the teacher, or when to use mistakes as helpful training opportunities." Likert's investigation also found that interpersonal competencies, such as those mentioned in Chapter 3, are also an important indicator of group productivity and job satisfaction. Employees often assess their worth by the amount of responsibility, leadership, and support that they are provided.

Box 8-4 Classification of Task and Relational Competencies

TASK COMPETENCIES

Problem Orientation
TC1. Analyze the group problem.

Criteria Establishment
TC2. Establish evaluation criteria.

Solution Activity
TC3. Generate alternative solutions.

TC4. Evaluate alternative solutions and conflict style.

TC5. Solution selection and confirmation.

Procedural Activity
TC6. Establish operating procedures.

TC7. Process reflection.

RELATIONAL COMPETENCIES

Interaction Management
RC1. Orientation: clarification, summarization, orientation.

RC2. Flexibility: directive style, adaptability, balancing participation.

RC3. Conflict management: integration-bargaining/consensus building/problem solving, accommodation, smoothing, avoiding.

Expressiveness
RC4. Ambiguity: documentation, equivocal, and relative words.

RC5. Objectivity: opinionatedness, self-orientation, irrelevant remarks.

RC6. Evaluation: agreement, offensive language.

Other-Orientation
RC7. Acknowledgments of others' input: self-referential statements, surveys information, seeks evaluation, recognizes ideas, seeks involvement of other group members.

RC8. Trust and Respect

Relaxation
RC9. Involvement: frequency of talk participation.

Source: From J. Kevin Barge and Randy Y. Hirokawa, "Toward a Communication Competency Model of Group Leadership," *Small group behavior*, May 1989.

Likert emphasized a principle of supportive relationships, where the supervisor focuses on developing an employee-centered, supportive environment. In his text, *New Patterns of Management*, he said that employees should see their work experience "as supportive and one which builds and maintains his/her sense of personal worth and importance."

PHASES OF GROUP DECISION MAKING

Another part of understanding group communication involves recognition of typical phases of interaction through which members progress when solving problems. Relationships that are gratifying move from loose, informal structures toward regular meetings and procedures. Once a collection of people has become a group, generally certain patterns develop.

Workgroups within organizations sometimes are temporary project teams or committees, but most often are configurations of people who have in the past and will in the future continue to work together. It is particularly fitting, therefore, to examine these continuing relationships as one might view a small society, a society that moves over time into different stages of development. To have meaning, a group must possess a sense of its identity, a structure, and a task. Regardless of the type of group, whether social, interpersonally supportive, learning, or decision making, the phases of interaction are usually similar. The following labels for the phases of group decision making were named by communication scholar B. Aubrey Fisher.

Orientation

The initial phase of interaction is called the orientation stage. This is a time of defining and testing group norms, and for securing member commitment. During this phase, the person suitable for the leadership position is usually determined. The group typically begins with introductions or some small talk. They are searching for initial signs of cohesiveness and structure. Although many functions of the orientation stage will be fulfilled at early meetings, every time the group meets some orientation behavior is involved.

Conflict

The conflict stage is next. We realize that many people have negative connotations when they hear the word conflict. Actually, conflict is quite healthy, and is a natural part of the group process. As was stressed earlier in this chapter, a group that has conflict has less danger of groupthink. Conflict in its simplest state merely means that differing ideas are put on the table, and discussion needs to determine which of these ideas is best suited for the group. Therefore, it should be said — and said loudly — that working with groups means working with conflict. People do differ. People do take sides. Some people are disagreeable. Some are more likeable than others. This

---

Box 8-5 **Productive Rather Than Destructive Conflict**

As a leader, you play an influential role in setting the tone for how conflicts will be handled. Here are a few tips for encouraging productive rather than destructive conflict:

1. Try to set up win/win situations rather than win/lose. Encourage group members to compromise so all parties feel like their voice is valued.

2. Limit discussions to issues, and avoid letting participants talk about people and personalities.

3. Encourage perspective taking. Use language such as, "that's a good point, but have you looked at that issue from another point of view?" or "thanks, I hadn't thought about this from another perspective."

4. Seat people who are known to have negative vibes *next* to each other. In a group meeting people tend to interact more with those *across* a table rather than those who are seated next to each other because it is easier to make more eye contact and see gestures.

---

phenomenon is particularly true for groups that must work together for a long period, perhaps years. A group in which members are afraid to voice disagreements is in more trouble than one in which disagreements are openly expressed. Discussion may help people work through conflict.

Emergence

Once a group has discussed the various options voiced during the conflict stage, members typically reach agreement on at least portions of the solution. Thus some or all of the solution begins to emerge. However, if no one feels comfortable with any part of the solution, the group must revert back to the conflict stage. The goal of the group is to reach consensus that the solution is an operational and satisfying one. If consensus cannot be reached, compromise, majority voting, or agreeing to differ may have to be the way conflict is resolved.

Reinforcement

The final stage of group decision making is often called reinforcement. This phase is characterized by collective agreement with the decision made. In essence, group members reinforce the solution that has emerged. It is very important for group members and the leader to check verbally and nonverbally to see if indeed there is genuine concurrence with the solution. If reconsiderations are not aired at this point, group members may carry tensions with them that can later undermine the successful implementation of the decision.

WE MEAN BUSINESS

Think back to your last group meeting. Analyze the meeting using these four stages of group decision-making. Did your group progress through the phases?

SUMMARY

Throughout this chapter we have developed the idea that each of us is a member of many different types of groups. Every group of which we are a part has certain norms and rituals known and adhered to by members. If members feel comfortable with these norms, it is more likely that they will feel interpersonal satisfaction and a sense of cohesiveness with other group members. On the other hand, if there is dissonance between a member's core beliefs and important group norms, there will undoubtedly be frustration and resentment.

Too much cohesiveness within a group can lead to the dangerous consequence of groupthink. In order to avoid situations in which members self-censor their critical thinking, wise leaders will explore all options to a solution.

The type of leadership that exists within a group can determine the task and interpersonal satisfaction of group members. Autocratic leaders tend to control interaction, and thus increase the danger of groupthink occurring. Democratic leaders encourage participation from his/her group members, and allow some freedom in decision making.

Almost every group progresses through the stages of orientation, conflict, emergence, and reinforcement. Keys to high-quality problem solving and decision making in the workgroup are creative ideation and rigorous analysis. High commitment to solutions hinges upon group involvement and democratically decided solutions.

SKILL BUILDER: DESIGNING A GROUP SYMBOL

Randomly assign class members to groups of four or five. Each group will need a posterboard-size sheet of paper, and one crayon or marker (preferably of differing colors) per group member.

Each group is to draw a symbol of their group. The decisions for what this symbol will be is solely up to group members.

Upon completion of the task, each group is to explain the group process involved in designing the symbol. Groups should describe their orientation, conflict, emergence, and reinforcement phases. They should also note emergence of leadership.

Display the completed symbols.

SKILL BUILDER: CLASSROOM CREATIVITY

Divide into 9- to 12-person groups in different sections of the classroom. Assign two people from each group to take turns listing ideas on a blackboard. Each group will randomly be assigned one of these topics:

1. Ways to study group communication
2. Moneymaking ideas for weekends while in college
3. Things that can be done to make school more valuable to high school students

First list as many ideas as possible without judging the effectiveness of the ideas. Then select the most interesting and workable plan. Sketch a brief plan for implementation. Each group will then present its plan to the entire class.

RESOURCES

Asch, Solomon. (1951). "Effects of group pressure upon modification and distortion of judgment." In Harold Guetskow (ed.), *Groups, leadership and men*. Pittsburgh: Carnegie Press.

Bales, Robert F. (1950). *Interaction process and analysis: A method for study of small groups*. Reading, MA: Addison-Wesley.

Barge, Kevin, and Randy Hirokawa (1988, November). "Toward a communication competency model of group leadership." Paper presented at the annual meeting of the Speech Communication Association, New Orleans, Louisiana, November 1988.

Bormann, Ernest G. (1975). *Discussion and group methods: Theory and practice* (2nd ed.). New York: Harper & Row.

Fisher, B. Aubrey. (1980). *Small group decision-making*. Chicago: Science Research Associates.

Gorden, William I., and John R. Miller. (1983). *Managing your communication: In and for the organization*. Prospect Heights, IL: Waveland Press.

Gouran, Dennis S. (1982). *Making decisions in groups: Choices and consequences*. Glenview, IL: Scott, Foresman.

Hirokawa, Randy Y., and Marshall Scott Poole. (eds). (1986). *Communication and group decision-making*. Beverly Hills, CA: Sage.

Janis, Irving J. (1982). *Victims of groupthink: Psychological studies of policy decisions and fiascoes*. Boston: Houghton Mifflin.

Likert, Rensis. (1987). *New patterns of study*. New York: Garland.

Ross, Raymond. (1989). *Small groups in organizational settings*. Englewood Cliffs, NJ: Prentice-Hall.

Schutz, William C. (1958). *Firo: A three-dimensional theory of interpersonal behavior*. New York: Rinehart.

Schutz, William C. (1966). *The interpersonal underworld*. Palo Alto, CA: Science and Behavior Books.

Shaw, Marvin E. (1981). *Group dynamics: The psychology of small group behaviors* (3rd ed.). New York: McGraw-Hill.

Sherif, Muzafer. (1936). *The psychology of social norms*. New York: Harper.

Chapter 9

Running Meetings and Team Building in the Workplace

Concepts for Discussion

- Running meetings
- Project teams and committees
- Support groups
- Negotiations
- Group creativity

- Team building
- Quality circles
- Ad hoc teams
- Natural workgroups
- Autonomous work teams

Meeting for Business and Health

Business consultant Peter Drucker has observed that managers waste too much time in meetings. Business people whose whole days are consumed by meeting after meeting may be more tired than if they had physically exercised. There are ways to cut down on meeting time.

- Prepare an agenda in advance. Put it in writing. Agendas are the chairperson's responsibility. Topics that should be addressed may be solicited by phone or invited by memo.
- Schedule meetings at regular times . . . Call them off when there is no need for them.

- Schedule meetings at times when they are most needed.
  — For motivation: Early in the week — perhaps first thing Monday morning.
  — For providing information that will enable work coordination — early in the week.
  — For long-range planning — an offsite, daylong retreat.
  — For checking on progress — late in the day, midweek.
  — Developing a working relationship — possibly meet for lunch, or even meet for a fitness workout. Protagoras in the fifth century B.C. conducted seminars while walking. President Harry Truman took guests and advisors with him on his morning walks. Presidents Carter and Bush were known for their runs with staff. Albert Einstein liked to walk with colleagues when exploring ideas about how the universe works! Some chief executive officers conduct meetings on the run.

Ken Thuebach, president and CEO of Alpine Log Homes in Victor, Montana, is one such individual. A running meeting, he says, begins with an exchange of significant information. Ground is covered and various scenes stimulate informal conversation, sometimes nonbusiness sharing of interests.

Meetings for business and health are possibilities for the adventurous.

Adapted from Nathan Edelson,
"The Manager's Journal," *The Wall Street Journal*, April, 1989.

In this chapter, we will focus upon meetings and teams. First we will describe rules for participation in formal meetings; and then we will discuss more common, less formal meetings. Following that, techniques will be presented for a work unit's responsibility for measuring and monitoring the quality of work performance and service. Finally, we will discuss several approaches to employer involvement and teambuilding: brainstorming, quality circles, ad hoc teams, natural work groups, and autonomous self-directed teams.

CHAIRING MEETINGS

Most leaders think of running a meeting in terms of parliamentary procedure: Calling the meeting to order, asking for the reading of minutes, taking up old business and committee reports, presentation of new business, and adjournment. Knowing parliamentary rules of order is essential to function effectively in the public sector.

The essential principle of parliamentary rules of order is that business is most efficiently and fairly deliberated *when a proposal is set forth and its acceptance is moved and seconded.* To do business, voter qualifications must be decided. Preconditions of membership are usually stated in the constitution and by-laws. Procedural matters such as whether a quorum is present must be determined in accordance with the by-laws. The chairperson should be addressed. Members should be acknowledged before speaking to the gathering, as in "Madam Chairwoman" and "Yes, Mr. Jones."

Motions that proposals or reports should be approved by a body must be seconded; and then are debatable, amendable, and voted up, down, or postponed, typically by majority vote.

Only one main motion at a time can be on the floor. Procedural motions, however, can intervene to either facilitate or delay action. Those who are experienced in parliamentary rules of order may help or hinder a group as they will. Some schools and civic organizations offer special courses in legislative procedures.

A brief listing of the rules for parliamentary order are diagrammed in the charts below. First we will present the rules of main motions and relevant questions such as: Can one interrupt a speaker to make a main motion? Is a second required? Is it debatable? Can it be amended? What vote is required, if any?

	Can One Interrupt Speaker?	Requires a Second?	Debatable?	Amendable?	Vote Required?
Main motions					
A general main					
motion	no	yes	yes	yes	majority
Specific					
main motions					
reconsider	yes	yes	yes	no	majority
Rescind	no	yes	yes	no	majority
Resume					
consideration	no	yes	no	no	majority

In addition to main motions, a number of other motions are designed to conduct the business of a body: (1) privileged, (2) subsidiary, and (3) incidental. These motions have an order of priority: privileged motions have the highest priority and secondary motions follow. Incidental motions, because they are meant for clarification and to facilitate the business at hand, carry no special order of precedence among themselves but should be decided immediately.

	Can One Interrupt Speaker?	Requires a Second?	Debatable?	Amendable?	Vote Required?
Privileged motions					
Adjourn	no	yes	no	no	majority
Recess	no	yes	no	yes	majority
Questions of privilege	yes	no	no	no	no vote
Subsidiary motions					
Postpone temporarily (lay on the table)	no	yes	no	no	majority
Vote immediately (previous question)	no	yes	no	no	two-thirds
Limit debate	no	yes	no	yes	two-thirds
Postpone definitely	no	yes	yes	yes	majority
Refer to committee	no	yes	yes	yes	majority
Amend	no	yes	yes	yes	majority
Postpone indefinitely	no	yes	yes	no	majority

	Can One Interrupt Speaker?	Requires a Second?	Debatable?	Amendable?	Vote Required?
Incidental motions*					
Appeal	yes	yes	yes	no	tie or majority
Point of order	yes	no	no	no	no vote
Parliamentary inquiry	yes	no	no	no	no vote
Withdraw a motion	no	no	no	no	no vote
Suspend rules	no	yes	no	no	two-thirds
Object to consideration	yes	no	no	no	two-thirds neg.
Division of a question	no	no	no	no	no vote
Division of assembly	yes	no	no	no	no vote

*No order of precedence among themselves. Each motion decided immediately.

Rarely is business conducted formally in the workplace. Workplace meetings generally are more or less semiformal and decisions are made by consensus. Only when there is a conflict do leaders resort to motions and roll call votes.

Leaders even in informal situations are most effective when they are process-conscious. They instinctively ask themselves and others such questions as:

- What is the purpose of this meeting?
- Who did or should call it?
- Who should be included?
- How shall "we" determine if this meeting is successful?
- When and where should it be scheduled?
- How far in advance should people be notified?
- Who should contribute to the agenda?
- Who should chair it and how will that be decided?
- How public or secret should it be?
- Is there time to send out an agenda?
- How formal should the setting and procedure be?
- Who will decide when the meeting is over?

The effective leader constantly asks what is necessary to (a) generate a high-quality product and (b) create maximum acceptance and commitment to whatever solution is decided. These two concerns prompt attention first to bringing together the best expertise possible; second, to allow thoughtful deliberations; and third, but not of lesser importance, to inclusion of all parties essential to creating commitment. The concern for expertise is a technological/knowledge problem; the concern for commitment is a political problem.

Once a meeting is convened, the leader(s) will do the utmost to balance the difficult job of keeping comments of the group on track and encouraging participation. A chair's role, therefore, entails keeping order, maintaining relevance, tactfully discouraging too much redundancy, and maintaining respectful discourse among those present. The concern for process is an unrelenting commitment to fairness, efficiency, and quality of group communication.

WE MEAN BUSINESS

Have you ever chaired a meeting, whether it be for business, service, or fraternity/sorority? Analyze how you approached this task. Did you follow the criteria included in this section?

Leadership in meetings is easiest when there is active followership. Active followers check whether comments are on-track; they avoid unnecessary tangents; they are rigorous and critical when necessary; they help the chair know when they are ready for closure on a topic; they ensure that there are plans for following up on the group's decisions. Effective followers, like effective leaders, are process-conscious.

WORKGROUP'S RESPONSIBILITY FOR MEASURING AND MONITORING QUALITY

Measuring and monitoring quality in successful organizations is a workgroup's responsibility. Workgroups are enlisted in formulating the organization's mission statements. Workgroups get involved in defining quality goals and standards. Workgroups are involved in the continuous process of making sure that specifications are adhered to. Federal Express handles a million and a half packages a day. Its 85,000 employees do not waste time in meetings, but they do interact in their workgroups. Quality is calculated mathematically in terms of service quality indicators (SQI), based on what customers want: Loss of a package is weighted by a factor of 10; one day late by 5; five minutes late by 1. Lowering the SQI is the road to fewer unhappy customers. Chairman and founder Frederick Smith said, "The bottom line is that to satisfy our customers, we must first treat our employees as customers," and he has stressed that "creating trust through open, candid communication is at the heart of this effort."

The basic ingredients to securing employees' cooperation begins with workgroups working out the answers to the questions: What do you expect of me? What do I expect from you? The essential elements in creating a package transportation system are accurate sorting, tracking, and delivery. The communication loops to make this happen are people-intensive. The handheld computer scanners that monitor the packages are meaningless without a committed, competent, communicative workforce.

KIVs/KOVs

Quality depends on a workgroup's ability to define key input variables (KIVs) and key output variables (KOVs). So often employees are simply ordered to perform certain task-behaviors. Just-do-it-and-don't-ask-why is not an attitude that modern organizations can afford. Involvement in discovering what KOVs are desired by internal and external customers generates knowledge about what is wanted in a product or service. It also creates a "want to" attitude in a workgroup to assess more carefully what are the essential KIVs to meeting those expectations.

Workgroups that are involved in studying the essential key input and output variables come to appreciate the analytical problem-solving process and the need for keeping records.

FISHBONING

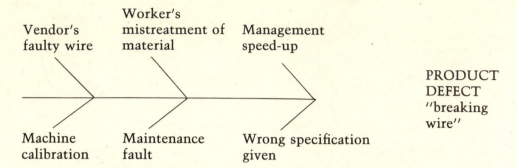

This is a "fish bone" diagram. Each of the six KIVs, or input variables (e.g., vendor's faulty wire) need to be examined to discover what causes the KOV, or output. In this case, the output included a product defect.

The analytical process is made easier when a work unit knows how to think systematically. Fishbone diagrams facilitate this process. For example, suppose your work unit was encountering broken wires in a lightbulb. This is an undesirable outcome variable. The work unit immediately pictures the various key input variables that might cause the wire breakage, and proceeds to check out possible causes.

Cause-effect diagrams facilitate workgroup communication and monitoring of the work process. They speed up detection of causes for unwanted problems and wanted solutions.

GROUP CREATIVITY

One of the most popular of all group activities in the business world is brainstorming. Brainstorming can be done by a group of one to 100. But it got its start in advertising as a group process. Alex Osborn, in *Applied Imagination: Principles and Procedures of Creative Thinking*, set forth four rules of brainstorming:

1. *Criticism is ruled out.* Evaluation of rules comes after ideas have been generated.
2. *Free-wheeling is welcome.* The wilder the idea, the better. It's easier to tame an idea than to think one up.
3. *Quantity is wanted.* The greater the number of ideas, the more probable some will be winners.
4. *Combination and improvements are sought.* Additions, turning ideas upside down, subtraction, multiplication, partitions, mixing ideas should all be listed as new ideas.

Box 9-1   **A Student's Voice**

A student who read about ''KOVs'' responded:

> I had a job at a yogurt franchise in Cuyahoga Falls, Ohio. When a customer ordered a medium cup, which was seven ounces of yogurt, we would fill the cup, weigh it out (it usually weighed 7.5–7.8 ounces) and then the manager had us record how much over each cup was filled in a ''Yogurt Waste Journal.'' In this way he could keep record on his KOVs and determine how much yogurt was being given away for free. In one year he had given out $3,000 worth of free yogurt.

Source: Kelly Christ, Kent State University, 1991.

Charles Clark, who worked with Osborn and wrote a book titled *Brainstorming: How to Create Successful Ideas,* listed over 60 major organizations that used brainstorming in the first publication of his book. He said that in 1956, 47 continuing brainstorm panels (usually of 12 persons each) held 401 sessions in which 34,000 ideas were produced. About 6 percent of those ideas were worthy of adoption or development. This meant an output of some 2,000 worthwhile ideas per year that might otherwise have remained unborn. These panels were conducted by Batten, Barton, Durstine, and Osborn, at that time the largest advertising agency in the world.

Brainstorming is designed to counteract negative thinking. Clark suggested that some companies adopt the green light as a metaphor for the "Let's go" of brainstorming. He also recommended follow-up sessions that evaluate ideas for their workability, which may be thought of as red-light sessions.

Ideas may lie fallow for several years before they find someone who will become their champion. That was true of the radio music box suggested by an assistant traffic manager employed by Marconi Wireless Telegraph Company who wrote a memo envisioning radio stations and receivers. Six years passed before David Sarnoff, who became CEO of RCA, then became the person to champion the idea of radio.

TEAM BUILDING

Throughout this chapter we have emphasized the idea of working collectively to reach decisions and to get the job done. Earlier in the text we spent considerable time talking about the development of shared meanings within the corporate culture and we discussed the importance of interpersonal relationships in the workplace. All of the pieces of this corporate puzzle fit together to spell one word—"team."

An organization with a team-building climate is characterized by many of the following behaviors. See if any of these sound familiar from earlier discussion: A corporate culture that follows the team approach is one in which top management actively seeks input from subordinates. Subordinates have confidence in the leadership of their superiors. Motivation is high. Attitudes toward the organization and its goals are positive. Maslow's hierarchical needs, ranging from physical and security to self-actualization, are met. Communication is open and extensive. Decision making and control are generally decentralized and occur at all levels through the group process. The emphasis is on collaborative problem solving. Does this sound like a system of which you would like to be a part?

WE MEAN BUSINESS

Do you remember Porter's definition of organizational commitment discussed in Chapter 1? How does commitment relate to the concept of team building?

Chris Argyris, author of *Organization and Innovation*, best summarized the criteria for team behavior and participation within organizations. He included the following criteria to serve as standards by which any group may test and review its own working relationship.

- Contributions made within the group are additive.
- The group moves forward as a unit; there is a sense of team spirit; high involvement.
- Decisions are made by consensus.
- Commitment to decisions by most members is strong.
- The group continually evaluates itself.
- The group is clear about its goals.
- Conflict is brought out into the open and dealt with.
- Alternative ways to thinking about solutions are generated.
- Leadership tends to go to the individual best qualified.
- Feelings are dealt with openly.

Quality Circles

Many of the features of team building discussed above play a part in a rather recent management strategy called quality circles, or QCs. Certainly our culture has shown a dramatic concern for management by, for, and of the people. Currently participative management techniques are being employed in an effort to let the employee's voice be heard. Many agree that this SHOULD be an inherent right of the modern American worker. Another

Box 9-2   # Japanese Values that Encourage Quality Circles

The Japanese grow up in a group-centered culture. They learn from youth to study, play, and work together. Here are some words that have special significance for the Japanese way of doing things:

Jaman suru: to persevere

Gom batte kudasai : please keep trying

Michi: an aesthetic sense that Japanese people share about the right way to approach work or any other activity worthy of one's time

O keikogoto: refers to the insight gained from the discipline of study, training, and personal improvement

Kaizen: describes a process-oriented way of thinking about constant improvement.

Source: Adapted from Linda S. Dillon, ''Can Japanese methods be applied in the Western workplace?'' *Quality Progress*, October, 1990, pp. 27–30

---

argument is that people feel that they have more of a stake in their company if they have a role in corporate decision making. Quality circles recognize and make use of the most powerful resource we possess—the people.

The Japanese recognized this fact and began using quality circles at the close of World War II. At this time, it was important for the culture to send a message to the world that "Made in Japan" meant quality.

There is little argument about Japanese industry's effectiveness in gaining major market shares in electronics, steel, and automobiles. That success has enabled this small nation buffeted by typhoons and with few natural resources to rise to extraordinary economic influence. Advocates of participative management have attributed Japan's competitiveness to a culture that is conducive to diffusing quality control processes into the workforce. The quality circle is praised as that vehicle. Yet there is contrary evidence. Robert Cole, quite an enthusiastic advocate of QCs after studying the Japanese workplace, stated that even in those plants with the best programs probably only "one-third of the circles are working well." Others have pointed out that only about 12 percent of the Japanese workforce is involved in quality circles and that they were instituted after, rather than before, the reputation for quality had been earned. With this caution in mind, the Japanese quality circle nevertheless merits attention.

Box 9-3   It's Magic!

Bill Merz puts a little "magic" into business meetings. Not only does Bill perform attention-getting magic at meetings held by companies such as Kodak, General Foods, and IBM, but he also designs tricks that executives can perform themselves at meetings.

For example, the president of the credit division of Dun and Bradstreet used magic to make a point. He told his director of sales to climb into a box and sealed it. Then he dramatically pulled out swords that he used to stab through the box again and again. The president said, "We're going to stab the competition. We'll jab our customers into seeing what a good job we can do," he announced. The audience held its breath. "What we're going to do is make our competition disappear."

Tricks such as this are used to liven up meetings and, according to Steve Solomon of Fuji Photo Film, "makes stars out of executives."

Source: Adapted from Maxine Lipner and Bill Merz, "Learning tricks of the trade." *Compass*, (1990).

In Japanese companies that have won the Deming Prize, the quality circle is part of an interactive company-wide quality effort. Ideas are not simply voted up or down. Rather they are tossed about in a "catchball" exercise in which those in a circle are asked to reflect upon, modify, and expand on them. Then these ideas, coupled with others that have been attached, are passed to other circles. At Toyota, across a 35-year period, the number of employees submitting suggestions has grown to 95 percent, an average of 47 suggestions per employee. Almost all suggestions of the over two and a half million submitted annually (96 percent) have been implemented.

Quality circles in Deming Prize companies are not simply low-level workgroups but are linked to middle and top executives' field visits and reports. Executives take time to make personal on-site visits and examine lower-level manager reports (jissetsu) on quality efforts and then to make their own jissetsu. Quality circles in these companies are part of a quality plan. Training for quality is vital to that plan and includes every level of employee.

American industry began its great concern for quality in the 1980s. By the end of the decade, quality circles had been tried in some 2500 work settings within the United States, with mixed results. Understanding why QCs were and are less integral to U.S. quality efforts than Japanese is traceable to cultural differences and to the history of management-labor relations. Consensual decision making is not a model consistent with the individualistic U.S. culture. The model of management in the United States has been more pragmatic than familylike. Those who had the capital and initiative called the shots. They were the venture capitalists that financed the digging of the canals, built the railroads, owned the coal mines, set up the steel mills, and managed the work force. Labor was an adversary once it became organized. United States labor unions were not just company-wide and therefore relatively controllable as they were in Japan.

Management's role was to create the technology, plan, and control; and to keep the pressure on for greater production. The union's role was to see that workers had safe working conditions, were treated fairly, and were rewarded. Quality got lost in this adversarial model. Quality circles, although strong enough to become the hot topic of the early 1980s, did not find as fertile a soil as they had in Japan.

Quality circles at Lockheed begun in 1974 grew to 30 by 1977, and resulted in an estimated savings of $3 million. The number of defects per 1,000 hours caused by the manufacturing process declined by two-thirds. A survey found that employees who were circle members had improved morale and job satisfaction. Some of the cost-cutting suggestions that came from the circles were: a two-step instead of a five-step process for a plastic mold that resulted in a $160,000 saving over the life of the government contract; a better assembly process for circuit boards that resulted in improved quality at $19,000 per missile; development of an ink mixture that would be retained longer on parts, a savings of $120,000.

Upon learning of other successes, other defense contractors adopted quality circles — Sperry, Northrop, Martin-Marietta, Hughes, Rockwell, General Motors, and Westinghouse. Nondefense companies also began quality circle programs. As the movement grew, the International Association of Quality Circles was founded. The American Society for Quality Control, through its Quality Motivation Technical Control Committee, also designed programs to encourage this new employee involvement approach.

How do quality circles work? They usually involve six to 12 first-level employees who meet for about an hour per week to discuss cost reduction and quality improvements for goods or services. Quality circles' focus must be on work related to circle members. A plant level facilitator may first train participants in problem solving, simple statistical monitoring techniques, and group dynamics. Circle leaders may be unit supervisors or one elected by the group.

A plant circle steering committee includes key people from manufacturing, quality control, marketing, finance, accounting, and representatives of supervisors and employees. This steering committee sets policy and procedures for review of and decisions pertaining to quality circle proposals. In this country, participation in quality circles is generally voluntary, and the pressure to participate varies from workplace to workplace.

Quality circle members decide their own agenda. Topics range across a wide spectrum pertaining to the tasks of a particular work group: cutting scrap, order filling, billing errors, inventory, housekeeping, product design, and operations. Studies have found that the chief motivation for management's starting quality circles is economic. Management's goal is to improve quality and lower costs. A secondary motivation in some cases is to improve employee morale so as to make the climate unfavorable to union growth or to minimize union influence.

Quality circles' limited success and frequent failures in the United States can be traced to several overlapping reasons: a tendency for managers (a) to see themselves as the only competent and legitimate decision makers and to devalue contributions of the rank-and-file employees, (b) viewing participation as just extra work that takes time-consuming research, (c) viewing circles as a tool of management used to address peripheral issues, (d) a rejection of democratic leadership, (e) viewing quality circles as dealing with problems that could not be solved for reasons of cost and expediency, (f) viewing meetings as jeopardizing departmental production targets, (g) feelings that QCs add more stresses than benefits.

WE MEAN BUSINESS

What norms do you think would be crucial to have as a part of the culture in order for a quality circle to be successful?

A General Electric plant that one of the authors visited has 13 quality circles. Many of the names of these circles tie into the lamps manufactured there. One group calls its circle "Watt's Up," another the "Arc Angels," and another the "Light Express." The "Trouble Shooters" was a group of ten women who for some two years had met for one hour per week. They had a relaxed friendly atmosphere that day. At one point they chided Neil, their facilitator, for referring to rejected lamps as "junk," a term he said at a previous meeting should not be used.

The Trouble Shooters examined defective bulbs that day. Their plan was to conduct a "show and tell" session to those on the production lines to raise consciousness about different kinds of problems. Their last project had been installing information boards on machines so messages could be readily available at shift changes. The Trouble Shooters also had created manuals of lamp specifications that were placed near each machine. Not everyone in this plant was a quality circle participant. Those who were said they believed their circles were worth the effort. QC project descriptions were prominently displayed on the bulletin board near the shop entrance.

A group approach toward improving quality and creating a commitment to excellence involves direct participation of the employees within an organization. Who knows more about a specific job than the people who work with the tasks every day? This is the basic premise behind the quality circle method. The success of the QCs relies on input from the employees to analyze, control, and solve problems that relate to their specific jobs in natural work groups.

Ad Hoc Problem-Solving Teams

Any organization can benefit from a number of ad hoc (temporary) task-solving teams. Cars are designed and produced better and faster when individual designers, engineers, machine operators, salespeople, and customer service mechanics are brought together under the same roof — and assigned to the same project. Special teams with members from different departments have found ways to reduce duplicate forms, to prevent pollution, to recycle, to cut waste, to improve phone service, and to reduce customer complaints.

Cross-department teams are vital tools in today's modern organizations. But their overuse also causes serious logistical and production problems: When to meet, where to meet, and how often to meet are inevitable issues and more difficult to resolve than for the natural workgroup.

Natural Self-Directed Workgroups

Each work unit should function as a team. Coworkers can interact here because they see each other frequently and teamness is most natural. Each work unit is concerned that it has the proper material, information, and well-maintained tools to do the jobs assigned. Each work unit is concerned about the skills of those in it, and therefore probably is the best judge of who can do the job — of who should or should not be hired and who should or should not be fired. And if there is more than one shift, each work unit must deal with turning over its workspace and machines to another shift.

Each work unit is concerned about the quality and quantity of the goods and/or services it can produce. Each work unit wants its producers to be pleased with what they deliver to the next work unit and/or the ultimate users of the goods and/or services produced.

When those in a workgroup are dissatisfied about any of the many variables that affect its productivity, that is the time for individual and collective problem solving. Sometimes that problem solving will involve contacting relevant parties outside the work unit. For example, in one plant that manufactured electric circuit boards in which one of us did a series of team-building seminars, there was a problem with warping. To solve this problem, representatives of this plant met with its several suppliers of fiberglass cloth, resins, and varnishes. Natural work units from each of these several companies were the ones most directly affected with the warp problem and they were the most knowledgeable about it.

Autonomous Work Teams

The San Diego Zoo is considered by many to be the best zoo in the country. It includes a 1600-acre wildlife preserve north of the city. These parks contain well over 5000 animals. More than three million visitors annually pass through its gates. During the peak summer season there are as many as 1800 employees. The Zoological Society Board of Trustees oversees a $50 million budget. The zoo's newest exhibits house the animals in bioclimatic

Box 9-4   **Team Building: Can We Change?**

Peek back into the early 1970s, perhaps before you were born. The setting is the world's fastest, most fully automated car assembly line nestled in the small town of Lordstown in northeast Ohio. Far above the industry average of 55, this assembly line cranked out 104 cars per hour. Regardless of this amazing difference, the Assembly Division at GM concluded that although the assembly lines were fast, they could go faster. That speed-up occurred after GM awarded the Lordstown workers for the outstanding quality of their work.

The Assembly Division was one of the last management systems in the U.S. still to use a strict version of Taylor's scientific management. In order to increase productivity, they increased the assembly line's pace, and doubled the workload for the workers that were lucky enough to have survived the layoffs. As a result, the remaining line workers were tired, bitter, and ready for revenge. They sabotaged the cars through such means as welding hammers into the bumpers or placing loose nuts and bolts in doors. Angry and alienated, the workers struck.

The strike at the General Motors plant in Lordstown, Ohio, has become well-known to many, especially those interested in productivity. It was a classic example of Taylorism gone wrong. It was viewed by many people as the struggle of the "little guy" to stand up to dehumanizing technology. However, some critics say that this idealistic stand was not much more than a group of frustrated workers "tired of running their fannies off." Regardless of the reasons for the strike, the outcome, 20 years later, has been a renewed vision and commitment to quality.

Today one man who knows exactly what it was like speaks of a much different Lordstown than the one most remember from 20 years ago. There's nothing about the face or stature of Charles Gamble that's not average. He's medium build, wears glasses, is gray at the side of his wavy head of hair. But when he talks about his job, he is anything but average. He has an enthusiasm for the union and a passion for the company in which he works. He believes in what he and his coworkers do and the quality of their work.

Charles Gamble has been a line worker at Lordstown for nearly 20 years. He grew

zones. Tiger River Run is one such project that is managed by an autonomous seven-member team. Each department was asked to offer its best people for Tiger River. Team members therefore came from Building and Grounds, Horticulture, Birds, and Mammals divisions. Rich Reese, an outside consultant, helped train and form the team in a series of workshops and planning sessions. A unique aspect of the project was cross-training to do each other's jobs and a management policy of consensus decision making. The building and grounds attendants cut food and the keepers wash windows. There's a sense of mutual responsibility and ownership for Tiger River. Formal meetings are few. Vacations and days off are negotiated.

up there and was a part of those early days. However, now he talks about pride, worker performance, and commitment to quality. Passionate about the changes that have occurred in the Lordstown plant, he tells of his own turbulent history in the plant:

> I was hired in May 1970. I've been thrown out. I've been dismissed. I've been permanently laid off. I've been accused of what used to be termed sabotage in the plant. I took part in all the events back in the early 70s. That GM and that Lordstown is GONE out there; it no longer exists. It's been buried. It's now a cohesive group working together in unity turning out, I think, the best quality product in the world.
>
> We've had problems where our products weren't selling because the quality wasn't good. We all realized that we were ALL at fault. You can't blame the other guy when you know that you're participating in the problem. So management told us about the way other companies were succeeding. But in their wisdom, they also began to accept the idea that we workers had ideas about what could improve productivity and build quality vans. We used to just keep them to ourselves. We had an adversarial relationship. When that relationship was put to bed, we were able to work together to put out a good product.
>
> How am I involved? My suggestions are taken seriously. If it's just an idea, every idea is looked at seriously. They're discussed with the employee that turns them in. If they're rejected, we are told why they're rejected. If they can be improved upon with changes, then we'll find a way to do that. And people are compensated for them.
>
> On every job that comes down the line, there's a piece of cardboard hanging on the front called a *pride ticket*, which means if you can't get something or you see something wrong on it, you write it up. That vehicle can't leave the plant until repaired. Who makes that decision? Me. What if a man putting in a bumper sees a smudge on it and he doesn't like it? Does he need to call a meeting to see if the bumper's thrown out? No. HE throws it out. He doesn't have to put it on because it doesn't fit HIS quality standards. So it's up to us, we all have a part in it.

The Lordstown plant is once again producing successfully. The important point to remember is that organizations CAN change. These changes take time and need cooperating parties in order to become the quality-producing organization they aspire to be.

Source: Lordstown speech by Charles Gamble, presented in a quality team-building seminar, Kent State University, 1991.

On a five-point scale (1 = low, 5 = high) the average *job satisfaction* score for those on the team before participation was 3.8; two years later, it was a solid 5. This high job satisfaction does not mean that team members could find no room for improvement. They wanted more animals in their care and professional exchange with other departments. They wanted to expand their territory by adding another member to their team. They had had some minor personality conflicts. They wanted more money for maintenance.

A before-and-after measure of *employee morale* demonstrates high approval of their autonomous workgroup experiment (10-point scale, 1 = low, 10 = high).

	Before	After
Animal Care/Exhibits	3.8	9.1
Guest Appearance	4.4	8.3
Job Enrichment	3.8	9.6
Quality of Work Life	6.0	9.8

The comments of the Tiger River Run team members support these numbers. They said, "Everyone here is happier and more productive . . . there is better support system here than before the team," and "In the past two years there has been one sick call. That says a lot for people wanting to come to work."

The Sun Bear Forest was managed in a semi-autonomous fashion. There was a team assigned to it but its ten members were assigned by their supervisors. That assignment was perceived by some of the team as just another job and as secondary to their home departments. Training was not as extensive as for Tiger River, and therefore the bird keepers were not well integrated into the Sun Bear project. The before-and-after measure of job satisfaction was not significantly improved, but team perceptions of exhibits, guest experiences, shared responsibilities, and quality of work life were.

These two autonomous teams managed bioclimatic zones. This is the way almost all zoos will be organized in the future. Many corporations are experimenting with self-managing teams, and we predict that companies increasingly will develop autonomous groups.

SUMMARY

Group leaders need a sense of process. Their effectiveness hinges upon advance consideration of who should be involved, and how the deliberations of a work unit or committee might bring together the necessary expertise and political will.

When a group is operating optimally in terms of fulfilling interpersonal and task needs, its success can probably be attributed to a sense of teamness among members of the corporate group. One approach to team building within an organization is through the use of quality circles.

Experience with QCs shows that a high percentage of their recommendations are adopted by management. The QC movement and other widespread use of employee participation programs by other names bear powerful testimony to the theme of this text; that is, those in professional and industrial careers need to develop competent communication skills.

The autonomous work team is the direction being taken by modern organizations. Modern organizations are committed to training employees to function as teams within their natural work units, and to work with other units to attack production problems that are interdependent and system-wide.

SKILL BUILDER: INVENTORY OF GROUP NORMS FOR COMMUNICATION IN MEETINGS AND ORGANIZATIONS

Directions Obtain permission from an organization to study its work setting. After observing a meeting, fill out the following inventory.

Time

1. Frequency — Number of meetings per week _____ per month _____
   Too few   About right   Too many
2. Length — Minutes per meeting _____
   Too short   About right   Too long
3. Promptness — Everyone on time   Some usually late

Who

1. Number of persons included _____
2. Are there more included than necessary?   Yes   No
3. Are there persons not included who should be?   Yes   No

Type

1. Staff — Number of meetings per week _____
2. Ad Hoc Committee — Number of meetings per week _____
3. Standing Committees and Task Forces — Number of meetings per week _____

Procedures

1. Agenda prepared — Rarely   Often   Always
2. Opportunity to add to the agenda — None   Ample opportunity
3. Adherence to agenda — Ignore   Flexible   Rigid
4. Completion — Usually complete   Rarely complete
5. Formality — Motions written   No motions written
6. Decisions — Majority vote   Consensus

Recognition

Must be recognized by chair to speak   No recognition necessary

Participation

Balanced; most speak about an equal amount of time   Some monopolize the time

Influence

Each person's ideas are equally valued   Opinions of persons in higher-status positions receive greater attention

Esprit de Corps

The staff or group enthusiastically exhibits a sense of unity/direction	The group is fragmented, with low morale and little sense of direction

Emotionality

Everyone must speak rationally	Feelings are not expressed
Feelings are expressed explosively toward others and/or the organization by some members	Members are encouraged to express their feelings

Workload

Excessive	Shared	Unevenly distributed

Conflict

There is no expression of difference	Conflict is used to improve quality of solutions	Conflict centers on personalities

Departments

Are aware of what other departments are doing	Are indifferent to other departments
Are unaware of other departments	Complete for funds with other departments
Are antagonistic toward other departments	Tolerate other departments
Make jokes about other departments	Cooperate with other departments

SKILL BUILDER: TEAM EFFECTIVENESS

Directions   Take copies of this questionnaire with you to a group meeting. Have each member answer the questions in order to assess to what degree each believes the group is a team. Discuss the results.

	Low						High
Contributions within the group are positive and constructive	1	2	3	4	5	6	7
Unified group, sense of team spirit, high involvement	1	2	3	4	5	6	7
Decisions made by letting everyone have his or her say	1	2	3	4	5	6	7
Commitment to decisions is strong	1	2	3	4	5	6	7
The group continually evaluates itself	1	2	3	4	5	6	7

	Low						High
The group is clear about its goals	1	2	3	4	5	6	7
Conflict is brought out into the open and dealt with	1	2	3	4	5	6	7
Alternative ways of solving problems are sought	1	2	3	4	5	6	7
Leadership tends to go to the individual best qualified	1	2	3	4	5	6	7
Feelings are dealt with openly	1	2	3	4	5	6	7

Trust
High suspicion -3 -2 -1 0 $+1$ $+2$ $+3$ High trust

Support
Every person for -3 -2 -1 0 $+1$ $+2$ $+3$ Genuine concern
him/herself   for others

Communications
Guarded caution -3 -2 -1 0 $+1$ $+2$ $+3$ Open, authentic

We don't listen -3 -2 -1 0 $+1$ $+2$ $+3$ We listen, under-
to others   stand, and are
                                                        understood

Objectives
Not understood -3 -2 -1 0 $+1$ $+2$ $+3$ Clearly under-
by team   stood by team
Team negative -3 -2 -1 0 $+1$ $+2$ $+3$ Team committed
toward   to

Conflicts
Deny, avoid, and -3 -2 -1 0 $+1$ $+2$ $+3$ Accept and work
suppress   through conflict

Utilization of Member Resources
Abilities, knowledge, -3 -2 -1 0 $+1$ $+2$ $+3$ Abilities, know-
and experience are   ledge, and
not utilized   resources are
                                                             fully utilized

Control
Imposed on us -3 -2 -1 0 $+1$ $+2$ $+3$ We control
                                                        ourselves

Environment
Pressure toward -3 -2 -1 0 $+1$ $+2$ $+3$ Free, supportive;
conformity   respect for
                                                         individual
                                                         differences

RESOURCES

Argyris, Chris. (1965). *Organization and innovation.* Homewood, IL: Richard D. Irwin, Inc., and The Dorsey Press.

Clark, Charles. (1958/1988). *Brainstorming: How to create successful ideas.* North Hollywood, CA: Wilshire Book Co.

Cole, Robert. (1980, September). "Learning from the Japanese: Prospects and pitfalls." *Management Review,* 22–42.

Dillon, Linda S. (1990). "Can Japanese methods be applied in the Western workplace?" *Quality Progress,* 27–30.

Ellenberger, J. N. (1982, April–June). "Japanese management: Myth or reality?" *AFL-CIO American Federationist,* 3–12.

Glines, Davis. (1989). *Semi-autonomous teams in the San Diego Zoo.* Unpublished report.

Gorden, William I., and Roger J. Howe. (1977). *Team dynamics in developing organizations.* Dubuque, IA: Kendall/Hunt.

Gorden, William I., and John R. Miller. (1983). *Managing your communication: In and for the organization.* Prospect Heights, IL: Waveland Press.

Labovitz, George H., and Yu Sang Chang. (1990, May). "Learn from the best." *Quality Progress,* 81–85.

Osborn, Alex. (1953). *Applied imagination, principles and procedures of creative thinking.* New York: Charles Scribner's Sons.

O'Toole, James. (1975, Spring). "Lordstown: Three years later," *Business and Society Review,* 64–71

Sturgis, Alice F. (1950). *Sturgis standard code of parliamentary procedure.* New York: McGraw-Hill.

Whitsett, David A., and Lyle Yorks. (1983). *From management theory to business sense: The myths and realities of people at work.* New York: American Management Association.

Chapter 10

Making Effective Use of Audiovisuals in the Workplace

Concepts for Discussion

- Preparing visual aids
- Types of visual aids
- New technology in the office
- Telephone communication techniques

All media work us over completely. They are so pervasive in their personal, political, economic, aesthetic, psychological, moral, ethical, and social consequences that they leave no part of us untouched, unaffected, unaltered. The medium is the message.

Marshall McLuhan and Quentin Fiore
The Medium is the Message

The old cliche is true: a picture is worth a thousand words. Therefore, it is a good idea to use well-designed visual aids in your presentations. These aids allow you to best show your organizational skills and knowledge. Susan Dellinger and Barbara Deane, in their book *Communicating Effectively*, say visual support should be used "because sight is the most powerful sense— almost six times as powerful as the other four: sight, 75 percent; hearing, 13 percent; touch, 6 percent; smell, 3 percent; and taste, 3 percent." This helps explain why charts, diagrams, and other graphic aids are an indispensable part of most business presentations. The theoretical principle is that two or more channels of communication can be more effective than a single channel.

Visual aids are used to clarify and present complex information. We need words first to explain the concepts, and then we use visual aids or pictures to assist our words. Words are the primary means of presentation; visual aids are secondary supports. So visual aids are just that—aids and supplements, not substitutes. In other words, we first describe or explain, and then we present the material graphically.

Visual aids are used only when they are needed to clarify a discussion, and not just for adornment. When the information is clear and the reader will not have difficulty interpreting it, visual aids could be superfluous.

The primary purpose of using visual aids is to present a picture of what the prose says. The "picture" can take many forms, depending on the message you want to convey to the audience. Visual aids convert and condense complex information into a pictorial form, helping the reader "see" relationships. Visual aids also emphasize points that deserve special attention or coverage. Because they can present a vivid image, visual aids are easy to understand, read, remember, and interpret.

Within this chapter, we will introduce you to the most popular types of visual aids and their specific advantages. We will explore some new innovations in electronic technology for the information age. Finally, we will discuss telephone techniques.

Here are the most common types of visual aids used in business presentations. Remember to consider your audience, their goals and interests, their current knowledge of the topic, and their previous experiences when choosing your visuals. Also, consider the purpose of your presentation, the room size, the setting, and your knowledge of the topic. We also preface this chapter with a bit of sage advice: Don't be overly dependent upon audio or visual aids. Equipment can fail. Electricity can go off. The technology you want may not be available or suitable for the place of your presentation. Prepare to speak well without use of aids should something go wrong! Also remember, aids must be prepared well in advance of a presentation. After you have considered these areas, you will be ready to choose the type of visual aid that best suits your purpose.

VISUAL AIDS

Flipcharts

A **flipchart** is a large pad of paper that is attached to an easel. It is most successful for small groups that are solving problems and interact frequently. Flipcharts are the most widely used medium in business presentations. They have several advantages that make them so popular. First, they can be prepared ahead of time or developed during your presentation. Also they are readily available, portable, and require no additional equipment. Finally, they can be left in place for further viewing if the need arises. Here are some tips to help you when using flipcharts.

If you prepare flipcharts ahead of time, make sure you are aware of the audience and room size to determine the size of print you should use. Printing should be neat, large, uncrowded, and colorful. Check before your presentation to make sure that your pages are readable. Remember to leave a blank sheet between each page that you write on to make sure that the marker does not soak through. You may want to write small notes to yourself in pencil next to your diagrams to serve as a memory device during your presentation. Large newsprint pads are good for listing ideas in small group meetings. And sheets filled with on-the-spot generated ideas can then be pasted with masking tape on the walls. This is a much-used visual tool for problem-solving work teams.

Chalkboards/Erasable Markerboards

A chalkboard is the most familiar audiovisual, since you probably began using one in elementary school. It is easy to use and can be prepared ahead of time or during your presentation. There are, however, several disadvantages to this medium. First, chalkboards are messy, so you have a tendency to be covered with chalk dust by the end of your presentation. Another problem is that you have to turn your back to the audience when writing on the board. Sometimes chalk and erasers are missing. Since you need chalk, make sure that you always carry it and an eraser with you if you are planning to use this medium. Try to avoid using the chalkboard unless absolutely necessary, as this is a dull medium. Not only are you most familiar with the chalkboard, but so is the rest of the audience. Most modern organizations provide erasable markerboards for training purposes. Nonpermanent felt-tip ink markers must be used on these surfaces. The effect can be colorfully attractive and professional.

Overhead Projectors

An **overhead projector** projects on a screen an image of words or pictures that are printed on transparent plastic sheets. This device is usually used when a good deal of information is presented to a small or medium-sized audience.

The transparencies can be easily and inexpensively made manually, by office copiers, or by thermal copy machines. Therefore, original data or reprints of material and illustrations can be used. The transparencies are portable and easy to change at a moment's notice. Be sure equipment is available and that there is backup equipment. Projectors are usually available in business settings; however, you should ensure before your presentation that there are large white walls or screens available situated so your audience can see well. This medium allows the presenter to interact with the audience, since s/he does not have to turn his/her back.

You may have a problem with legibility since the lettering is sometimes very small. Our advice is to avoid many statistics and words, and rather to represent data in graphic form. Do not use standard or even capital letters produced on typewriters or word processors. Graphic centers can help your aids to be colorful and more easily read. This medium is not recommended for large audiences unless you use a powerful projector and a very large screen.

A final benefit of transparencies is that overlays can be nonprofessionally created with magic marker and can be made in advance or on the spot. This means that material can be highlighted or emphasized by using different colors on different transparencies that are placed on top of each other. If you plan to use overlays, it is a good idea to tape each to a cardboard frame before your presentation, so they do not slide around and prevent light-slippage around borderless materials. Warning: Do not use too many or hastily put on one transparency after another. Overdependence upon them detracts rather than enhances a presentation. We have seen effective presentations that use no more than one transparency.

Films

People misuse films when they are unwisely substituted for live communication. Films are appropriate when you want to show objects, people, or events in motion. If you use films, make sure they are short, interesting, and current. One of the problems with the use of training films is that so often someone in the audience has seen them before. Always preview a film to make sure it fits into the purpose of your presentation. Prepare questions and points you want the audience to consider about the film, such as: Was the material realistic? With whom in the film did you identify? What are the most valuable points in the film? What would you do differently if you were a character in the plot, or if you were the writer or director? Also, make sure the room will be equipped with a screen and that you will be able to obtain a projector and backup equipment.

Films are beneficial because they promote audience interaction; however, they are very expensive to produce. Therefore, you should consider your budget if you are planning on making your own film. A good rule to keep in mind is that over half of your presentation should be spoken, so do not let a film take your place!

Filmstrips

Although filmstrips are rarely used these days, some years ago they were a good visual aid for instructional purposes. This device allows the viewer to move at his own pace and self-instruction is usually sufficient. Our advice is to avoid them because they are so far from the state of the art in visual aids.

WE MEAN BUSINESS

Look in magazines, periodicals, and newspapers and note how visual aids are used. Do they present the data effectively? Why or why not?

Videotape

Videotapes are gaining popularity in the business world. They are easy to make or rent, and the cassettes can be changed and reused frequently. Material can be recorded and then played back exactly as it occurred; it can be edited, added to, or changed at the last minute. Other advantages include: tapes are portable, easy to copy, and can be distributed widely.

Videotapes are frequently used for recruitment purposes to attract potential employees and as training devices for new employees. They are used when employees need to learn through role-playing how to sell or demonstrate new products. A disadvantage of videotapes is they generally can only be used for small audiences, since they are played back on a TV screen (unless the business has larger screens that can be used).

35mm Slides

A slide is an image of a picture taken by a camera that is projected on a screen. Slides can be color or black-and-white, depending on the film that you use. Since they can be projected on large screens they can be used with an audience of any size. Most corporations have their own media department, so slides can be inexpensively made by professionals. If you plan to use slides, make sure their quality is good or DO NOT use them at all.

When using slides, try to plan what you are going to say before your presentation. This will prevent you from groping for words on the spot. Make sure that all of your needed equipment is available and is preprogrammed before you begin your presentation. Be sure to run your slides before your presentation to ensure they are in the correct sequence. Again, we advise backup equipment. Too often we have seen projectors jam, bulbs blow, and speakers fumble with apologies because they cannot find an extension cord or something else goes wrong.

Handouts

Handouts, or hard copies of data on paper, are beneficial when you are presenting a lot of statistics or complex information to your audience. This medium relieves the audience from taking extensive notes and allows them to carry material with them for future reference. Since the data is in front of them, it is easier to follow than by ear alone. An audience can then pay closer attention to what you are saying. You also can include illustrations, graphs, and tables so the material is concise and easy to read. Let the handout serve as your guideline; refer to it but do not read the information. Leave detailed examination of the handouts up to the audience. Be sure that your handout does not contain too much information. Overload can distract your audience and turn them off from reading it. A tip: Try cartoons and colored paper.

Bar and Line Graphs

Graphs are special kinds of charts that show quantitative relationships. They are ideally suited to show trends, such as growth or decline in sales over time. They are useful because they can represent a large amount of data without becoming cluttered. The two most common types are bar graphs and line graphs. The simple bar graph is perhaps the most effective graphic device for comparing quantities. The length of the bars, whether vertical or horizontal, indicate quantity.

The quantitative axis should always begin at zero. The gradation spaces and the width of the bars should be equal. If you want to show how different factors contribute to a total figure, subdivided bar charts are desirable. Bilateral bar charts can be used to show positive or negative differences. The bars of these graphs begin at a central point of reference and may go either up or down. Bilateral bar charts are especially good for showing percentage change, but you may use them for any series in which positive or negative quantities are present.

Here are some guidelines to use that will help you prepare effective bar charts. Always represent time on the horizontal axis of your graph, running from left to right. Arrange the bars in a sequence that best suits your purpose. You might choose the order from high to low, low to high, in alphabetical order, or in order of importance. Make sure that the numerical values you are representing are clear. Sometimes this means putting the numbers adjacent to the bars. In some cases the figures will fit inside the bars themselves.

A simple line graph illustrates the movement of one variable, or more specifically how a relationship changes in a given period of time. A multiple-line graph shows changes in more than one variable.

In constructing line graphs, keep the following points in mind. As with bar graphs, always indicate time on the horizontal axis. Clearly label each line on a multiple-line graph. For maximum interest and clarity, use different colors or designs for each line. Whenever possible, limit the number of lines to a maximum of three. Use a scale that makes the desired point without distorting your data. Keep the scales on the graph uniform. If you use abbreviations or symbols within the graph, make sure they are labeled and easily deciphered.

Pictograms

A pictogram is a variation of a bar graph. It uses pictures or symbols rather than lines or bars to represent data. Although pictographs attract attention because of their novelty and eye appeal, they can easily mislead readers and distort data if they are not planned properly.

Present simple information when constructing a pictogram. Use representative symbols and pictures that are easily recognized by the reader. Show quantities by number of units rather than by differences in sizes. Present units that are identical and of equal size.

Pie Charts

Pie charts are used to show how the parts of a whole are distributed. As the name implies, the whole is represented as a *pie*, with the parts becoming slices or wedges of the pie. The slices may be distinguished by color, crosshatching, and/or labeling. Careless use of pie charts can distort your data.

Observe these guidelines as you construct pie charts: Place the segment you most want to emphasize at the top of the pie or begin at the "twelve o'clock" position. Viewers tend to read a pie chart in a clockwise direction; hence they will begin reading at this wedge of the pie. Arrange subsequent items clockwise in the desired order of emphasis. Identify each segment and the percentage it represents. You should not use more than eight slices in your pie graph. Finally, be sure that all of the wedges total 100 percent.

Maps

When you wish to show a representation that is dependent on geographic relationships, **maps** are your best choice. Maps are useful for comparing quantitative data such as sales in different geographical locations. Companies frequently use maps in annual reports to show distribution of dealers, stockholders, products, resources, and sales.

Tips

Now that you are aware of the reasons that visual aids are effective, let's discuss some helpful hints that you should remember when you use visual aids in your presentations.

- Be sure that you have used the right type of visual aids. Since there are a wide variety of forms available, you must consider the purpose and content of your speech and the characteristics of your audience before you choose a form to use.
- Be sure that you talk to the audience, not to the visual aid. Also, you should display the visual aid only when you are discussing it. After

you are finished with the visual aid, set it aside to prevent audience distraction.

- Make sure that everyone can see your visual aid and the print can be read easily. Consider the audience and room size when you are choosing the type of visual aid that you will be using. Be sure you give the audience adequate time to read and comprehend the information.
- Keep the visual aid simple by portraying only one main idea in each form that you use. If the message is too complex, the audience will lose interest in your presentation. A cluttered visual sends messages of unprofessionalism and lack of preparation.
- Label all of your variables and use concise headings to explain the material. Titles are also beneficial because they can summarize your purpose.
- Print your visuals neatly. Use a ruler and pencil first. Use colors that are attention-getting but not distracting.

INVOLVING PARTICIPANTS IN ON-THE-SPOT-GRAPHICS

Graphics should not be limited to the art department, nor should they be restricted to advance preparation. The process of group communication can be enhanced by on-the-spot graphics.

Equipment

The equipment needed is simple:

- walls on which newsprint pads or wrapping paper may be taped.
- it is best to use large sheets 28 inches wide.
- masking tape is ideal because it is easily removed. Be sure to test the surface with the tape to make sure no damage will be done.
- several colored, wide-tipped nonpermanent markers (El Marko, Papermate, etc.).

Techniques

The techniques also are simple. Variations in form, color, lettering, and recording of group ideas and decisions lend insight to the process. Several variations should be in a leader's repertoire, such as:

- Use of diagrams to illustrate roles of participants. Circles, squares, triangles, rectangles.
- Use of lists. When recording ideas, one should be faithful to what is said and urge the contributor to shorten his/her remarks rather than changing it for him/her.
- Use emphasis by printing in large block letters, shading in or outlining with color, indentation, underlining, arrows, stick figures, mini-pictures for cues, etc. Your imagination is the only limit.

Hints

Write, or better still, print distinctly and large. Write in a straight line; leave plenty of space. Margins may be used to add notes. Don't overemphasize techniques. Don't worry about your artistic ability. You already know enough to do group graphics.

Benefits

On-the-spot graphics offer special benefits to group processes. They help focus attention and prevent memory lapses. They involve participants. They center the problem-solving process on the problem and away from people. Joint ownership thus is encouraged and cooperation is displayed graphically.

Possibilities for Graphing

The equipment, techniques, and hints for on-the-spot graphics, to be sure, must fit the momentary needs of the situation. Likely a leader will be offended if another in the group always insists on grabbing the magic marker and takes over the graphing job. But groups can be introduced to on-the-spot graphics by volunteering for the task in advance when special problems arise.

A leader, because of his/her role as initiator and structurer of ideas, is in the best position to acquaint a group to on-the-spot graphics. Others may then take turns assisting in this role.

What lends itself to group graphics? The most natural first suggestion is Agenda Posting. An agenda may be posted in advance and submitted for prioritizing or modification, or it may be built from items contributed on the spot by the group.

- Listing is a second natural for group processes: brainstorming, "to do" lists, criteria, parties who should be contacted. The possibilities are many.
- Memory Notes serve a valuable function for a group. Seeing the ebb and flow of group topics, like a flowchart a debater or lawyer might keep, enables a group to monitor its progress.
- Diagramming of a situation—a system's input, throughput, and output—facilitates a group's perspective. Sometimes an actual map or a calendar may enable a group to visualize who is responsible and the time frames that are set. Colored markers may be used to make notations on the map or calendar.
- A matrix or grid may be used in a number of ways to indicate relationships or responsibilities, such as which employees are assigned certain functions and who should be consulted before acting, etc. A matrix also might be used to compare options A, B, C with respect to manpower, cost, time, and work.
- Sometimes symbols or figures may be used, such as a thermometer, building, or the human body. Most importantly, on-the-spot graphing should be flexible and fun.

NEW TECHNOLOGY IN THE OFFICE

New technology is constantly being introduced in the business environment and the end of this Information Age will probably never be in sight. These changes have created challenges for the employees of companies as they constantly have to keep in touch with new developments in the field. As research is conducted and new products are created, the office environment becomes more automated.

The result of these innovations is that better information will be available to employees. Ultimately, improved decisions will be made and the company will be more efficient and effective in producing products and services.

The more you, as future professionals, can learn about this terminology, the more marketable you will be. Systems are being designed with you the user in mind. Therefore they are increasingly user-friendly. Office functions are performed in each individual's work station, and often they are linked together to make the organization a single operating unit. With all the new equipment that is available now and currently under development, the work stations of tomorrow will be much different than they are today.

Let's look at some of the technology that is creating new trends in the business world.

Teleconferencing

Teleconferencing is the interaction of two or more groups of people in different locations who communicate via one of several forms of electronic transmissions. There are three main forms of teleconferencing: audio, written, and video. This process began in the 1970s, but is gaining popularity as travel and accommodation expenses increase. In addition to the amount of expenses, businesses lose time and productivity when employees are out of the office.

Companies use teleconferencing in order to have shorter, better organized meetings and increased participation of members, since time is money. Teleconferencing makes decentralization of large companies easier, and it allows other resource people to get involved.

According to Robert Johansen in his book *Teleconferencing and Beyond*, the following prerequisites are needed for successful implementation of a teleconferencing system:

- top management support.
- openness to innovation on an individual and organizational level.
- commitment of an effective advocate.
- identification of needs that can be met through teleconferencing.
- a sound training program.
- adequate start-up and continuing funding sources.
- availability of information about suppliers and equipment.

Now that you have the guidelines for the implementation of a teleconferencing system, let's discuss the three types of teleconferencing that exist. The simplest form is audio teleconferencing, which is the interaction of three or more individuals or groups who use voice communication over telephone lines. This process is aided greatly by the use of speakerphones, which allow a roomful of people to hear the communication. Audio teleconferencing is used for training sessions, business conferences, and instructional programs.

The second form is written teleconferencing, which is the interaction of many people using computer terminals. This process is beneficial because messages are transmitted instantaneously and they can be stored for later use. Computers allow the users to have a written agenda of the meeting; they can send figures as well as illustrations using computer graphics; and they can connect to an electronic blackboard or video screen. This way the messages can be viewed by several people in the same room.

The final form of teleconferencing, video, is the most sophisticated and most expensive type. Video teleconferencing allows audio interaction of individuals and groups, as well as full visual capacities over closed-circuit television. The signals are transmitted by cable, microwave, or satellite. This form is generally needed by specialized users for interviewing, recruiting, personnel purposes, and performance reviews. Some large companies have teleconference rooms available in their headquarters and large branch offices. Many of them rent out their facilities to smaller organizations that cannot afford to have their own teleconference rooms. A few motel chains have even installed these facilities in their motels so companies can rent them out and hold their meetings there.

There are currently several drawbacks of video teleconferencing, so research specialists are working hard to create new advances. The current disadvantages include: high cost, lack of equipment compatibility within the facilities, lack of enthusiasm of participants, and the complexity of the technology that is used.

Electronic Mail

Electronic mail involves the interconnection of computer terminals to which many people have access. Each participant has an electronic mailbox where messages can be sent. The messages are left in storage until an inquiry is made. The receiver can respond, store the message in a file, or destroy the document. The primary advantage of this process is that critical communications can be sent within seconds, instead of waiting several days for the postal service. Senders save on paper and mailing costs.

A personalness in electronic mail is a surprising development. Co-workers separated by great distances can contact each other. They can ask the unseen network for help, send notices, even convey heartfelt sympathy upon learning of a death. Sometimes those who monitor the personal functions become aware that interpersonal messages are usurping so much time that the business purpose of the technology must be reasserted.

Another new form of electronic mail is **voice mail**, which allows an ordinary telephone to become a small communication center. Messages can be sent across telephone lines anywhere in the world. Voice mail also uses the mailbox storage system. Receivers enter their optional, personal password in order to hear their messages. This system can also be computer-based, if messages need to be stored.

Voice mail has several advantages over regular telephone conversations. First, it prevents "telephone tag," where senders keep missing each other's calls and have to leave messages. Another advantage is that voice mail increases a worker's productivity. A worker does not have to wait in an office for an important phone message he/she is expecting. Voice mail also is always available, so it offers its users continuous accessibility. Finally, it eliminates message typing or dictation, since it is spoken by the sender into the mailbox.

As with any new technology, the results are not yet perfect. Neither voice nor electronic mail is completely private, unless you use a personal password. If you do not, anyone can press a few buttons and have access to your mail. Another problem is that these forms of communication are often too convenient. For instance, if you become very upset with someone you may send them a message that you will later regret. Therefore, always think before you speak or write when using voice or electronic mail.

Facsimile Machines

Facsimile machines, or **fax machines**, allow users to send exact images of printed documents over telephone lines, by satellite, or by microwave signals. Previously, fax machines cost a good deal of money, but new developments have made them easy to purchase even for small businesses. New innovations have occurred that now allow regular paper to be used.

Fax machines are very easy to operate, so they require no special user training. The user simply turns on the machine, dials a telephone number, presses a button, and then sends the desired documents through the machine. Automatic transmission fax machines are now available, so that users do not have to feed in the documents. Some new machines also have automatic phone-answering capabilities and portable transceivers attached to them, so that they can be used anywhere outside the office where a telephone is available.

When using fax machines over telephone lines you should remember that telephone rates are cheaper at night. Therefore, if the document does not have to be sent immediately the user should send it at night and save the company money. The average fax call for a company is 30 seconds (dependent on the number of documents being sent). Contrast this to the average telephone call, which lasts at least five to seven minutes.

WE MEAN BUSINESS

Visit a company that has recently implemented an integrated office automation system. Talk with an information manager who knows the design of the office. Ask questions about what integration problems were encountered, how they were overcome, and what difficulties still remain for the company.

Computer Graphics

New computers, such as Apple's Macintosh, are designed with graphics in mind, because pictures are gaining importance in business. Software programs allow users to create statistical diagrams, tables, charts, graphs, company logos, and other pictures on their own computer terminals. This data can then be stored or printed for further use or reference. Many of these devices can be used in business presentations to allow better audience comprehension of your speech topic.

According to Roger Hart, in his article "Add Impact with Graphics," there are two types of graphics that can be produced on a personal computer —analytical and presentation. Analytical graphics software is not used for creative purposes as much as presentation software is. It is used to create charts and graphs of data that are usually given in rows, such as statistical figures. For instance, spreadsheets can be useful for accountants. They are not useful for presentational purposes, though, because your audience has difficulty seeing small data changes or new trends that may be developing.

Presentation graphics are more complex because they allow the user to create sophisticated pictures. Some programs even translate material from spreadsheets into graphs or charts, and allow the use of animation, or create three-dimensional figures.

In order to create graphics on your personal computer, you need several types of equipment. Input devices include: a mouse, a touch pad, light pens, video cameras, drawing pads, or optical character readers and image scanners.

Graphic information can be stored in a computer that is designed for graphics by two methods. The first method is by mathematical relationships, whereby the user creates relationships using angles, arcs, lines, or points. The second method is bit mapping, which involves translating each dot of an image into a special code that the computer can understand. Professional meteorologists employ such chartmaking in televised weather reports.

Optical Character Readers and Image Scanners

An **optical character reader**, or OCR, scans printed or typed documents and converts them into electrical signals. The typed material is then stored in a computer storage device such as a floppy disk, magnetic tape, or a compact disc. These devices can scan a page in 15 to 25 seconds, instead of the typical hour for a typist. A single typing error does not require that the full page be retyped.

Most OCRs can read any style of typeface, and new machines can even decipher handwritten pages. The problem with these machines is that they require a great deal of storage space, since so much material can be easily saved. Even though you may have never heard of an optical character reader, most of you are familiar with another form of an image scanner that is found in grocery stores. The devices at the checkout counter are image scanners that scan an item's price and update the store's inventory records.

Compact or Optical Discs

Compact discs, or CDs, that have gained popularity in the music industry in recent years are currently being used to store computer software and data. CDs can be attached to personal computers and store vast amounts of information. Therefore, CDs are gaining a great deal of popularity in the business world. Computer CDs are identical to their audio counterparts, so they cannot be erased or updated. Therefore, they are called CD ROMS, which stands for read only memory.

According to Lawrence J. Magid, in his article "Compact Discs Open New Era," the CD's memory is fascinating:

> A single CD can store up to 600 megabytes of information. That's more than 600 million characters, or the equivalent of roughly 400,000 double-spaced typed pages. Once a company has invested about $1,500 to produce a master, it costs as little as $2 a disc to make further copies.

CDs are much less expensive than books and can be easily carried around in a briefcase. A manager could carry a CD-equipped laptop computer with him and have a large collection of visual, audio, and statistical data at his fingertips. A form of a compact disc that is available is called a videodisk, which is used for training and instruction in businesses and schools. This medium is useful for companies that continue to use the same training procedures over time. With these disks, users can interact by simply responding to questions on a keyboard, and the computer will tell the user if his or her response is correct.

Telephone Techniques

The telephone is the most frequently used form of communication in the world, next to face-to-face interactions. Telephones can make communication personal. They are very fast and easy to use. Since we use them every day, we often take for granted the way that we speak to others. Therefore, an important part of building communication competence involves practicing telephone communication skills. The following sections will give you guidelines on how to communicate properly on the telephone.

Office Identification   If your company's switchboard operator identifies the name of the company, be sure that you identify yourself in the form that is specified by your supervisors. Most offices prefer their employees to identify their department and their full name — "Accounting Department, Jason Hackworth speaking."

Speak Clearly   Be aware of your speaking rate and tone of voice. Use words that are easy to comprehend and make sure that complex information is understood by the receiver. The mouthpiece should be held about an inch from your mouth for best results.

Practice Good Listening Skills   Do not interrupt the speaker, but be an active listener. A good listener will summarize the information that he or she has received to make sure both parties understand.

Be Courteous   Use the caller's name whenever you get the opportunity because most people like to hear their own name. Answer calls promptly and be friendly when you speak.

Screening Calls   It takes practice to know which calls you should handle yourself and which you should send through, if you are screening calls for your superior or coworkers. Remain tactful if the superior is unavailable and ask if you can take a message or have the superior return the call.

Taking Messages   Keep a pad of paper close to your phone, so that you can write down a message. Write down the name of the caller, the time of the call, the caller's phone number (including area code), and any other information that the caller wants you to deliver. Initial the information in case your superior or anyone else has further questions about the message. Such information also may be typed into a computer.

Dealing with Problem Calls   If a caller becomes unpleasant when you cannot send his or her call through, you should put the call on hold and ask your superior what he or she would like you to do. Remain tactful and friendly, even if you become upset.

Planning Calls in Advance   Before you make an important call, make an outline of the call on paper. This way you will be less likely to leave out important details. You want to sound articulate and organized because this communication may serve as a first impression.

Check Time Zones   Be aware of the time zone when you are placing a long-distance or overseas call. A map (with area codes and time zones) can be found in most telephone directories.

Box 10-1 **Memo to Workers: Don't Phone Home**

Companies are monitoring phone calls. For 18 months, Citicorp's South Florida subsidiary used a personal computer hooked up to a digital PBX to scan all the telephone calls that were made by employees. The system discovered that one software developer spent approximately half of each day on the telephone.

Because of situations such as the one described above, more companies are purchasing call-accounting systems in order to improve the quality of job performance. American Express has installed a system that reports the length of calls, the frequency of calls, and how rapidly the phones are answered. This system gives the supervisors a good opportunity to trap employees who are abusing their telephone privileges.

According to Jeffrey Rothfeder, "most employees rank improving the quality of job performance as the No. 1 reason for purchasing a call-accounting system." One report indicated that the government spends over $100 million a year on personal calls. Private companies spend about the same amount on employees' personal calls, while a major corporation may spend up to $1 million a year.

To discourage this habit, some companies post lists of the names of the most frequent phone users on bulletin boards for everyone to view. This embarrasses employees and they have a tendency to stop making personal calls because they do not like to see their names in bold print. Action is taken when employees do not respond to the bulletin board approach.

Rothfeder cautions that "there's a downside to this approach . . . Even some employers argue that, when abused, it can lead to employee stress and lower morale."

Source: Adapted from Jeffrey Rothfeder, "Memo to Workers: Don't Phone Home," *Business Week*, January 25, 1988, pp. 88–90.

WE MEAN BUSINESS

Practice using these skills when making or receiving your next business-related telephone call. Make an outline on paper of what you plan to say before you place your call.

Telephone Techniques to Avoid

Improper business telephone communication sends signals of unprofessionalism. In order to not give a negative first impression, avoid the following telephone techniques.

When using the telephone, <u>Do Not:</u>

- Reprimand someone. Use face-to-face communication.
- Talk on the telephone when you have an office visitor. Ask if you can return the call.
- Use the telephone when you have vital information to tell someone. The receiver needs to see your face, so that he can respond to your nonverbal cues.
- Discuss emotional issues.
- Make a long-distance call when you can send a quick letter. Save your company money.
- Talk too loudly or too rapidly.
- Try to change your personality and be someone you really are not.
- Attempt several tasks while you are on the telephone. The listener appreciates your full attention.
- Transfer a call to avoid a person or issue. Make sure that you are friendly and direct the caller to the right department or person.
- Chew gum, play your radio in the background, or make funny noises.
- Tape record the conversation unless you get the caller's permission. Once they agree to be recorded, verify her/his permission on the recording.

SUMMARY

Making effective use of audiovisuals in your presentations can be the difference between turning on or tuning out your audience. Well-designed visuals help demonstrate organizational skills and knowledge. Throughout this chapter we introduced you to the most common types of visuals including flipcharts, chalkboards, overhead projectors, films, videotape, slides, handouts, bar and line graphs, pie charts, pictograms, and maps.

Keep in mind that visual aids are just one means of support. They should always be secondary to the oral message. Speakers who overuse visuals or use them as a crutch are easily singled out. When designing your visuals, make sure that they will be easily visible to all audience members, including those in the back of the room. Refer to each visual and discuss it, but only display the visual during the period when it is directly being used.

The Information Age continues to be exciting as new technology is introduced for the home and workplace. Although you may not come into contact with all of these machines, we wanted you to become familiar with some of the newest innovations in the office. It will be interesting for you to note use of this equipment in offices where you interview. We talked about teleconferencing, electronic mail, facsimile machines, computer graphics, optical character readers, and compact discs. We hope that these time-efficiency machines and equipment will help make your career more challenging.

Finally, telephone communication was discussed. We spend a great deal of time using this piece of technology, yet little literature is devoted to discussion of proper communication on the telephone. Here we have provided tips for proper phone communication. Pay close attention also to the behavior to avoid.

Every day the workplace becomes more complicated as new technology and visual aids are introduced. Increased knowledge of the equipment available can give you the edge in job productivity and creativity.

SKILL BUILDER: ON-SITE EXPERIENCE

Visit a company that employs the innovations we have discussed in this chapter. Practice using these machines, so that you are aware of the capabilities.

SKILL BUILDER: MEDIA MIX

State the desired audiovisual mix for the following types of organizational presentations.

1. The introduction of a new product at a trade show.
2. A speech to upper-level management on the progress of an important project.
3. A speech to new employees on company policies and benefits.

Consider the production time required, the type of medium you would use, the audience characteristics, and the approximate costs of your presentations.

RESOURCES

Aronoff, Craig E., Otis W. Baskin, Robert W. Hays, and Harold E. Davis. (1981). *Getting your message across.* St. Paul, MN: West.

Dellinger, Susan, and Barbara Deane. (1980). *Communicating effectively: A complete guide for better managing.* Radnor, PA: Chilton.

Fruehling, Rosemary T., and Constance K. Weaver. (1987). *Electronic office procedures.* New York: McGraw-Hill.

Hart, Roger. (1986, July). "Add impact with graphics." *Administrative Management,* 38–43.

Johansen, Robert. (1984). *Teleconferencing and beyond.* New York: McGraw-Hill.

Koehler, Jerry W., and John I. Sisco. (1981). *Public communication in business and the professions.* St. Paul, MN: West.

Krevolin, Nathan. (1983). *Communication systems and procedures for the modern office.* Englewood Cliffs, NJ: Prentice-Hall.

Kupsch, Joyce, and Sandra Whitcomb. (1987). *The electronic office.* Mission Hills, CA: Glencoe.

Leech, Thomas. (1982). *How to prepare, stage, and deliver winning presentations.* New York: Amacom.

Long, Richard J. (1987). *New office information technology: Human and managerial implications.* New York: Croom Helm.

Magid, Lawrence J. (1989, April 10). "Compact discs open new era." *St. Louis Post-Dispatch,* 5BP.

Paznik, Jill M. (1986, July). "Optical character readers and image scanners can reduce workload." *Administrative Management,* 23–28.

Rosenblatt, Bernard S., Richard T. Cheatham, and James T. Watt. (1982). *Communication in business* (2nd ed.). Englewood Cliffs, NJ: Prentice-Hall.

Rothfeder, Jeffrey. (1988, January 25). "Memo to workers: Don't phone home." *Business Week,* 88–90.

Smith, Harold T., William H. Baker, Mary Sumner, and Almon J. Bate. (1985). *Automated office systems management.* New York: Wiley.

Chapter 11

Organizing Presentational Speaking in the Workplace

Concepts for Discussion

- Choosing a topic
- Analyzing your audience
- Establishing the specific purpose
- Writing the thesis statement

- Organization
- Introduction
- Conclusion
- The forms of proof

Title: "Here Comes the King!"

Purpose: To convince the audience that Anheuser-Busch is indeed a company that deserves tribute.

Thesis: Anheuser-Busch deserves tribute for its constant dedication and attentiveness to its employees, product quality, and social responsibility.

Why Me? I have had the opportunity to witness Anheuser-Busch's dedication to their employees, products, and community firsthand while working for the past two summers in the Corporate Quality Assurance Department.

Why You? Anheuser-Busch is a large company whose diversification in a wide variety of subsidiaries provides employment opportunities that are very real to graduates like us every day.

The excerpt above illustrates the planning stages necessary to make a presentation most effective. Indeed, a lot of work is involved before you even write a word of your speech. This is what we are going to discuss in this chapter. We are going to guide you step by step in what we have found to be the most successful at building a good talk. Often the biggest stumbling block is the issue of CHOOSING A TOPIC. Once your topic has been chosen, it is essential to ANALYZE and ADAPT TO YOUR AUDIENCE. Once this is accomplished, you need to ESTABLISH A SPECIFIC PURPOSE STATEMENT, and WRITE YOUR THESIS STATEMENT. The final stages of analysis include what we call WHY ME? AND WHY YOU? So let's show we mean business, and follow these steps to success.

CHOOSING A TOPIC AND ANALYZING THE AUDIENCE

Often the most troublesome part of a speech assignment is figuring out what you are going to speak about. When choosing a topic, you want to find a subject that will be interesting and appealing to both you and your audience. Here are some suggestions:

Step 1: Talk About Something That Interests You

This may seem rudimentary, but often students overlook this objective in order to just "get the assignment done." We believe that everything you do should be done with purpose. This way you will gain knowledge and confidence that will help you attain your future goal. Try to link the purpose of your presentation (inform, entertain, give tribute, persuade) specifically to your major, extracurricular interests, hobbies, or ambitions. If possible, try to talk about an area in which you have personal experience. When you can add narratives and examples from your personal experience, it enhances your credibility and audience interest. When choosing a topic, ask yourself this question: If I am not interested in this topic, why should my audience be?

Step 2: Analyze Yourself—Methods of Solo Brainstorming

In order to find out what interests us, we must analyze ourselves. Individual brainstorming generates ideas for topic selection. (Brainstorming, as was discussed in Chapter 9, is a method of gathering many ideas without judgment in a short amount of time. You simply write down the first ideas that come to mind.)

Michael and Suzanne Osborn's text *Public Speaking* suggests making columns on a sheet of paper that are relevant to your specific purpose. The columns may have headings such as: Events, Values, Goals, Problems, Activities, Work, and People. Once you have chosen the headings that most apply to you (you may also make up your own), set a timer for three to five minutes. Within this time limit, list at least five items underneath each heading. Study this list. Do any of the items trigger interest? If so, star those items.

WE MEAN BUSINESS

Practice brainstorming for speech topics using the above headings.

If you wish specifically to target activities in which you have taken part, you can make a longer list of just one or two of the columns. For example, if you want to trace back your membership in extracurricular and cocurricular activities during college, you could make a list that included each activity. If you wanted to chart all the companies to which you have thought about applying for employment, or that you had heard good things about, you could use this more concentrated style of brainstorming.

The method of solo brainstorming should be tailored to specifically meet your needs and the speaking occasion. You may learn a lot about yourself from this method of gathering data quickly. Once you have gathered the information, then it is time to go back and select those topics which most apply to the purpose.

Step 3: Analyze Your Audience and Check the Setting

How many of you have ever heard a public presentation? Probably each of us has at one time. Let us ask you another question: How many of you enter that public speaking situation with the attitude, "Make me want to listen. I dare you." We admit that when we are members of an audience, we are occasionally guilty of this attitude, for it is common. As audience members, we expect the speaker to adapt his/her message to us, to meet our needs, and to link to us in some fashion.

Perhaps the wisest lesson we have been taught in terms of adapting to our audience, was provided by Carolyn Dickson, president of Voice-Pro Consulting Agency. Carolyn is a former opera singer who has struck gold with her theories, which integrate techniques of vocal training plus business tactics for effective public speaking. Corporations come to her for her innovative techniques and training. Carolyn's first lesson is a simple one. She calls it the idea of "flip-flop-focus." The premise behind this statement is that speakers typically focus first on themselves, therefore concentrating on feelings of nervousness. "Everyone's looking at me" or "I can't wait until this is over" are common statements internalized by speakers who focus first on themselves. This is when Dickson suggests a speaker should flip the focus because our focus should first be directed to how we can best meet the needs of the audience. If we follow Dickson's philosophy and concentrate on the audience first, we would be concentrating on feelings such as "Does everyone look interested?" and "Am I meeting the needs of the audience?" If speakers focus on audience concerns, nervousness should be reduced. Primary focus should be directed toward the audience, and secondary focus directed toward your self-presentational skills.

When planning a presentation, it is wise to ask yourself the question "Why You?" This question asks why you, the audience members, are assembled for this presentation, what your needs are, and how you can best benefit from hearing this presentation. Our students actually write out their analysis of "Why You" for every presentation (see example at beginning of chapter).

A speaker and her/his audience want something from the other and, hopefully, they can provide something for each other that is mutually gratifying. The executive may want to convince the city fathers to create an industrial park. The city politicians may want greater tax revenues. The central concern we face as speakers is twofold: my interest and their interest. It is important to remember that the underlying intention of a presentation is to make my interest your interest, just as a salesman should remember that the customer's interest must be his/her interest. We believe that this can be accomplished in an honest and ethical manner. We will divide steps for analysis into three general categories: demographics, situational features, and how these, in turn, can be used to adapt to your audience.

Demographics Audit It is important to analyze certain variables of every speaking situation.

- Gender — Is the audience represented equally by both sexes? Is it predominantly male or female?
- Age — Does the audience represent a specific age group (18 – 23, 35 – 50, over 65)? Is the audience a mixture of the above ages? Can I use language that will appeal specifically to this age level (slang, jargon)?
- Education — Does everyone in the audience have a high school diploma, or a college degree? Do some have advanced degrees? How can I appeal by using language or issues relevant to the education level of my audience?
- Ethnic/Religious — Do the audience members represent a variety of ethnic and religious backgrounds? Will this make a difference in my appeals? What if they are all of the same religious/ethnic background? How can I link their treasured traditions to my topic?
- Socioeconomic — Do members of the audience belong to different social classes (lower, middle, higher)? Are there white-collar and blue-collar workers? How can my issue be important to each?
- Shared membership — Does the audience have a shared affiliation; a reason for coming together on this speech occasion? Is this a club or group function?

- Geography/locale—What do you know about the geographic location where the speech is being presented? How can you gain knowledge about this locale to help link to the audience? What sources could help you research information about the area?

Situational Audit   Situational factors are important to analyze as well. Situational features include: time of day, lighting, temperature, weather, size of room, size of audience, sound system, and any other factors that may affect the success of the presentation. Whenever possible, go to the room where you are scheduled to speak and investigate as many of these situational factors as possible. Check ahead of time if sound or audiovisual equipment is necessary, AND that it is functioning properly.

Attitude Audit   Some final suggestions for analysis include:

- Attitude—Try to assess what the overall attitude is toward your topic. Does the audience feel positive, negative, or neutral?
- Information—How much information about this topic does the audience already have? Try to find out ahead of time, so that you can assess whether or not you will have to include definitions of terms, or at what level you can speak.
- Needs—Can you determine any specific needs that the audience may have? What do they want to get or feel from this presentation?

Hostile Audience   It is very important that you assess the attitude of the audience toward you as a speaker (credibility, reputation), toward the situation (are they forced to be here, voluntary) and toward the topic (pro or con). If you face a potentially hostile audience, the most effective tactic is to develop your credibility. Throughout the speech, emphasize your knowledge about the topic, your belief in the purpose of this speech, and passion for the topic, and your morality ("I am a good person"). These messages of credibility, or ethos, should be woven throughout the speech. Careful selection of facts and clear, logical reasoning need to supplement and complement the speech.

In 1990 Barbara Bush teamed with Raisa Gorbachev to give the commencement address at Wellesley College. There had been much controversy about their choice as commencement speakers. In fact, 150 out of the 2200 students at Wellesley signed a petition to keep Bush from speaking. However, with finesse, Bush delivered a speech that was wildly applauded by the students of the elite women's school. Dana Kennedy of the Associated Press said that Bush "received her loudest cheers" as she closed the speech by saying: "Somewhere out in this audience may even be someone who will one day follow in my footsteps and preside over the White House as the president's spouse. I wish HIM well!"

Box 11-1 **Women, Speak Up!**

You were ignored during an important meeting. Again. You were outshouted, interrupted and generally discounted while people who didn't know half as much as you got the boss' full attention.

You're a knowledgeable, assertive woman. You know what you're talking about. So why can't you command other people's attention at work? Perhaps it's because you sound like a wimp, even though you don't feel like one.

Do you smile all the time—even when what you're saying isn't the least bit humorous? People who constantly nod and smile in agreement are quickly dismissed as being too eager to please.

Do you spend most of your time nodding and making encouraging noises while other people talk? This can be a good method for encouraging people to keep speaking, so it's definitely not a good device to use when you want to do the talking.

Do you cover your mouth, play with your hair, glasses, earrings, or nibble your fingernails while you talk? These nervous gestures distract people and give them the impression that you're flighty, scattered, and unsure of yourself.

Now check how you start your sentences. Do you give people good reasons not to listen to what you're about to say? ''I probably don't know what I'm talking about, but. . . .'' ''You probably won't want to hear this, but. . . .'' This may be a dumb idea, but. . . .''

Watch how you end your sentences, too. Do you turn statements into questions by raising your voice? ''We're going to meet after lunch?'' vs. ''We're going to meet after lunch.''

We often end our statements with actual questions that seek approval, as well. ''We're going to meet after lunch, aren't we?'' or ''We're going to meet after lunch. Is that all right?'' or ''We'll meet after lunch, don't you think?''

Are you using subjective, overblown adjectives such as gorgeous, wonderful, great, adorable, terrible, awful? Are you cluttering your speech with fillers such as ''You know,'' and ''Like'' and ''Well''?

Pay attention to the tone of your voice, too. Is it too soft to be heard? Or so shrill that you sound childish? Does it come from your diaphragm or through your nose? Do you sound authoritative or like a small, yapping dog?

If people aren't taking you seriously at work because you've picked up some bad communication habits, the good news is that they aren't hard to break. You've already taken the first step, after all, which is to be aware of the problem. And your next step is to make a firm decision to begin to sound like the knowledgeable, competent, assertive person you are.

Source: From Niki Scott, ''Speech must grab Attention,'' *Lansing State Journal*, November 2, 1989.

> ## WE MEAN BUSINESS
>
> What demographic, situational, and attitude factors are important to your specific presentation?

Adapting to the Audience Now that you have answered the questions above that are relevant to your particular speaking situation, you are ready to adapt your ideas to the audience. Here are four guidelines to establishing common ground:

- Begin with the level of information you think they have.
- Link yourself to them. Find information/demographics/attitudes that you share.
- Make the audience feel important.
- Gain support and familiarity with the audience. We find people credible whom we can relate to.

Step 4: Establishing the Specific Purpose

Once you have selected your topic and analyzed the audience, you are now ready to begin writing your presentation. But don't start writing that introduction yet! Before you begin writing the actual speech, there are a few more items you need to accomplish. The first is writing your specific purpose statement.

Classroom presentation assignments will almost always include a general purpose. Your professor has either asked you to inform the audience, persuade, entertain, sell, give tribute, or give a speech of introduction. So for these assignments, your job is made simpler. But you still have the responsibility to realize what it is you more specifically wish to accomplish during your presentation. This is your SPECIFIC PURPOSE.

Your specific purpose statement is somewhat like a behavioral objective. As the speaker, you must determine WHAT measurable thing you want to happen, WHO you want to perform it, and WHEN. Here are some examples:

- I want my audience to laugh at my stories of how our company came into being, so they will tell their friends these stories. A further outcome from this speech should be a legend that will be passed on by members of the Chamber of Commerce. (The general purpose for such a specific purpose might be to entertain, inform, or inspire.)
- After hearing my presentation, the Research and Development Department will allocate $25,000 toward a more economical and safer process of. . . . (Persuade)
- After my address to the City Club, at least 25 persons will give a pint of blood in this current Red Cross Drive. (Persuade)

- To convince the audience that Anheuser-Busch is a company that deserves tribute. (Tribute)

Keep in mind that your purpose statement must reflect a realistic expectation and a clear focus of your general intent.

WE MEAN BUSINESS

Practice writing purpose statements for a speech about corporate fitness and labor relations.

Step 5: Writing the Thesis Statement

The thesis statement reflects the core idea. That is, it is the one declarative sentence that states the main idea of your presentation. It is essential that your thesis statement be remembered. In order for a message to be remembered, it must be repeated. A statement must be attractive in order to be easily repeatable. Prepare a clearly phrased statement of what you want to accomplish before you try to encapsulate that desired goal into a repeatable thesis sentence. For example, President John Kennedy wanted the nation to be inspired enough about his idea of a Peace Corps that it would urge Congress to support it and individuals would enlist in it for service at home and abroad. Once he had decided this would be a central goal for an address to the country, he and his speech writers put their thinking caps on to encapsulate that idea in an appealing thesis statement. They succeeded. They created a sentence we remember years later: Ask not what your country can do for you, but what you can do for your country.

Your thesis statement can include the main topics of discussion within your presentation. Or it can simply contain a brief sentence, such as in Kennedy's appeal. Here are two examples of thesis statements for speeches of tribute:

- The pride is back at Chrysler because of its quality products, employees, and corporate leaders. (includes preview of main points of discussion)
- Hallmark Cards, Inc., is a company that truly cares enough to send the very best.

WE MEAN BUSINESS

Develop a thesis statement to correspond with the purpose statements written earlier.

Step 6: Organization

The disorganization or organization of a message has both an intellectual and psychological impact upon the audience and the speaker her- or himself. An audience usually can recognize a disorganized presentation, and in doing so, the speaker's credibility is lowered. People desire order. Without structure, relationships are unstable and unsure. Presenters should strive to make their message clear, logical, and attractive.

A message, like a house, may be designed in a number of ways. Most importantly, like a house it should suit, if not express, the personality of the owner and should complement the land and the community. And as with houses, there are a number of stock designs. Their economy enables quicker and often more assuredly tasteful design than do entirely custom-built homes or speeches. And since the stock design for a speech, unlike the prefab home, is only a broad framework, there is ample opportunity, in fact necessity, to tailor each speech to the personality of the presenter and the liking of the community. Therefore, with this preface in mind, let's look at a list of design formats:

1. *Time Sequence* (Past, present, future, or any chronological order);
2. *Space Sequence* (Geographical divisions, such as East, West, South, and North, or regions);
3. *Topical* (Dividing topic into items or categories rather than by points in time. These categories could be persons, places, or processes.)
4. *Causal* (Moving from description and analysis of causes to effects OR from description of current conditions (effects) to a description and analysis of the causes thought to have produced these effects)
5. *Parties Involved* (Proponents, opponents, indifferent, etc.);
6. *Journalistic* (Who, what, when, where, and why);
7. *Reflective Thinking* (Locating a problem, defining, assessing cause, setting up criteria for a solution, considering how well alternative solutions satisfy the criteria);
8. *Medical Diagnostic-Prescriptive* (Ill, blame, cure, and cost);
9. *Military* (Attacking the enemies);
10. *Q-A* (Answering the questions in the mind of the target audience);
11. *Residues* (A process of analysis and elimination of possible solutions until the best one is left);
12. *Motivational* (Attention, need, satisfaction, visualization, action);
13. *Narrative* (The story of how I became interested and involved in this cause, field, etc.);
14. *Negotiation* (What we want, what they want, and what we might trade off);
15. *Justificatory* (Reasons why we had to do it, or how the devil made me do it);
16. *The Journey* (The account of getting around detours and roadblocks, and choices of roads to a destination);
17. *Problem-Solution* (Or a series of parallel problem-solutions);

18. *Extended Analogy* (Comparisons between a known experience and the experience advocated).

These stock designs reveal a lot about the speaker to the audience. For example, a speaker who selects an attack-the-problem design sometimes puts her/himself into a posture of a lone warrior against a giant establishment (reforming the tax structure is such a posture). At other times it positions the speaker on the side of the establishment, waging war upon the foes of that institution (such as the federal government's war on crime). In either case, the audience asks: Who does the speaker think s/he is, what kind of power does s/he have, and how does s/he view us, as friends or foes? The "Attacking Metaphor" implies destruction of the enemy. Therefore, one speaking for business might wisely use the attacking design for a speech against inflation, but not in a speech attacking the Department of Labor, unless one truly desires its destruction.

The medical metaphor, on the other hand, positions the speaker in the role of the wise doctor able both to diagnose the disease and to prescribe the remedy. The target audience is compelled to wonder if the doctor views them as ill, and if so, why the speaker thinks he is so wise as to know their illness and to prescribe their cure. Very few doctors solicit the advice of the patient, and consequently the audience may feel excluded from genuine involvement in working out their own solution.

The medical analogy's strength is its familiarity. All of us can follow such a four-step sequence: (1) seeing the symptoms, (2) naming the illness, (3) analyzing the probable cause, and (4) prescribing a cure. And this is the strength of most stock designs: they readily call a structure to the surface in the mind of the audience. And this structure consequently provides the enabling climate for thought about the message.

Time and/or spatial sequence probably are the most familiar. All of us move from minute to minute, week to week, and year to year. Thus there is order in a presentation that begins with the origins of a problem and traces its growth. Similarly, we live and travel through space. It is natural, then, for us to think in terms of the spatial parts of informational and instructional communication. And it is adventurous, yet easily understandable, to think in terms of reaching a destination across distance.

The "Journey" does not pit the speaker against an establishment, but rather suggests that the speaker and audience can travel together. Together they can find ways around detours and one day come singing down the yellow brick road into a new and better land.

There are many other ways a message may be partitioned. One of the attractive and challenging designs is the scientific. To those living in a scientific age, testing an hypothesis serves as an understandable problem-solving approach. In such a case, the speaker proposes a theoretical postulate and follows this with a plan for testing this theory. The plan may involve a group decision to pilot-test the idea. Such an approach, perhaps, is the most convincing format for business proposals, because this suggests a cautious, conservative, reach-test mentality.

Closing this list of stock designs is the extended analogy. People find analogical thinking both insightful and stimulating. One speech that lingers in the memory of one of the authors after some 20 years compared getting a Ph.D. to courtship and marriage. The speech suggested several phases for comparison, such as the similarity of going steady, to beginning a master's program; proposing, to selecting a chairman for one's thesis committee; engagement, to candidacy for the doctorate; and the wedding to taking comprehensive examinations.

Analogies come in varied species and sizes. We do not believe that the use of metaphor (or analogy) cannot be learned. The ladder of success, for example, has a number of rungs. Any businessman can take this ladder and from his own experience, entitle those rungs, and find vivid illustrations for them.

An analogy simply is giving something a name that belongs to something else, and in so doing often it makes a persuasive comparison or insightful leap. It may stretch the imagination by either making the familiar strange, or the strange familiar. It was Alexander Graham Bell who derived the idea for the telephone from the tiny hammer, stirrup, and anvil bones of the inner ear. An internal communication consultant, for example, might illustrate how a business could improve its communication system by comparing it to a beehive queendom or to a computer. Suffice it to suggest that the extended analogy is yet another framework for the major address.

Step 7: Now You Can Prepare an Introduction

Earlier in the chapter, we introduced the notion that listeners decide very early within a presentation whether or not they care to listen. So, it is the speaker's responsibility to begin with an introduction that will create a desire from within the audience to WANT to listen. How can you accomplish this? There are some very simple guidelines that you can follow to create an effective introduction.

Link to Audience Interest   Remember always to keep in mind the needs of your audience. The Spanish scholar Gracian said that "A speech is like a feast, at which the dishes are made to please the guests and not the cooks." The ancient philosopher Cicero pronounced that those who wish to be persuasive must "shape and adapt themselves completely according to the opinion and approval of the audience." Keeping this in mind, you must find a way to alert and capture the attention of the audience. That is, within the first few moments of your presentation, you must say something that will link to the interests of your audience. Several examples of attention-getter strategies include:

- ask a question
- tell story, example
- refer to historical event
- use a gimmick or slogan
- refer to the occasion
- make a personal reference
- present a startling fact
- present a quotation
- tell an appropriate joke
- point to common beliefs
- issue a challenge
- appeal to self-interest of audience

Announce Your Topic After you have planned an effective attention-getting strategy, the next step involves announcing your topic. The audience needs to know very early in your presentation what your topic and purpose will be. Again, be sure to angle your approach so that it meets the needs of the audience. You should be able to assess these needs by following the suggestions for audience analysis listed earlier in this chapter.

One strategy that helps an audience clearly hear the purpose of the presentation is the use of a preview. While preparing an introduction, ask yourself whether the purpose of your speech is already very clear, or whether including a preview of the main points would help the listeners follow and remember important parts of the message.

Almost every speech should include a preview. Previews help the listeners understand where you are going in your talk, and help them follow along as you move from point to point. The preview most often serves as a transition between the opening section of your speech and the development section.

Often the preview falls after the thesis statement, as in the following example:

> "(**Thesis**) After extensive research, I created a new product called HOAT bran. (**Preview**) In order to see how this healthy alternative treat can provide you with all the health benefits you'll need for a longer, healthier life, let's first examine the problems with existing products on market, and then talk about the many benefits and advantages of eating HOAT bran." (Kim Hutchinson, student)

Establish Credibility A third purpose of a speaker's introduction is to establish credibility. According to James Golden et al., in their text *The Rhetoric of Western Thought*, "It is the source's perceived relationship with the message which seems to be the prime persuasive factor." Source credibility will be discussed in more detail later in the chapter.

A final responsibility of a speaker's opening remarks involves a declaration of the thesis statement. Your thesis statement, which represents the core idea of your presentation, usually should be clearly stated within your introduction. At appropriate junctures in the text, that thesis sentence may be repeated to punctuate your examples and reasoning.

The student speech "Here comes the King," featured at the beginning of the chapter, incorporated many of the elements discussed above. Her introduction reads,

> When we hear the phrase, "Here comes the King," to most of us, images of royalty appear in our minds. But, if you're from St. Louis, your thoughts probably turn to beer. And if you are lucky enough to have been employed by Anheuser-Busch as I have been for the past two summers, then you would also realize that Anheuser-Busch is the King of employment opportunities in the United States. Anheuser-Busch deserves tribute for its constant dedication and attentiveness to their employees, product quality, and social responsibility. Now let's look at some reasons why Anheuser-Busch has gained this royal status.

Box 11-2 **What an Audience Likes**

When speaking before a group, you may have a "captive" audience, but just because you are, by fact, the speaker does not mean that you have automatically "captured" their interest or attention. Like most people, your audience likes to be treated well. In fact, they expect you to respect the honor they have given you by asking you to be their speaker. They are right; and here are some tips to help you achieve this goal.

An Audience Likes

—Simple English. This is a prime essential. Don't use many words that are strange to you or your audience.

—Simple phrases. Short sentence structure. Frequent pauses and rests. The audience likes to absorb one idea at a time. Simplicity is your guide.

—Knowledge of the subject. Don't attempt anything you are unfamiliar with unless you have done some research.

—A speaker who sticks to his time. Complete your talk in the time allowed. Keep faith with your audience and your chairman. Speak to influence and please your audience.

—Sincerity! Don't bluff! The audience will spot a phony a mile away.

—Enthusiasm! Let yourself go! State the facts! No speaker was ever criticized for being enthusiastic.

Source: "Members' guide to speak-up Jaycee," *Lessons in Effective Public Speaking*, revised 1967. The United States Jaycees.

Step 8: Preparing a Conclusion

The conclusion of a presentation in many ways parallels the introduction in reverse order. Within the entire presentation, an effective speaker guides his/her listeners step-by-step, smoothly, with transitional summaries of main points and ideas. Thus it is imperative that the speaker signals the move to the conclusion of the presentation. Assumptive language, such as "As you can see . . .", "Clearly I have shown . . .", "I trust that now we can all agree . . .", works much more effectively than the standard, unmotivating transition, "In conclusion, I'd just like to say that. . . ."

After you have signaled you are moving to the close of your presentation, again remember to restate and reinforce the thesis statement. One key to success in presentational speaking is creative redundancy. Tell those of us in the audience once, then tell us again! When judicious repetition of the thesis statement echoes throughout the speech, the audience will be more likely to remember the statement.

An essential responsibility of the conclusion is to heighten the motivation or desired response you wish to elicit from the audience. Keep in mind your purpose. Do you want us to feel angry, frightened, elated, hopeful, or committed? Heightening this emotion can be achieved with a short, moving story; quotation; and change in rate, volume, or intensity of voice.

A speaker should provide a sense of closure consistent in style with the rest of the presentation. If your presentation is persuasive, be sure to leave us with a clear, desired response. If your purpose is motivational, motivate us to some "feeling" during your close. Please refrain from using "That's about it" to close your presentation.

Step 9: Meeting Audience Expectations

The effectiveness of a speech is best measured by how well a speaker meets audience expectations in each phase of composition and delivery. What those expectations are, of course, will be unique to each occasion, but certain audience expectations are common to most occasions.

Outlining   What should be accomplished in a major speech? The presentation is a means to an end. The process of designing is thus a matter of making an idea attractive enough to get a fair hearing. To achieve this, the speaker searches for ways to establish his/her own credibility and create a listening experience that will cause identification with his/her concern. To achieve this rhetorical experience, the speaker should carefully consider how he or she will meet certain cognitive and psychological expectations of the audience. An outline that is designed to meet the reasonable and emotional expectations of an audience focuses on the receiver rather than the subject alone. With this attitude in mind, let us present a checklist of expectations in an audience-centered outline.

An Outline of Audience Expectations

Opening Phase: We, the audience, expect

- to be recognized in greeting
- some expression of goodwill, friendliness, and concern for common ground
- attention to what interests us
- an announcement of the subject
- sound reasons for its selection
- a modest explanation of why you, the speaker, are competent in this subject area

Box 11-3 **Outline of Tribute Speech**
by Jackie Norfolk

Purpose: To give tribute to Wal-Mart and to show how it is a success for Sam Walton, the associates, and the public.

Thesis: Looking in a three-way mirror, one can see how the views of Sam, the associates, and the outside world intertwine, making Wal-Mart a rapidly growing and energetic company.

Why you/me: I have worked at Wal-Mart for ten years and still enjoy my job. As approaching graduates, we are all interested in success; not only in personal success, but in working for a successful organization.

I. Introduction

We all view success differently. For the past ten years I have worked for Wal-Mart, and even after ten years, I still enjoy my job. As approaching graduates, we are all interested in success; not only in personal success, but in working for a successful organization. Through Wal-Mart, I not only get the chance to work for a successful organization but also feel personal success. I'd like to tell you how Wal-Mart is a success, not only for me and the other associates, but also for Sam Walton, the founder, and for the general public. Looking in a three-way mirror, one can see how the views of Sam, the associates, and the outside world intertwine making Wal-Mart a rapidly growing and energetic company.

II. Body — Main Points
    A. Sam Walton views Wal-Mart as being a way to serve others.
    B. Wal-Mart associates view the company as one large family.
    C. The public views Wal-Mart as a profitable business venture which maintains low prices.

III. Conclusion

Getting back to the three-way mirror, success at Wal-Mart is viewed differently. Sam views it as being able to serve others, the associates view it as being part of a large, growing family, and the public views it as a profitable business venture which maintains its commitment to low prices. All of these views intertwine and focus on one important aspect: making people happy. So let's put our hands together for the people and success at Wal-Mart.

Development Phase: We, the audience expect

- a core idea — a clear, concise statement of your thesis — to put it into a memorable, motivating phrase
- a preview, a partition of the major areas or points you will cover. We expect structure and order
- cues or transitions signaling when you begin a new point
- explanation, illustration, and evidence to support each point
- internal summaries of a point and transitions to the next point
- to be reasoned with
- to be genuinely emotionally moved, but not manipulated
- to be honestly and ethically treated as equal; to get some cues about why we can trust the speaker
- the development phase of the message to have meaning for us

Closure Phase: We, the audience, expect

- to quickly have the highlights of the message recalled
- to hear again a memorable motivating phrase which symbolizes the core thesis
- to hear a clinching argument
- to be invited to talk back, to question, and to test the ideas presented

Transitions   Transitions are words, phrases, or sentences used to guide the audience smoothly from point to point within a speech. Effective transitions bridge between what has previously been said and what is about to come. Transitions should be used between the opening and the development phases of the speech and between the development and the closure phases of the speech. In addition to these places, transitions should be used to signal the audience that you are moving from one main point to the next.

Following is a list of possible transitions to use within presentations:

Building on this point (argument) . . .

Because of the problem outlined above . . .

In a similar vein . . .

In addition to . . .

Therefore . . .

First . . . second . . . third . . .

Since we have seen . . . it is necessary next to consider . . .

As we will see . . .

It follows that, then . . .

If . . . then . . .

Not only . . . but also

In contrast . . .

THE FORMS OF PROOF

Aristotle, an ancient Greek philosopher, was a product of Plato's academy. Aristotle's views on rhetoric are considered by some scholars to be the most important work on persuasion ever written. With this in mind, we would like to introduce you to one of Aristotle's fundamental ideas, namely his notion of the forms of proof in public speaking.

> Ethos — proof that depends on the believability of the speaker.
> Pathos — proof that is designed to appeal to emotions and sway a listener's feelings.
> Logos — proof or reasoning used to demonstrate that a thing is so.

Ethos

In more recent times communication scholars have discovered that ethos, or source credibility, is comprised of five components. The three major factors that influence ethos are audience perception of competence (knowledge about topic in the field of study), trustworthiness (honesty and ethics), and dynamism (nonverbal and verbal expressiveness in delivery). Additional factors that influence initial credibility are attractiveness and coorientation. Perceived physical attractiveness includes the ideas that the listeners: (1) like the speaker, (2) find the speaker warm and friendly, (3) enjoy the smile and direct eye contact of the speaker, and/or (4) find the speaker in some way physically attractive. Coorientation includes a feeling of identification with or closeness to the speaker, or a feeling of having something in common with the speaker.

An audience may perceive someone as credible because it likes the way a speaker talks or dresses. The factors of attractiveness and coorientation are considered only minor factors because they only affect credibility initially. Hopefully, if the speaker is not competent or trustworthy, we will dismiss our earlier opinion that this speaker is credible because he/she is from our hometown and wearing a sharp suit!

Source credibility thus comes from the reputation that precedes one and is generated in the audience by the content and delivery of the speaking in the many ways one "proves" one's credibility. Expert testimonies are widely used to confirm ethos of a source.

Earlier in the chapter we mentioned the strategy of "Why You" in terms of analyzing your audience while planning your presentation. There is a flip side to this question. To be successful in preparing your presentation, you must also ask "Why me?" That is, why am I credible and prepared to give this presentation? Look at the criteria for being considered a credible source. How can you show that you are indeed competent and trustworthy, etc.? (See the sample at the beginning of the chapter.)

Box 11-4 **What It Means to be Professional**

In the future, the passport to a good job will be knowledge. A first-rate education will be necessary to get a good job, high salary, and respect. The best-known business consultant, Peter Drucker, labels such well-prepared people ''knowledge workers.''

Education to become a knowledge worker, Drucker asserts, should ''equip students with elementary skills of effectiveness as members of an organization.'' These include: the ability to present ideas orally and in writing, briefly, simply, and clearly; the ability to work with people; and the capacity to shape and direct one's own work.

Source: Adapted from Peter F. Drucker, ''How Schools Must Change,'' *Psychology Today*, May 1989, pp. 18–20.

Pathos

Pathos is pathetic proof stimulated in the audience commonly referred to as emotional appeals. The premise underlying this form of proof is that we are all moved to a great extent by how we come to ''feel.'' Those who use emotional appeals try to help the audience respond with emotions such as anger, fear, happiness, etc. For instance, one may tell a story about a young boy whose life was saved because someone signed the back of his/her driver's license to donate an organ. Thus, he/she may use this appeal as a way to capture attention and arouse the level of need and concern necessary to make the theme ''Donate organs'' persuasive. Narratives work effectively to elicit pathos because they enable one to experience vicariously.

Logos

This form of proof is concerned with how we form and structure arguments. The use of statistics and facts helps us to support a reasoned strategy to show extent and amount. For some speakers, the selection of supporting material appears to be instinctively right. That which interests them inevitably interests their audience, and that which is convincing to them is likewise convincing to their audience. The purpose of providing information is to lessen their uncertainty and to enable them to make wiser choices and successful predictions for them and their organizations.

A speech is more than an idea and yet more than a good outline. It is a personal sharing of thoughts and feelings with another being. What is it that for a few minutes compels an audience to listen with empathy, discrimination, or appreciation?

Listenability is attributable to many factors both internal to the listener (his physical state—i.e., hunger, fatigue, sexual excitation) and to the generation of psychic tension (his fears, arousal of pleasure-seeking drives, or ego concerns). The listenability or interest level depends most of all upon its relevance. Do the ideas, examples, illustrations, testimonies, statistics, analogies, and explanation carry meaningfulness to the listener? In plain words, does it hit close to home? This is why a speech at its best is not an essay readable time after time.

The sensitive speaker chooses support that springs from experience and observation. Speech materials emerge from years of working with tough problems, with lovable and difficult people, with facts and figures, new products and old standbys, from heated conversations with colleagues and unusual vacations, from stories and poems memorized as a child, from movies and headlines in today's paper. The interest level depends upon the variety of supports and upon its fluctuation between the concrete and abstract. A presentation composed of one long story after another would tire an audience to fatigue by its detail just as a presentation composed of high-level abstraction would bore them to slow death.

A premise or point is made not merely by its statement, but by its support. The supports selected generate the feeling or belief desired only if they are relevant and believable to the listener. Let's consider the address from the perspective of the listener. First he/she expects the opening, then the development, and finally the closure. The development section must look good to him or her. He/she must see the core idea and surrounding it, the explanation, illustration, and evidence (testimony, statistical research). The eye of the listener thus sees the speech in this way (see Figure 11.1).

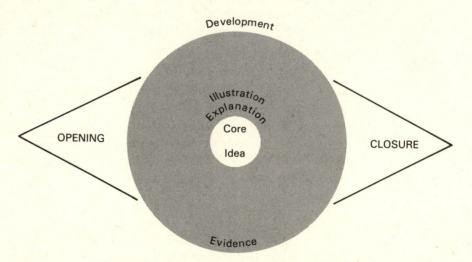

THE EIE MODEL

Figure 11.1 Explanation, Illustration, Evidence

The EIE models what the witness of a presentation must see in order to feel and/or believe. The target audience requests of the speaker: "Explain to me what you mean; illustrate, show me what you believe or feel by a live experience; and present the evidence, lay out the facts, expert opinions and data which cause your beliefs and feelings."

Explanation   In every career people give orders, follow instructions and find it necessary to be able to explain what they are doing or think should be done. A physician with some 40 years' experience put it this way: "The chief communication skill I must use is being able to give patients an explanation." Whether in a one-to-one or a one-to-many situation, explanation is essential to developing a message. The key to presentation of supports is the ability to tie them to the subordinate premises, and the more important linkage to the central thesis of the message. For example, suppose that the central thesis was: "Put your money in a savings and loan institution." The speaker might first seek to establish a subordinate premise: "'Don't worry about the future' is bad advice." Through explanation these two are tied together. He might say:

> Today, I'm here to explain the benefits that can be yours by investments in savings and loans. But I know my message faces a giant propaganda machine that holds great appeal. This message comes at us 15 to 20 times an hour. What is it? Bluntly it shouts, "Don't Worry About the Future." Let's see if you've heard that message as I have. Yesterday, for example, I counted the number of times I heard such bad advice in a half-hour of television. In the dozen spot ads I witnessed, these are the words I heard at least once: "Now . . . buy it now! Buy now, pay later! You only go around once! You deserve the best. The money is as close as your phone! If you can't afford it, we can help you."
>
> I suggest that such propaganda leads to irresponsible behavior and often very sad consequences: Debts that are not paid. A young generation that doesn't think about the consequences of a venereal disease epidemic. Short-sighted expediency demands that a government owes me a living. The fable of the grasshopper who fiddled all summer while the ant stored food for winter presents a choice for this audience.

In the paragraphs above, explanation and transition have been used to weave relationships together. Transitions help move from one thought to another. Sometimes these transitions are brief rhetorical questions such as, What is it? or, How does that affect us? Other times transitions are introduced with, "But . . . ," "In addition . . . ," "Let's consider . . . ," etc. The transition is the speaker's tool for proceeding in a conversational fashion with his listeners.

Perhaps the most important transitional device is the signpost. The signpost serves as a signal that there is something coming. Sometimes the signpost is a simple "First," "Second," or "Third"; other times it is a "Next . . ." or "Now, let's . . ." or "Let's draw our attention . . . ," "Let's focus on . . ." or "In conclusion let me recap. . . ."

Explanation develops an argument by describing relationships. It weaves together what has been said in a former paragraph to what is being said at the moment. It may introduce an example and evidence, and then it ascends from the concrete up the ladder of abstractions to consider the wider implications.

Good explanation is also interpersonal. The speaker reveals his interdependence with the listener. In an address to the 16th Annual Management

Conference at the Graduate School of Business of the University of Chicago, David Rockefeller, university trustee and president of the Chase Manhattan Bank, talked about youth and the profit motive. Look at the following excerpts to see the extensive use of personal pronouns:

"**My** instinctive response—and probably **yours** too— . . ."

"What **we** as businessmen must do . . ."

". . . the best of **our** young people . . ."

"**We** must show beyond dispute . . ."

". . . **you** and I know that business . . ."

"But despite this, I believe it is clear to **all of us** . . . for **our** time."

Illustrations An illustration may be a factual account of something that actually happened, or an invented story of something that probably could happen. Illustrations present the most effective means for dramatizing a premise. A factual illustration consists of a story narrative of an event (see the personal story of Charles Gamble in Chapter 10). As in the first line of a news article, it should include the who, what, when, and where; and in the subsequent story, enough description of the interaction that the audience can provide some reasonable explanation of why. Imagery, movement across a period of time, and actual or paraphrased dialogue may be liberally utilized. Illustrations affect the teller as well as the listener.

Evidence Statistics go beyond individual cases to averages, percentages, and significance. The closest thing that the social sciences have to proof lies in a carefully drawn representative sample or data of a total population. The speaker, when using statistical data, must realize that his audience's ability to understand is directly related to its ability to visualize. Therefore, when presenting figures, a presentation not only should to be repeated but should be made graphic. Visual aids may help and comparisons will help. In addition to saying, for example, that 50,000 persons are killed annually and several hundred thousand are injured on American highways, a speaker may state that the odds are that three out of every five persons in this room will sometime in their lives be involved in an auto accident.

In a speech to the Society of Automotive Engineers, Semon E. Knudsen, as chairman and CEO of White Motor Company, made creative use of the hypothetical illustration to present statistical data:

Let me give you a hypothetical illustration of what I mean. On the Alaskan North Slope, in the Prudhoe Bay area, there are proven reserves of about ten billion barrels of oil. That sounds impressive, and many of us have been comforting ourselves with the thought that this great oil find will solve our energy problem if we can only get the oil piped out. But let's take another look.

At the present time, we are consuming—in the United States alone— between six and seven billion barrels of oil a year. And our consumption of oil is increasing at an annual rate of 6 or 7 percent. Now, suppose we had all that Alaskan oil pumped out of the ground, shipped, refined and in storage tanks. And suppose we decided to use it up so as to improve our balance of payments and strengthen the dollar. If we followed this course of action, all of that Alaskan oil would be gone in eighteen months. So even if we get that Alaskan oil out, and even if we find other equally big fields on the North Slope, in offshore areas, and in other parts of the world, the rate of use throughout the world is so high and growing so fast that we must ultimately find other sources of energy to take over much of the energy load being carried now by petroleum.

Semon Knudsen, ''The Interchange of Technical Information,''
Vital Speeches, 1973.

Testimony is the opinion of someone who should know, possibly an authority in a field or at least a person who has witnessed an event. As in court, the validity and admissibility of the testimony depends upon the credibility of the expert witness. Therefore, when using an opinion, some care should be given to establishing the expertise of the witness and/or his ability to observe. One of the authors once listened to a funeral sermon in which the only support used was testimony. The clergyman read brief statements from 40 famous persons affirming their belief in immortality. The event was moving and persuasive because of the credibility of the famous people, despite the fact that none of them had yet actually experienced their own deaths nor did they claim to have seen any one person come back to life after his body died.

Credibility   The name of the game is credibility. All supports must withstand the critical judgment of the target audience. What does the intelligent listener ask? What tests of reason and common sense does he use? Credibility is generated (a) when the speaker has a reputation for honesty and competence, (b) when the supports that he uses are consistent with other knowledge, (c) when the supports appear to come from reputable sources, (d) when the supports appear to be adequate in number, up-to-date, and representative, and (e) when the presenter conveys sincerity, both verbally and nonverbally. There is some evidence that a dynamic speaker is evaluated by an audience as more credible than a less forceful speaker. This criterion probably relates to the fact that intensity of emotion is associated with conviction.

For a more elaborate description of qualities that motivate, study Chapter 13 on motivation, persuasion, and evidence.

WE MEAN BUSINESS

What type of support(s) persuade(s) you most?

SUMMARY

Public speaking is an art. Building an effective presentation requires a commitment from you, the speaker. Just as in mathematics, there is a formula for creating a presentation by using the strategies outlined in this chapter.

Regardless of the occasion, a speaker must plan a clear purpose statement, a thesis statement, analyze the audience (why you), show how he/she is credible (why me), structure logical arguments, and keep in mind the responsibilities of the introduction and the conclusion.

But merely providing an organized framework will not satisfactorily move the audience to accept your message. The language selected to articulate the arguments and the types of supporting material chosen must be tailored to the specific audience. Audiences depend on some blending of ethos (source credibility), pathos (emotional appeals), and logos (logical arguments). It is up to the speaker, through careful audience analysis, to determine what this "blend" should be.

SKILL BUILDER: ANALYZING YOUR AUDIENCE

You have been asked by the following audiences to deliver a presentation on physical fitness. How would you answer these questions for each audience?

Audience

• Senior citizens — Sunday afternoon
• Musicians' club — Tuesday evening
• Faculty meeting — Friday afternoon
• Football team — 3:10 practice
• Fraternity meeting — Sunday evening

Questions

• What DEMOGRAPHIC and SITUATIONAL factors would be important to consider
• Answer "why me/why you"
• Write a purpose and a thesis statement
• Create an opening paragraph

RESOURCES

Aristotle. (1954). *Book 1 of the rhetoric.* (Robert W. Rhys, trans.). New York: The Modern Library.

Berquist, Goodwin F., William F. Coleman, and James L. Golden. (1978). *The rhetoric of western thought* (2nd ed.). Dubuque, IA: Kendall/Hunt.

Deer, Roger. (1974). "The Lamb Electric Story." Rotary Club Address.

Gorden, William I., and John R. Miller. (1983). *Managing your communication in and for the organization.* Prospect Heights, IL: Waveland.

Kennedy, Dana. (1990, June 2). "Bush charms graduates." *Lansing State Journal*, 1A.

Knudsen, Semon E. (1973). "The interchange of technical information." *Vital Speeches*, Vol. 39, 40.

Osborn, Michael, and Suzanne Osborn. (1988). *Public speaking.* Boston, MA: Houghton Mifflin.

Voice-Pro Consulting Agency. (1985). Seminar on improving public speaking techniques, by Carolyn Dickson, president.

Chapter 12

Speaking Situations in and for the Workplace

Concepts for Discussion

- Tribute speech
- Sales presentation
- Speech of introduction
- Oral briefing/status report
- Facing the camera

- Talking to the press
- Types of delivery
- General principles of delivery
- Ten tips on delivery

Three things have to be coordinated and not one must stick out. Not too much intellect because it can become scholastic. Not too much heart because it can become schmaltz. Not too much technique because you can become a mechanic.

Vladimir Horowitz
New York Times Magazine

What is the number one fear that most Americans share? Surprisingly enough, the answer is not fear of falling, fire, or flying in planes. The number-one fear in America is of public speaking. Why do we dread this event? Public speaking of some sort will probably be a part of your career, and may well be the key to your success. Few things are as powerful as the right words themselves, and almost nothing is more powerful than a persuasive individual.

Within this chapter we will introduce you to the most common types of speaking situations you may encounter in the workplace. The focus of this portion of the text is on the speaking situations themselves, and how to organize your ideas best to fit the unique purpose of your presentation. Reference points for details on organization can be found in this chapter, and discussion about the use of evidence can be found in Chapter 13.

The first portion of this chapter will focus on the most common speaking situations in the workplace, including the tribute speech, sales presentation, speech of introduction, oral briefing, and team presentation. The final part of the chapter will be devoted to the discussion of delivery tips. Although tight organization of a speech is vital, delivery of a speech gives the words life and meaning!

SPEAKING SITUATIONS

The Tribute Speech

Pride is the message every business must peddle. As we have stressed throughout this book, we want to be proud of the place where we live and work. At home, we take time to plant flowers and cut the grass, and don't like it when weeds grow. Weeds show neglect and lack of pride in our home. Such is the case in the workplace. Pride is an important asset, and is an asset that businesses cannot afford to ignore. So, an important part of the personal side of upkeep of our work setting is to show our commitment to this place to others. How far should we go in this selling process? We must do a good job, for our businesses are at stake! Think about places where you shop regularly. What attracts you to these stores? Do you feel a sense of pride from the employees? As an employee, you should be able to articulate this pride for the place you work. One of the authors remembers a student in class who worked for Wal-Mart Stores. The young woman gave a speech of tribute to Wal-Mart. In the speech you could sense her devotion, and it was contagious. Members of the class remarked about the language she used and her clear sense of pride. She began, "We all view success differently. For the past ten years I have worked for Wal-Mart, and even after ten years I still enjoy my job. . . . Through Wal-Mart, I not only get the chance to work for a successful organization, but I also feel personal success. . . . Wal-Mart associates view the company as one large family." Her speech created the urge for this instructor to shop at a Wal-Mart store for the first time (the student's speech outline is presented in Chapter 11).

A speech of tribute affords us the opportunity to reflect upon our sentiments and achievements. It allows us time to share our goodwill and a little bragging. The message within a tribute speech must be both affirmative and personal. For college-course purposes, an assignment to write a tribute speech can be an excellent way to research and learn more about a company where you currently work or wish to be employed. We use this speech in our course for this purpose. Students are required to research the company and interview members of the organization, and from this data, prepare a presentation. You may find this a rewarding way to find out more about a company where you wish to interview.

Once in the workplace, you may also be requested to give such a presentation. There may be times when it is necessary to persuade the public that your organization is first in its field or just simply a great place to work. Acceptance speeches also typically include some information of praise for the organization as a whole.

Whether the speech is written about the place you wish to work, the community where you live, or the place where you are employed, the message should be personal. Your listeners are interested in you — in your ideas and in your feelings. *Do* use the word "I"; it gives you credibility and a link to your topic. *Do* share your experiences and dreams for this place, too.

The story, or narrative, is one of the best forms of support to use within a tribute speech. Usually stories begin with some reference to when and where an event took place and your connection to it. That is, did it happen to you, one of your friends, was it told to you by someone involved in it, or did you come across it in the newspaper or some other way? Following this orientation, the story usually proceeds in a chronological order, describing the people involved and their relationships. Think about speeches you have heard. What was your favorite part of the speech? It may well have been the portion when the speaker stirred and stimulated the audience with the aid of a story.

The speech of tribute can be organized in a variety of different ways. The "Reasons why" format allows the speaker to develop two to three reasons why a corporation, town, or idea deserves applause. This format is easy to organize and easy for the audience to follow. For example, the young woman who spoke about Wal-Mart used the following thesis statement: "Looking in a three-way mirror, one can see how the views of Sam (Walton), the associates, and the outside world intertwine to make Wal-Mart the rapidly growing and energetic company it is today." Her three reasons were then previewed after this thesis statement.

Reason One — Sam Walton views Wal-Mart as a way to serve others.

Reason Two — Wal-Mart associates view the company as one big family.

Reason Three — The public views Wal-Mart as a profitable business that maintains quality at a low price.

This format is simple but effective. When using this format, it is important to remember that you must provide at least one form of support for each main point. You have the luxury of choosing from statistics, analogies, testimonies, examples, or stories. Try to vary the types of support used throughout the presentation, but don't forget the popularity of the story.

The "One reason why" format is even simpler, though it does not provide the depth shown above. If you were to give a public relations speech about your community, for example, your thesis could be, "I think this is a great town because of its senior citizens." Two or three stories about the achievements or kind deeds rendered by this class of citizens completes the one reason format. The formula is direct: One Reason + Three Illustrations = Point. The point is not so much proven as it is affirmed. The person who makes such a speech, of course, is stroking the senior citizens. This format is effective when you have one concise point that you can easily illustrate with a few examples.

Another format option is what we call the "Fantastic time." This speech consists of a simple statement such as: "It has been a fantastic year," and could be followed by a list of several events. Each event would then be humanized by a short account of some person responsible for making that event a success. "It has been a fantastic time" can be completed by any length of time, from one week to 50 years. The important thing is that the stories illustrate some warmly human concern.

Recently one of the authors gave such a speech. As advisor to a sorority on campus, she was asked to summarize the year's activities at our annual Parents' Day banquet. This year she used the "fantastic year" formula. Recognition was given to many young women whose contributions made the "fantastic year" possible. Modern business is greatly concerned about its public image. Public and private industries want consumers to understand the efforts and costs of services. The tribute speech is a vehicle to accomplish these goals and more. It is important to remember while organizing this presentation that you are representing not only yourself, but the organization about which you speak. Whether you write this type of presentation as a college student hoping to work for a particular company, or as a business leader dreaming for hopes of commitment from members of the community, the speech of tribute helps the company story to be told.

The Sales Presentation

Chapter 13 details strategies for using evidence effectively to persuade. This portion of the text will focus more specifically on suggestions for building an effective sales presentation.

Before beginning this section, we want to emphasize that the form of persuasive speaking we are advocating involves careful collection of evidence with which to support an argument. We want to stress that knowledge and trustworthiness (see discussion on credibility in Chapter 13) are central elements of ethical persuasion. As we begin discussion of the sales presentation, please keep in mind even though we equate "closing the sale" with success, ethics and credibility should be integral parts of this close.

While giving toasts to a business and professional speaking class at the final meeting, one student toasted the sales presentation assignment. As a finance major, at first she did not understand why she should be expected to deliver a speech whose purpose was to create and sell a product or service. After organizing and delivering the presentation, however, she changed her mind. "Everyone is involved in persuasion of some form," she told the class. "Whether persuading an employer to hire us or selling our boss on a new proposal, everyone needs to practice these skills." We agree. Public speaking is an art, and refining these skills is never a useless exercise.

Sales power lies not only in the quality of a product but also in how the sales message is structured and delivered. When attempting to make any type of sale, as with any type of presentation, you need to consider first the audience. Your job is to make the audience forget that they are simply buying a product or service. Instead, the audience is buying satisfaction or fulfilling a dream. Joe Girard is considered one of the greatest car salesmen in America. In his book, *How to Sell Anything to Anybody*, he describes how he does not sell cars, but rather sells dreams. Similarly, a buyer does not purchase a television and VCR, he buys home entertainment. One creative salesman used this scenario in his sales pitch to sell life insurance. This example, which appears in Charles Irvin's text *How to Sell Yourself*, shows how powerful language can be. Life insurance policies are usually treated as morbid, but the following example shows how life can be breathed into a product through persuasion.

> A life insurance policy is just . . . legal phrases until it is baptized with a widow's tears. Then it is a modern miracle, an Aladdin's Lamp. It is goods, clothing, shelter, education, peace of mind, comfort, undying love and affection. It is the sincerest love letter ever written.

When structuring your sales presentation, it is important to consider your audience. Tailoring benefits to meet the specific needs, wants, and desires of your audience is a strategy that makes the message more personal. A successful salesperson should listen to the clients to determine their needs. Then, he or she can demonstrate reasons why the idea, product, or service will benefit them by satisfying these needs. For example, when selling memberships at an athletic club, the membership director needs to individualize his or her sales presentation for each prospective member. A senior citizen has different needs than a young adult. A senior citizen can be persuaded that benefits of membership might include increased endurance and stamina. Although these would also be important to a young adult, he or she might be more interested in building muscle tone and improving physical appearance.

The sales presentation can be effectively organized using the Monroe Motivated Sequence of Persuasion. This sequence involves moving the audience through stages that help them realize there is a problem that can be solved by accepting your idea, product or service (Chapter 13 discusses this model in more detail). The sequence includes five steps: attention, need, satisfaction, visualization, and action.

The attention and need stages are the "problem" portion of a persuasive presentation. During these phases, through careful linkage with the particular audience, the speaker captures the attention of the audience and then convinces them that there is some need that is not currently being fulfilled. The speaker then moves to introduce their product, idea, or service as the satisfaction or solution to the problem. The next stage, visualization, includes ethical evidence and appeals about the features, advantages, and benefits of adopting this idea, product, or service. The action stage is where the persuader moves the audience to "buy."

A strategy to remember while structuring this section is what we call "FAB." FAB stands for features, advantages, and benefits of an idea/product/service. This formula can be used to sell yourself in an interview, to sell an idea to an audience, and to persuade a customer to purchase your product. FEATURES refer to the product's physical characteristics. What are the ingredients? What are the stages of the solution? What special features does this service or product uniquely provide? ADVANTAGES are product characteristics that are a result of the special features. This section also refers to comparisons to other products on the market that claim to be similar, and then shows how your product's performance is superior.

William Gorden and John Miller, in their text *Managing Your Communication*, stressed that you need to demonstrate and point up each of the product's advantages. Proving your product's BENEFITS means that you must construct and be able to defend logical arguments about how a product or service will benefit users. Most companies supply their force with proof of product advantages such as statistics, research findings, testimonials, and case histories. One of the best ways to show a product's features, advantages, and benefits is by a live demonstration. Customers want to see the products they are going to buy.

The final step of Monroe's Motivated Sequence is "action." The hardest part of a sales presentation is closing the sale. There are seven types of closures from which to choose. These descriptions should help you to select the types that you think are ethical and most suited to your occasion. More than one closure can be combined when appropriate.

The Assumptive Close is probably the best-known and easiest to use. The language used and the nonverbal cues sent can imply that you assume the customer is going to agree with your sales pitch. The customer is given options from which to choose, but among those there is NOT the choice to say yes or no. One who uses the assumptive close might ask, "That style looks very attractive on you. Would you like to buy one in each of the three colors?" This approach assumes success and removes the yes/no choice implied in simply asking, "Would you like to buy a sweater?" When assumptive language is used, customers are more likely to be led to the conclusion you desire. If you have successfully built a case that the audience agrees with to this point, the use of assumptive language can then likely lead them to accept your conclusions. However, some people resent an assumptive close. They don't want to be treated like children. So if you use assumptive questions, do so in a playfully-serious way.

A very similar method is the Minor Point or Closing on a Choice method, but in this case the audience's decision is still tentative. Once again, the structure of the request for making this choice is crucial. The best way to elicit positive results is to present two choices that imply some degree of "yes." A salesman might ask: "Which home do you feel would fit your needs, the colonial or the ranch?" "Will you have to have this by Monday? Our regular delivery for your area is Wednesday. Will you be home on that day?" As with the assumptive close, the language selected is crucial to the successful closing of the sale.

The Last Chance closure is a popular method used by many in sales. Humans tend to value that which there is a great demand for, but a limited supply. Thus many store owners use the last-chance appeal to increase sales. A customer may inquire, "Is this the last brown briefcase you have left?" The salesperson skilled in this approach will probably send a message that indicates that the customer should take advantage of the chance to buy now, before another consumer purchases the briefcase.

Another popular method of closing is the Return Back method. This method is similar to the rebuttal part of a debate. The salesman agrees with the customer's reservations, but then answers the argument with another benefit of the product. "That is a good point, but . . .", "I am glad you mentioned that, however . . .", "This is an interesting point, but when you consider . . ." could be language employed in this closure.

At the end of a presentation, an effective way to reinforce your arguments and build agreement with your conclusion is to Summarize the Advantages of your claim. Watch for examples of this on shows such as "L.A. Law." Attorneys summarize their appeals in the closing argument addressed to the judge and jury.

A closure that can effectively be woven within the others mentioned above is the Emotional Close. (Pathos, or the effective use of emotional appeals by targeting appropriate emotions such as love, anger, or fear, was discussed in Chapter 12.) Such appeals could be used in a closure as a means of anchoring needs of audience members and linking the fulfillment of those needs to acceptance of your claim.

The final type of closure to be discussed is the Direct Appeal. Although not as strong as the basic needs described above in the emotional close, many do respond to a plea such as, "You need the product. You want the product and deserve it." Before using this strategy in isolation, however, attempt to use a more logical appeal.

The strategies outlined above can be helpful for use in a wide array of persuasive presentations. Here is a final suggestion to keep in mind while preparing: Remember your audience. We keep repeating this theme, and hopefully you are recognizing its importance. Think in terms of the customer. Concentrate on his/her needs and desires and speak in language that shows this concern. The more reference you make to a customer's needs, the more successful are your chances to make a sale. Use as many "you" phrases

---

Box 12-1 **Public Speaking Seminars for Business**

Schools of public speaking are as old as the schools of rhetoric in classical Greece. But such schools are not something only in ancient history. Currently, Communispond, based in New York, is the largest public speaking training organization for business. It focuses on helping those whose jobs demand communication to present themselves more professionally. Thousands have gone through its two-day training. Videotaped feedback assists this instruction.

Other smaller companies in most major cities conduct similar training. Voice-Pro is one such company in Cleveland, Ohio. Reid Buckley, brother of William F. Buckley, the sophisticated host of "Firing Line," has his school in Camden, South Carolina. His two-and-one-half-day seminars help executives deal with the press. A simulated news conference with working journalists is part of the training. Videotapes also record students' performance. The cost for the seminar is $1490.

Source: Adapted from Amy Docksen, "Lesson No. 1: Lean Back in Chair, Roll Eyes and Wag Tongue Briefly," *The Wall Street Journal*, April 24, 1989, p. 1.

---

as possible. Some "you" phrases include: You benefit by . . . , You're right . . . , You have a good idea. . . . "You" phrases may also be in the form of questions, such as "Is this your problem?" and "What is your opinion?" Happy sales!

Salespersons should always remember that their job is to provide potential customers with enough information to make a decision that is in their own best interest. The motivated sequence should not be used to manipulate mind and emotions, but to enable potential buyers to weigh the benefits and costs in light of their own needs and ability to pay.

WE MEAN BUSINESS

Make a list of "you" phrases. The language may be directed as a question or a statement.

Speech of Introduction

Have you ever been to a public presentation, whether it be a commencement address, campus or community speaker, or television address, where the keynote speaker was introduced by another before he or she came to the podium? This is a common ritual in professional speaking.

If you are in charge of organizing a speaking event, it may well be your responsibility to deliver a speech of introduction. Here are some guidelines to follow when organizing this brief speech. The purpose of an introduction is twofold: first, to help the audience feel warmly receptive to the speaker and second, to help the speaker feel comfortable with the audience. The introducer wants to make sure that the information presented is enough to sufficiently develop credibility, yet is not so complimentary that it embarrasses the speaker or usurps her/his time.

The first part of the introduction should present the speaker's name, first and last. Make sure that you have checked for correct pronunciation of the first and last name BEFORE presenting your introduction. You are setting the tone for the speaker's presentation, and it would be extremely unprofessional to begin with a mispronunciation of her/his name.

Background material often is available about the speaker. Be sure to check its accuracy by going over this information with the speaker. You may wish to make a biographical data sheet for the speaker to complete. Some speakers will even provide an introduction of themselves that you may use. Provided that it is not excessively long, you may present those introductory remarks and even add a personal word of your own. From this material, prepare your remarks in 50 words or less to accomplish the two goals listed above. If the speaker you are to introduce cannot provide you with a written "bio," do some informal probing. For example, notice the artifacts (trophies, photographs, certificates) in his/her office. Chatting for even a few minutes before you present the speaker often elicits human-interest items you might find relevant to your introductory remarks.

Keep in mind that this introduction will set the mood for the performance. As Bruce Gronbeck, Douglas Ehninger, and Alan Monroe stated in their text, *Principles of Speech Communication*, the virtues of such a speech are tact, brevity, sincerity and enthusiasm. Generally, the speech of introduction should contain the following elements:

- Present the speaker's first and last name loudly and clearly, with correct pronunciation.
- Stir interest in the speaker's topic.
- Establish the credibility of the speaker with background information and personal experience with the topic.
- Restate the topic and speaker's name clearly.
- State the title of the speech and welcome the speaker to the podium.

If you follow the guidelines listed above, you will be successful in writing and delivering this brief yet important form of public speaking. However, one must avoid several common pitfalls when introducing the speaker. These are:

- Stealing the spotlight by speaking on the same topic or by being so clever that the speaker seems dull.
- Exaggerating the speaker's qualifications so much that he/she is embarrassed.
- Forecasting his/her success. Do not set a speaker up by telling the audience what a great speaker they are going to hear.

Box 12-2 **Sample Introductions**

1. Universal Pictures presents . . . a great fan, Laurie Smith. Laurie is a junior at Northeast Missouri State University where she studies mass communications. Last year Laurie produced her own music video and is currently working to produce videos to be shown during Homecoming Week, highlighting each day's activities.

    She is a great fan of the movies and hopes to work in the film industry as a producer or director.

    And now, with her tribute titled, "Here's Looking at You, Universal," is Laurie Smith.

2. Have you driven a Ford lately? I would like to introduce to you someone who drives one every day and loves it! Debbie Belford is a senior personnel management major who has experienced firsthand the culture of Ford Motor Company through her father's employment at the St. Louis Assembly Plant for the past 21 years. Please welcome Debbie as she shows us that at Ford, quality really is job #1.

3. Ladies, gentlemen, baseball fans, St. Louisian Steve Gold will now do a pitch for the St. Louis National Baseball Club, Inc. He is a marketing major and avid baseball fan, especially for his hometown team. Steve's marketing degree will hopefully land him a dream job for this organization. And now with his speech of tribute, "Up to Bat for the St. Louis Cardinals," Steve Gold.

- Overused introductory language, such as "We have with us a person who needs no introduction . . .", "We are gathered here . . .", "It is indeed a pleasure . . .", "Without further ado . . ."

One speaker suggests a surefire way to get an appropriate introduction: "Write it yourself and hand it to the person who asks, 'What shall I say about you?'" When you then rise to speak and acknowledge the kind words of introduction you can say in all honesty, "I appreciate those fine words of introduction; you read them well, just the way I wrote them."

The Oral Briefing/Status Report

So far we have discussed persuasive presentations in which the object is either to give tribute and recognition or to sell an idea, product, or service. Persuasion strategies and uses of evidence in persuasion will also be discussed in Chapter 13. Now let us talk about an equally important type of presentational speaking event: the informative speech in the business setting.

The purpose of this type of presentation is largely to present information to a specific audience. It is our opinion that the motivated sequence pattern is not an appropriate format for informative presentations. Informative presentations are best organized along topical, chronological, or spacial partitions (see Chapter 11).

H. Lloyd Goodall, Jr., and Christopher Waagen, in their text *The Persuasive Presentation: A Practical Guide to Professional Communication in Organizations*, define a briefing as a meeting that informs an audience, presenting information and ideas. The briefing is a forum for discussing and summarizing facts in a short amount of time. The format for the briefing is less structured than the presentations discussed thus far, because the briefing may not be a regularly scheduled event. The goal of the briefing is to introduce new information or to explain in easily understandable terms information that is being questioned.

The oral briefing is often an informal and unscheduled type of informative presentation. Keep in mind the word "brief" when thinking about this form of speech. Briefings occur all the time within organizations, from informal updates to formal synopses. The purpose of a briefing is to present a synthesis of material in a concise manner within a short period of time.

Briefings can occur in dyadic or group settings. Often these briefings are informal. Examples of informal briefings include updates at staff meetings. For instance, one might be asked to speak weekly about a certain agenda item at a meeting. People who attend this meeting will expect a brief report on the activities involved in this item. Another way a briefing is used is in the form of requests from management to "stop by" the office and brief him/her about the status of a project or an idea.

When structuring a briefing, try to plan in advance the main point of your report. When preparing, ask yourself questions such as: What is the main idea that you want the audience to know? Are there one or two illustrations that might help the audience understand this point? What are future directions, implications, or conclusions from this briefing?

The **status report**, is an oral or written presentation that is given to inform the audience about the current condition of a project. A person may be requested to give a status report at weekly, monthly, or semiyearly intervals. The information within the status report is important to the audience involved. Some questions you can ask yourself when writing your status report include:

- What is the subject of the status report?
- What is the history of the project? (You will need to decide how much of this will be important to tell at each status meeting.)
- How do I define the current situation? (How is the report being interpreted, are we on track, etc.)
- What do I want to get out of the status report? (Personal goals)
- Who is going to receive the status report and what does this individual or group think about the subject? (Audience attitude—positive, negative, neutral)

Both of the above situations call for an organizational pattern and checklist such as that discussed within Chapter 11. Be sure to assess the needs of your specific audience and link the topic and its relevance to them. You must have a clear, brief thesis statement that indicates the central theme of your report. Your introduction, body, and conclusion sections should be easily identifiable, even if you are called to give an informal presentation. Finally, each point must be supported by some sort of evidence.

Much of the communication in the workplace is in the form of team briefings, status reports, or some type of informational format. There is a very fine line between simply providing information and actually being involved in persuasion. Many people argue that when giving a status report, you are actually persuading the audience to approve of the status of your project and support you. This is true! All communication carries with it some message of persuasion.

The Team Presentation

Often corporations will call on committee groups, or a panel of experts in a certain field, to give a presentation together. Since most of you have probably been a member of a group, you are probably aware of some costs and benefits of group work. Group communication in the workplace was discussed in Chapters 8 and 9. In this section, we would like to bring some common types and procedures of team presentations to your attention.

A common type of team presentation is the **symposium**. The symposium is used when a group of people are making a variety of presentations on the same topic. For example, one of our business and professional speaking classes held symposiums about the issue of whether a "Made in the U.S.A." label indicates quality or not. A moderator is selected to introduce the topic and to deliver introductions of each speaker. The moderator also provides transitions between each presentation so it runs smoothly.

Each speaker then presents a prepared speech about his or her designated aspect of the topic. The symposium speeches on quality were split into topics such as defining quality, measuring organizational commitment, evidence of quality in the corporate culture, and summarizing the overall arguments. Brainstorming could be used as a method of determining topics and the most effective sequencing of each speech.

All of the speeches should be carefully planned and rehearsed. We tell our classes to practice within their symposium groups. This serves many purposes. First, it allows you to hear the information presented by other speakers so that you can avoid duplication and be assured that everyone is on the right track. Some groups like to weave a theme throughout all of their presentations, and hearing each presentation could give ideas for such a theme. Second, this gives you the opportunity to plan diverse types of visual aids. For instance, it would probably not be a strong strategy only to use bar graphs. You do want to make sure, however, that your visual aids are as uniform as possible. That is, that they are consistently professional, large enough for the entire audience to see, and uncluttered. You may wish to elect one or two persons in the group to make the visual aids. Brainstorm ways that you could keep attention with variety. See Chapter 10 for ideas on how to create effective visual aids.

Finally, practice increases competence and confidence. Take advantage of this built-in audience! Critique each other's speeches in areas of content and delivery. Practice your critical listening skills. There is so much you can learn from this experience. Usually symposia are followed by a question period. Practice asking and answering questions of each other that may come up from your audience.

A **panel discussion** is a more informal type of group presentation. Like a symposium, panels usually have a moderator who introduces the topic and speakers, and directs discussion to various members of the panel. The moderator wants to make sure that each person on the panel has a chance to speak, and that one or two people do not monopolize the panel. The moderator also controls questions and comments from the audience when there is a forum period.

Panel discussions involve a lot of impromptu speaking, and are similar to the kind of communication you may experience during the question and answer period after a public speech. A panel is like a conversation with other people listening. Therefore, members may divide eye contact between the panel and the audience while they are speaking. But politeness dictates attentive listening and turn-taking. The moderator as well as members should encourage each other to speak loudly or repeat if some remarks are presented with low volume.

Although much of the speaking is spontaneous, Stephen Lucas, author of *The Art of Public Speaking*, cautions that panel members do need to prepare before the panel meets. As he said, although you will be speaking off-the-cuff, it is vital that you study the topic ahead of time, analyze major issues, and sketch out the points that you want to be sure you cover during the talk. An effective panel discussion is one in which the members and the moderator have reviewed the key questions they want to address beforehand and the order of discussion. Usually they will have found some points where their opinions genuinely differ. Conflict is good. An audience enjoys disagreement. Therefore, do not avoid it. Presentation of alternative methods of analysis and solutions encourages rigorous thinking and spurs audience involvement. Remember that you too can learn from others' ideas. You are not there just to present a fixed point of view.

Group presentations can be rewarding if everyone within the group works together. Be wise in choosing a moderator. Remember that the performance of each person reflects the message of competence given for the entire group.

FACING THE CAMERA

Organizational representatives had better get some training for appearing on television. It is unwise to wait until a crisis, be it a chemical spill or a nuclear disaster, when the media will force your appearance, to seek professional advice. Here are some tips that are far superior to "winging it." They will only help if you arrange for practice and feedback in a nonthreatening situation.

- Prepare. Know your facts and how they were gathered, when, and where. But don't overload your listeners with statistics. Short examples are easier to remember and more interesting. Never try to bluff or fabricate. It is much better to say "I don't know" than to be trapped in an exaggeration or an unfounded claim. Good interviewers can sniff out lies and fabrication. Rehearse, rehearse, rehearse. Practice answering questions put forth by your coworkers. Before you speak for your organization, go through the proper organizational red tape to get whatever authorization is necessary.
- Deliver your message with conviction. Use simple words and emphasis. Avoid rigidity in voice and gesture. Don't preach or play tough on the one hand and don't pussyfoot and gesture limply on the other.
- Package it small. Prepare to say what you have to, that which is essential, in 60 seconds. Don't feel you must provide an elaborate preparatory statement. There will be time later, if at all, to elaborate.
- Don't get angry. Even if an interviewer tries to picture you and your company in a bad light, don't reply in anger. Rather, focus on the positive. Avoid sarcasm and never try to clown. Assume a serious yet friendly demeanor.
- Don't hang back. If several are being interviewed or are there to participate in a discussion, don't wait to be last or have to be coaxed to join in. Of course, talking over another is rude and makes it impossible for others to hear clearly, but you do need to assert yourself. The reason you are there is to present your opinions. So stay alert.
- Remember the central message you wish to present. Do not be sidetracked. Return to your theme. Say it in another way.
- Dress conservatively. Solid colors and pastels, are better than whites. Leave the flashy jewelry and the glitter at home, unless you are in show business.
- Don't speak to the camera. Rather, talk to the interviewer unless your host invites you to speak to the audience. In that case, speak directly to the lens.
- Prepare visual aids. Keep them simple and uncluttered. Use color and symbols rather than detailed graphs. Use no more than one or two aids for a short presentation.
- Prepare a press release to accompany your presentation.

TALKING TO THE PRESS

Executives must speak with the media. It is their responsibility in good times and particularly in bad. When the corporation sponsors a tennis or golf tournament, it is its task to praise the competitors and winners. When the corporation beautifies the community with works of art, words of tribute may be brief but are expected. It is easier for those lower in the corporate structure to represent the company in good times than in bad.

At times of crisis, the public as well as a company's employees want to hear from the chief. Serious problems unfortunately are not so rare. Accidents may injure employees and/or the public. Corporate lying, cheating, and stealing may have occurred. A downturn in business may result in layoffs and plant closings. Reporters are charged with learning the facts and interpreting the causes and implications of the bad news. Plant officers and corporate executives should get to the scene and ferret out the facts. They may be candid about what they don't know.

Johnson & Johnson received high marks for its handling of the Tylenol scare. Cyanide had been found in some Tylenol capsules. The product immediately was pulled from shelves all over the country. CEO James Burke frequently appeared to tell what he knew. Exxon's CEO Lawrence Rawls did not fare as well in the eyes of the press or public after the *Valdez* struck a reef, dumping 260,000 barrels of crude oil in Alaska's Prince William Sound. Perhaps Exxon's image would be seriously damaged no matter what Rawls had said. But Rawls seemed to hide from the press and appeared not to take responsibility for the spill. Ten days after Exxon apologized and declared the company had acted "swiftly and competently" to clean up the spill. But no Exxon official would admit that company employees had been in error. On "CBS This Morning," Rawls said it was not his job to know technical details of the cleanup plan.

In discussion of the poor performance of such executives as Rawls, a *Fortune* article advised that executives should learn the vocabulary of reporters (see Box 12-3) and plan in advance how to talk with the press. This is not a problem that can be shuttled off to public relations.

Ideally, executives develop a positive credible relationship with the media before a crisis. Executives serve as a primary source for an organization's news. They understand that reporters must meet deadlines and need to ask tough questions. They need to understand that not everything written will be accurate or positive. They need to identify with the public's need to know. They need to respond promptly and not to be so wary of saying something that might put the organization in a bad light. Stratford Sherman in *Fortune* stresses that corporate spokesmen, when talking to the media, should "Tell the truth—or nothing" and "If you screw up, admit it candidly. Avoid hedging or excuses. Apologize, promise not to do it again, and explain how you're going to make things right." We add to this sound advice that one's demeanor and communicator style should not be rigid, aloof, or

---

Box 12-3 **Meeting the Press**

Establishing ground rules with reporters depends upon knowing the reporter's working vocabulary.

- Off the record—means comments may not be published. Don't go off the record casually or with anyone you don't have reason to trust.
- Not for attribution—applies to information that may be published, but without revealing its source. Specify when that applies to your company as well as to you.
- Background—usually means not for attribution. Clarify this with the reporter before you give out information.
- Check with me before you use it—means just that. You have the right to expect the reporter to check back. You have the right when the reporter checks back to correct errors and misunderstandings, but not to withdraw statements you now regret. Again, it is good to clarify before you talk and to be specific about to what "check back" applies.
- Read it to me before you use it—means you have an advance warning of what is to be in an article, but no right to correct errors.
- No—means no, that you have refused to answer a reporter's question. May be used if used judiciously.

Source: Adapted from Stratford P. Sherman, "Smart Ways to Handle the Press," *Fortune*, June 19, 1989, p. 75.

arrogant. In troubled times, contrition, empathy, and passionate concern are particularly needed.

DELIVERY

The actual presentation of a message is very threatening and traumatic for some, but for most is exciting and exhilarating. No book can give you confidence nor can it, in and of itself, cure an extreme case of stage fright. But mastering the skills of speech construction that we have outlined throughout these chapters can help you feel more competent, and therefore, more confident. We are going to explain the four most common modes of delivery, and then provide some tips for making your delivery the best that it can be.

Box 12-4 **"All the World's a Stage"**

"All the world's a stage," wrote Shakespeare, who could just as easily have added, "and every player on it has stage fright."

Stage fright is natural and can even be helpful. Psychiatrist Isaac Marks commented in his book *Living with fear* that "Athletes have performance anxieties . . . (called "butterflies") and when . . . the butterflies aren't there, they don't perform at peak levels. Dancers and singers make it look easy, but moments before they go on, they say, it doesn't feel easy."

One of the most important points to remember is that you do not have to possess fantastic oratorical powers in order to be persuasive. Remember that Winston Churchill's voice was somewhat croaking, and Eleanor Roosevelt's voice was shrill. John F. Kennedy had a heavy New England accent; and Dwight Eisenhower spoke in a halting monotone. Yet each went down in history as memorable orators.

Source: Adapted from Scot Morris and Nicolas Charney, "Scaring off stage fright," *Psychology Today*, July 1983, p. 84.

Types of Delivery

What was the last public speech you heard? A classroom lecture . . . the President giving a press conference . . . a church pastor giving a sermon. How did these people deliver their presentations? Did they use limited notes, an entire manuscript, or was the speech memorized? Let us define for you the most common types of delivery styles.

The **manuscript mode** of delivery is the use of a script with your entire presentation written out. This method is necessary when exact wording is very important. Politicians use the manuscript method when delivering statements at press conferences or official policy speeches when specific language is essential. If you were running for president of the student body at your university, for example, you would probably do well to use the manuscript mode. But for most public speaking situations, the manuscript style is not necessary. It definitely has interpersonal drawbacks, since it is hard to establish a relationship with your audience if your eyes are on your paper. It is also difficult to sound spontaneous and conversational when using this method of delivery.

To combat the problem of reading from the page, some use the **memorized** mode of delivery. Although this method may ensure that again your language can be carefully planned and rehearsed, there is one big danger — you may forget. We do not advocate the use of the memorized style. Except for professional actors, memorizing always sounds memorized! There is a certain "canned" quality associated with memorizing that limits fluctuation in voice and restricts rapport with the audience. You can usually spot speakers who have memorized, because they typically look over the heads of the audience, fearful that if they make eye contact they will forget their message. We also note that speakers who memorize often look as if they are following a word-for-word script, and we can almost see them "reading" the script in their mind.

Impromptu speaking is the third approach to delivery. As we defined earlier in the text, impromptu means that you are speaking without prior preparation. Public presentations should NOT be given impromptu, although some students have attempted to do so! This IS the delivery style that you will be using during most of your employment interviews, and daily on the job. Your boss may ask, "Dan, what do you think about the new program?" Your response, though it must have some sense of organization, will be impromptu.

When you are placed within a situation where you are called upon to use this style of delivery, don't panic! Remember the three parts of any speech: the introduction, body, and conclusion. What is the central idea of your answer? Practice of this mode of delivery will help these organizational skills be second nature. Janet Stone and Jane Bachner, authors of *Speaking Impromptu*, suggest that you decide on your conclusion first, and then arrange the rest of your talk to lead up to that conclusion.

The final mode of delivery is **extemporaneous**. This type of delivery style is the one we advocate most for effective and conversational delivery. Extemporaneous delivery means that the speaker has carefully planned and outlined the presentation, and then uses key words to trigger thoughts during the actual presentation. We suggest that speakers write cues for the introduction, body and conclusion section on a 3×5 or 4×6 note card. Practice many times with this note card only, so that you are familiar with the cues you have selected.

With careful planning and rehearsal, your speech will be well prepared, although NOT completely memorized. Because you have only memorized KEY IDEAS, not complete sentences, you will have much more leverage to "fill in the blank" when you do forget (we say when, not if — all speakers forget something!). Extemporaneous and impromptu competence go hand in hand. By memorizing ideas only, you can establish eye contact with the audience, use space to get closer to your audience, and use more natural, conversational vocal variety. When you do forget, you use the impromptu skills that you are practicing for interviewing.

One of television's earliest popular speakers was Bishop Fulton John Sheen. Bishop Sheen employed extemporaneous delivery. He outlined and wrote out in detail much of what he planned to say. Then he practiced with and without his key-word outline until he could tear up those notes. He said, "If I can't remember what I am going to say, how can I expect my listeners to remember?" Some speech instructors follow Bishop Sheen's policy and prohibit their students from taking any notes to the platform. Most of their students are pleasantly surprised that they can speak on their feet without such crutches.

We believe that the goal of effective delivery is to be as conversational as possible. As Saundra Hybels and Richard Weaver say in their text, *Communicating Effectively*, some of our models for effective public speaking come from those who have big, booming voices and dramatic gestures. But more and more, the trend is moving toward achieving a conversational quality in our public speeches.

Speaking conversationally means that we speak to our audience as though we were in an interpersonal situation. The audience feels more involved, for they feel included in the message and not just talked AT.

WE MEAN BUSINESS

Practice saying the following phrases from Oscar Wilde's play, *The Importance of Being Earnest*: "That is a matter that surely an aunt should decide for herself." Practice using the whole range of your voice, high and low.

Adapted from Carolyn Dickson, Voice-Pro Consulting Agency.

General Principles of Delivery

When practicing your public presentation, keep in mind the following principles and adopt those with which you feel the most comfortable.

Adapt to the Size of the Room and the Audience   The larger the room, the louder the voice and the broader the gesture; the greater the distance from the audience, the more dramatic the presentation should be. You want to make everyone feel included in the presentation, so make sure they can hear and see you.

Adapt to the Mood of the Occasion   The voice expresses the emotions in the rate and tension. The body communicates mood by its rate of movement, tension, or relaxation of gesture and muscle. Remember that nonverbals speak. They play an important part in delivery of a message. Space speaks. Generally, movement toward someone, approaching, signals interest and intensity of concern for communication. Retreating provides a time for relaxation or variety. Contrast in movement and voice focuses attention. Time speaks. A change of rate of delivery provides emphasis. Speaking much longer or shorter than the expected period may irritate. The body speaks. The muscle tension reveals, by rigidity or relaxation, attitudes of confidence, concern, anxiety, or disinterest. We read each other's "body language," and unless the nonverbals are congruent with the verbal message, our attention is drawn to the nonverbals and doubt rather than trust is aroused.

Use Appropriate Language   Remember that you are in a formal environment, and pay strict attention to grammar and articulation. You may even wish to tape-record your speech to become conscious of habits such as clipping word endings or overuse of contractions. For example, it would be much preferable to say "I am going" than to say, "I'm goin'." Also, try to avoid using fillers such as "like" and "you know."

Ten Summarized Tips for Delivery

A speaker may break some of the rules because there are so many variables at work. Likely we all can name friends who hold down a good job despite faulty speech, and can also point to prominent national figures whose distinctive voices or mannerisms helped rather than hindered them: a nasal voice, slouch and drawl, a stoic immobile expression. The tips prescribed here, thus, may be considered advice from the experts for most speaking situations. Just remember that a presentation may be successful in spite of breaking one or several of these do's or don'ts, and the more successful you are, the more tolerance an audience has for your deviance from the rules.

1. Approach the platform with confidence. Sometimes, if the mood is one of excitement, you may even hurry to the platform to express your eagerness to greet the audience. Select clothing that will be appropriate and comfortable.
2. As you reach the speaker's stand, make contact with the chairman, accept his introduction with a handshake or nod, and greet any other person on the platform.
3. Next, look over the crowd; pause to concentrate on your verbal greeting and the first words of your message. Don't look at your notes again!
4. Take charge. The platform is yours now. But the room belongs to the audience, so if in doubt, check to learn whether your voice is easily heard in the back row. If possible, check out the room before your speech.
5. Acknowledge. Take notice of the situation, but do not strain to make a joke of it or somebody.
6. Avoid a long introduction. Build common ground quickly and get to your topic.
7. Use a key-word outline. Except for rare policy speeches do not read a manuscript. Rather, work from a 3 × 5 card with key words to aid recall of important ideas, supports, and quotations. Do not try to present a speech from memory. Impromptu talks are destined for failure. The first suffers from canned, overprepared action; the second suffers from lack of preparation. Practice your presentation

from beginning to end at least twice. Try saying it different ways. If possible, work in a room where you can talk out loud to an imaginary audience.

8. Do not keep your audience in the dark about your intention. Preview the topics you intend to cover.

9. Make your body work for you. Move to demonstrate a transition into a new point, but avoid pacing or fidgeting. Use your hands, head, and eyes to convey feelings, to describe, and to illustrate. Movement causes the eye to follow. Keep gestures up, make them definite, and do not hurry them. Maintain good posture. Suit your movement to the size of the room.

10. Stop at the end of a point. Make your transition and begin the next. Repeat or rephrase once, but do not overexplain.

SUMMARY

Possibly some of you feel that once you leave this college, your experience with public speaking ends too. However, for most of you this will not be the case. Almost everyone in the professional world will be called upon to speak to an audience, whether it be to three or 300.

This chapter introduced the most popular types of speaking situations in the workplace. Some of you will be called upon to give tribute speeches. Hopefully this will be a chance for you to boast about the place you work or live. Tribute speeches can also acknowledge exceptional people, and providing such a forum is rewarding. Recall that Aristotle said, "To praise a man is akin to urging a course of action."* Whether you are specifically seeking a career in sales, marketing, computers, management, or education, persuasion will be a part of your work.

The other presentations we described were the speech of introduction, oral briefing, and team presentations. These presentations have a more informative flavor. The speech of introduction is probably best handled when written yourself and handed to your introducer. This way you avoid embarrassment or distortion of information.

The oral briefing and status reports will be a part of any career. These presentations, whether formal or informal, require organization just like any other presentation. Team presentations can be a great way of gaining new ideas from members of a group, critiquing others, and inviting creativity. Members of panels and symposiums need to communicate regularly, have a clear definition of goals, and practice together.

Delivery has been discussed in various chapters of the text. This nonverbal portion of the presentation is an important element in packaging you as a competent communicator. The only way to reduce stage fright and increase

---

*We also add "woman or organization."

confidence is to understand communication principles and to practice, practice, practice. The modes of delivery that we advocate most are impromptu (though not for formal presentations!) and extemporaneous. Careful practice of these styles will increase your ability to be conversational in your delivery style.

SKILL BUILDER: ORAL BRIEFING

Following is an example of a briefing assignment. This briefing requires observation of a group meeting, where the reporter will focus on a specific aspect of the meeting to brief others about. The reporter is asked to identify within the group meeting either:

A. The major points of discussion
B. Any resolutions or plans for change or improvement

In addition to the above, the reporter is asked to choose one of the following categories to study and report on from his/her observation:

A. Leadership (answering questions such as)
   1. Was there a designated leader? Was this person REALLY the leader? Was there another who emerged as leader?
   2. Was leadership important to guide this group? Did the leader make the decisions, or did the group have input? How were decisions reached (compromise, consensus . . .)?
   3. How was the morale of the group? Did the leader try to make sure everyone was interacting, vocalizing, and satisfied?

B. Commitment
   1. Did the members seem committed to the group? Did they seem glad to be there? Interested? Proud?
   2. What was the climate like? Was it friendly and positive, or "let's hurry up and get out of here"? How was time used (was there a lot of time off-task?)?
   3. Did group members seem to have a personal stake in decision-making, or not seem to care?

C. Nonverbals
   1. What was the seating arrangement? Were there any indications of power?
   2. Describe facial expressions, posture, use of space, etc. Did all these factors show responsiveness and enthusiasm, or impatience, disinterest, and disgust?
   3. What were members doing while another was talking (doodling, wandering; or attentive, leaning forward)?
   4. How interested were the voices of the group members (animated and excited, or monotone and bored)?

Although the speaker is basically reporting, or giving a brief explanation of the happenings at this group meeting, add a little "color" to the briefing by observing one of these three areas (leadership, commitment, or nonverbals). Create a theme based on this observation, and organize your presentation around this theme.

Possible themes include:

"Leading the way to productivity"—Effective leadership within a group, and how this leadership can lead to a productive meeting.

"Commitment to quality"—Evidence of group commitment to quality in their decision making and to the group as a whole.

"Bored at the board meeting"—Nonverbal dissatisfaction rules as the overall atmosphere at the meeting.

SKILL BUILDER: CLASSROOM FLEA MARKET

One sales experience that is clearly a face-to-face, buyer-consumer activity is the flea market. The merchant must select, display, and price a product. She or he must show or demonstrate features, advantages, and benefits of the product. Too often in the classroom students practice only one sales presentation. A classroom flea market provides audiences for several presentations by each student in a relaxed, festive atmosphere.

Step One

Each student selects a product and makes a poster listing its major features, advantages, and benefits.

Step Two

One-third of the class sets up their products at various points in the classroom, hall, or outside. The rest of the class mills about from site to site listening to each merchant's presentation.

Step Three

Sealed bids are then handed to those merchants whose products are desired. The high bid wins the product. And the process begins again for the next group.

Step Four

Debriefing. What sold? Why? What presentations were particularly fun and persuasive? Why?

RESOURCES

Busby, Rudolph E., and Randall E. Majors. (1987). *Basic speech communication: Principles and practices.* New York: Harper & Row.

Girard, Joe. (1977). *How to sell anything to anybody.* New York: Warner Books.

Goodall, H. Lloyd, Jr., and Christopher L. Waagen. (1986). *The persuasive presentation: A practical guide to professional communication in organizations.* New York: Harper & Row.

Gorden, William I., and John R. Miller. (1983). *Managing your communication: In and for the organization.* Prospect Heights, IL: Waveland Press.

Gronbeck, Bruce E., Douglas Ehninger, and Alan H. Monroe. (1988). *Principles of speech communication* (10th ed.). Glenview, IL: Scott, Foresman.

Hybels, Saundra, and Richard L. Weaver II. (1989). *Communicating effectively* (2nd ed.). New York: Random House.

Irvin, Charles E. (1957). *How to sell yourself.* New York: The American Press.

Lucas, Stephen E. (1989). *The art of public speaking* (3rd ed.). New York: Random House.

McCroskey, James C., Virginia P. Richmond, and Leonard M. Davis. (1986). "Apprehension about communicating with supervisors: A test of a theoretical relationship between types of communication apprehension." *The Western Journal of Speech Communication, 50,* 171–182.

Osborn, Michael, and Suzanne Osborn. (1988). *Public speaking.* Boston: Houghton Mifflin.

Sherman, Stratford P. (1989, June 19). "Smart ways to handle the press." *Fortune,* 75.

Stone, Janet, and Jane Bachner. (1977). "Speaking impromptu." In Janet Stone and Jane Bachner, *Speaking up: A Book for every woman who wants to speak effectively* (153–161). New York: McGraw-Hill.

Chapter 13

Motivation, Persuasion, and Evidence

Concepts for Discussion

- Motivation defined
- Persuasion defined
- Identification and self-persuasion

- Persuasive strategy
- Evidence and persuasion
- Researched variables
- Applying persuasion theory

The new buzzword in employee motivation is "ownership." Says Harvard Business School Professor J. Richard Hackman: "If you want me to care, then I want to be treated like an owner and have some real voice in where we're going."

Ownership sometimes goes a step further by seeking to help employees feel like entrepreneurs. Alfred West, founder and chairman of SEI Corporation, a $123-million-a-year financial services company in Wayne, Pennsylvania, with 1100 workers, divided his company into entrepreneurial units. West gave each group of employees a 20 percent interest in their unit. If the unit flops, the members receive nothing beyond their salaries. West commented, "I'm an entrepreneur, and I want more people like that here."

Adapted from Jeremy Main, "The Winning Organization," *Fortune*, September 26, 1988, p. 49–60.

This chapter presents a need-based theory of motivation. Following that, we provide a discussion of persuasion theory, and then conclude with definitions of evidence and an explanation of how it is used effectively.

WHAT IS MOTIVATION?

In the work setting, **motivation** is a term whose meaning is similar to persuasion. Motivation is an internal impetus to move toward desired means and ends. To motivate someone to buy is to create a desire for a product or service, for certain benefits and advantages. Employee motivators are often referred to as carrots and/or sticks. Carrots reward with promotions, bonuses, trophies, and status symbols such as better office equipment, higher wages, stock options, etc. Sticks or kicks may include unwanted assignments, disciplinary actions such as reprimands, suspensions, demotions, fines, reductions in salary, and threats of discharge.

Figure 13.1 Managers can choose either a carrot or a stick when working with employees.

Motivation is usually considered internal, something inside us embedded in emotions and values. **Persuasion** is wrongly considered external, something that someone else does to get approval of our intellect. We do not believe, however, that motivation lacks cerebral activity or that persuasion lacks emotion and value-embedded activity. Rather, we are complex human organisms. Both heart and head are present, if not at work, during all activity. Just as every utterance has a content and relational aspect, and denotative and connotative element, so does a persuasive attempt engage both the intellect and emotion.

WE MEAN BUSINESS

What internal motivations drive you? What are your most powerful motivators?

Abraham Maslow is credited with the well-known need theory of motivation. Individuals are explained as having physical, social, and self-actualization needs. Physical needs include hunger, health, safety, and sexual expression. Maslow reasoned that until these basic needs are satisfied there will be little interest in any higher-order needs. Social needs entail belonging, inclusion in family, social, and working groups. Gaining recognition may meet a social need for belonging, and also be a symbol of achievement. Self-actualization is conceptualized as the highest order need humans possess. Self-actualization is represented in the U.S. Army slogan "Be all that you can be." Achieving intellectual goals, earning degrees, developing skills, and career accomplishments satisfy self-actualization needs. Building character and virtue, enjoying, and/or creating things and aesthetic activities (music, drama, art, dance, gardening, volunteering, organizing, etc.) are self-actualization needs. The ancient classical philosophers unknowingly were referring to self-actualization when they spoke of the human need for the good, the true, and the beautiful.

Psychologist Clayton Alderfer encapsuled Maslow's need theory in three words: existence, relation, and growth (ERG). However, he differed from Maslow in that he reasoned that one does not have to satisfy lower-order needs before higher-order needs come into play. His studies found that people universally and continuously seek to satisfy existence, relational, and growth needs. If we add spiritual needs to Alderfer's motivational formula, we have the acronym ERGS, an easy reminder of motivational need theory.

The salience (importance and immediacy) of one's needs determines personal involvement; and personal involvement, in turn, determines our willingness to process persuasive messages.

WHAT IS PERSUASION?

Persuasion involves changing attitudes. Persuaders' weapons are symbols. Threats, force, guns, and bribes are not persuasion. Persuasion is a communicative process.

We are influenced by many things that are not persuasion. A car bears down upon us and we hurriedly get out of the way. But that is not persuasion. People are affected by the presence of others. How hard we try in a race is influenced by the fact that others are in it. This is known as social facilitation, not persuasion.

Doing what one would not do alone because of the facelessness of or urging of a crowd is known as mob psychology. Such behavior as lynching, gang rape, or mass suicides as was the case in Jonestown, Guyana, indeed are tragic. "Group mindlessness" is dangerous. Sometimes people can be persuaded to do terrible things. Persuasion in the work setting, however, rarely involves rabid crowd behavior. But some sales meetings and corporate rallies are "under the influence" of the presence of others.

A number of variables interact at the moment of a persuasive attempt: The resistance or agreeableness of the target, the legality and reasonableness of the request, the power of the persuader and persuadee, and the long- or short-term consequences of doing or not doing what is asked. These contextual variables affect one's effort to persuade and a target's willingness to be persuaded by certain others.

All this is to suggest that persuasion is not a simple, discrete, intentional matter. People tend to fit into roles and to follow scripts. The sales department sells. Accountants account for. Supervisors supervise. If the script of the department manager is to process orders received from sales within 24 hours, s/he will "persuade" the workforce to stay the additional hours necessary to get out big orders. Allen Bradley, a leader in electrical controller manufacturing, has such a policy. Employees accept the manager's "script" that comes with an announcement that 5000 rather than 1200 controls must be shipped that day.

But let's suppose the person who packs the controls has been suffering from upper back strain and that he/she has been working ten-hour days. He/she may then talk to the manager and his/her coworkers about the extra pain the 24-hour delivery rule is causing him/her. He/she may search his/her mind for reasons to make exceptions to the 24-hour rule that would be persuasive to management. What he/she would say would depend upon the contextual variables such as the disposition of the manager, fear of losing the job, personal relationship with the manager, the company's policy about physical strain, and whether or not there is a union that has established policies about these matters.

What the person who packs the units decides to say probably will partially be derived from "scripts" he/she has used before to influence superiors. Perhaps these will be scripts used as a child with his/her parents, with teachers, or with previous bosses. We learn what works for us and then tend to apply that to new situations as seems appropriate. We are more comfortable using familiar scripts than in writing and learning new ones.

Wise communicators endeavor to understand contextual variables. They know that they and others in a workplace are expected to follow organizational policies, traditions, and job descriptions. They discover scripts about the way things are done in that place, and they seek to demonstrate that they know the scripts and roles they are expected to play. This is the job of role-taking. Those who role-take well will have more credibility when they try to influence a change.

When we try to influence change in the work setting, we are trying to shape our roles and those with whom we interact. Our role-making efforts are persuasive attempts to rewrite the script for our worklife. Thinking of persuasion within the work setting as role-making provides a metaphor that suggests:

- First learning well one's assigned role and script.
- Seeking to understand the contextual variables in the setting. This means studying the traditions, rules, and motivations present.
- Trying to make the role work.
- Seeking to make minor changes in keeping with the organization's values and mission.
- Realizing that rewriting a whole script rarely occurs and only happens when the assigned script fails. That failure usually is seen in terms of problems of quality, productivity, waste, and/or employee morale.
- Rewriting a script for others entails getting others involved. Within the work setting, employee involvement (EI) programs are paths to systematic change.

WE MEAN BUSINESS

Does thinking of persuasion as role-making and rewriting scripts have applications for the work setting? What might some applications be?

IDENTIFICATION AND SELF-PERSUASION

Persuasion does not always follow a straight line from stimulus to response. In fact, most often persuasion is a subtle, unconscious, taken-for-granted process. Children adopt role models and seek to become like them. Young employees tend to focus upon certain individuals employed where they work whom they respect or envy, and unconsciously follow their example. The work organization socializes new members by elaborate rituals and indoctrination. New hires are taught to respect the significant symbols in the work setting, its leaders, the organization's history, and its buildings. What captures our attention persuades. We imitate that which we admire.

In the first chapter on corporate culture, we discussed persuasion via the process of identification. Identification is the symbolic process through which the individual is bonded with others.

Self-persuasion may seem contradictory to those who view persuasion as something one person does to another. To be sure, a salesperson may make a product attractive — even appear fabulous. Some may follow the FAB technique of sales, (discussed in Chapter 12); that is, to present a product's features, advantages, and benefits. Other salespeople may talk their way out of a sale by false promises and discourteous behavior. Internal talk also goes on within the prospective buyer. That internal talking to oneself clarifies, tests, and evaluates the sales pitch. It is inside our minds that we process and persuade ourselves to open that pocketbook, to buy impulsively, or to persuade ourselves carefully that we can or cannot afford to part with our money. Even after we buy, inside our bodies we feel uneasy about parting with our money. We feel dissonance. It is then that we reiterate the reasons why we bought and reevaluate the wisdom of our purchase.

Those who would persuade should remember that they cannot persuade others. Rather, their role is to provide quality information and reasons that will be used by the target persuadees to persuade themselves.

No neat formula is available for making a message persuasive. The researchers have conducted many tests of different message structures. They have sought to learn whether strongest arguments are more effective when placed at the beginning, middle, or end of a speech. They also have compared the persuasive impact of one-sided verses two-sided messages and refuting the opposition's arguments before or after presenting one's own case. Other questions the researchers have asked are: Should a speaker draw specific conclusions? Will light, moderate, or heavy fear appeals persuade? How much evidence should one use? Will humor help persuade? Will obscenity excite or inhibit acceptance of a message? Should language be qualified, opinionated, or intense?

Professors Dominic Infante, Andrew Rancer, and Deanna Womack, in their text *Building Communication Theory*, say that conclusions drawn from these studies "are very tentative, and subject to numerous qualifications." Advanced courses in persuasion will enable one to understand and experiment with the complexities and nuances of constructing influential messages.

TEN PRINCIPLES OF PERSUASION

Our purpose here is to set forth basic and overlapping principles about how the persuasive process works. The first principle developed in this chapter is that persuasion is an internal self-adjustment process in response to manipulation of symbols. The second principle is that persuasion is not so much a matter of changing one's mind as it is a process of identification with others who think and behave differently. The third principle is that when ego-involvement of a target of persuasion is high, change will be very difficult. This means, for example, that uncommitted voters will be easier to persuade to vote a certain way once they learn about a new candidate than will those individuals who are already active in a particular political party. The fourth basic principle of persuasion is that dissonance is necessary for change.

Shoes that pinch make us go shopping for new shoes. Stress and tension make us seek stress reduction. Finding that our behavior disturbs our superiors causes sleepless nights. Discovering that our ideas are inconsistent leads to rethinking our opinions.

The fifth principle is that people are pleasure-seeking and pain-avoiding creatures. The sixth principle is that which meets basic needs is persuasive. All of us have needs for safety and security, for hunger, thirst, and physical satisfaction. We also have psychological needs for belonging and inclusion, for being wanted and loved, and needs for achievement and creativity.

The seventh principle is somewhat contradictory: People are persuaded by both that which reduces and increases uncertainty. Reducing uncertainty increases one's control and makes life more predictable. But if life becomes too predictable and routine, life is boring. Therefore, for such times, increasing risk has its unique appeal.

The eighth principle is that people are creatures of their culture's conditioning. People tend to be ethnocentric. They think their cuisine, their country, their religious beliefs, and their values are best. New attitudes become more acceptable when they are shown to be supported by one's cultural values. Authority and legitimacy accorded to a proposal enhance its persuasive power. That is why marketing groups seek endorsements. Procter & Gamble has employed this marketing endorsement tool for Crest toothpaste. On the tube outlined in red is this quote:

> Crest has been shown to be an effective decay-preventive dentifrice that can be of significant value when used in a conscientiously applied program of oral hygiene and regular professional care.
>
> American Dental Association.

The more an endorser's credibility is based upon knowledge that has been certified by a society's institutions, the greater is her, his, or its influence.

The ninth basic principle is that some people are more influential than others. They are role models because of their wealth, expertise, popularity, and power. They have status and they are the movers and shakers who are needed to raise money for the Heart Association, children's hospital, or passage of a tax for a school levy or sports stadium.

The tenth principle is the opposite of the ninth. That is that the underemployed, the poor, the homeless, the less educated, and the inarticulate have little power or influence. They too have needs. Their pain often goes unnoticed. Poverty stinks. That which stinks is usually avoided. Rarely is "stink" persuasive until it comes close to one's doorstep. Spokespersons for the homeless have sometimes resorted to dramatic vigils on the mall near the halls of Congress. Their visibility there is calculated to persuade passage of appropriations for the homeless. It is in the best interests of the larger society to be ever aware that the silent and oppressed should also be given opportunities to speak.

WE MEAN BUSINESS

Analyze yourself. Imagine yourself in the roles of consumer and seller. How are you most easily persuaded?

We live in a time when many want our attention, time, money, and commitment. It is in our own self-interest to be tough-minded about getting the facts and in understanding how evidence is used. As consumers and advocates, we need to ask: What is evidence? When is evidence persuasive? How does one apply persuasion theory?

A PERSUASIVE STRATEGY—MONROE'S MOTIVATED SEQUENCE

There are a number of other effective organizational formats (review Chapter 12), some of which you may use to partition your speech of tribute, sales, or persuasive presentation.

One of the strongest strategies for organizing an effective persuasive presentation is by use of Monroe's motivated sequence of persuasion. Alan H. Monroe, the first author of *Principles and Types of Speech Communication*, claimed that although each person has individual differences, most people are largely persuaded or influenced in the same way. That is, there are certain strategies that audiences accept with higher certainty.

The motivated sequence consists of five stages:

- Attention—As we discussed in Chapter 11, speakers must capture the attention of their audience within the first moments, or audiences will not tune in. Attention can be gained by carefully targeting your message to the specific audience, by establishing your credibility and linking yourself to the topic.
- Need—The need section is one of the most crucial to the success of your persuasive campaign. Within this section, you have the burden of proving to your audience that they indeed have a problem, which your idea, product, or service can uniquely solve. Create dissatisfaction with existing conditions. For example, one student who created a new hair product for a sales presentation outlined the following problems: (1) Appearance is so important to us, and we spend a lot of time and money on our hair to ensure that we are attractive. (2) Surveys have shown that visits to the hairdresser take 30-45 minutes, and may cost as much as $2000 a year for a four-member household. (3) Time is a valuable resource to us. A lot of time is spent going to the hairdresser or shaving. (4) The condition of our hair and skin is also

---

Box 13-1 The Monroe Motivated Sequence

I. Introduction to the speech
 A. Attention
  1. How can you grab audience attention?
  2. How can you focus audience interest on the subject?
 B. Need
  1. What is the problem or need facing the audience?
  2. What does the audience already know about it?
  3. How clearly can you make the audience feel the need?
II. Body of the speech
 A. Satisfaction
  1. How can the audience need be satisfied?
  2. What are the characteristics of the satisfier?
  3. Where can the satisfaction be secured?
 B. Visualization
  1. What are the benefits to the audience?
  2. What will happen when the need is satisfied?
III. Conclusion to the speech
 A. Appeal
  1. What must the audience do to get the satisfier?
  2. When must they act?
 B. Closing line

Source: R. Busby and R. Majors, *Basic Speech Communication*. Harper & Row, p. 296.

---

important to us. Be sure to DEFINE the problem adequately and EXTEND the needs so the audience is logically (and strategically!) led to your solution.

- Satisfaction—The satisfaction stage is where your solution is introduced. The solution in this case is simply to purchase or agree with your product, or agree with the proposed idea, or service. Be sure that your thesis is strong, clear, assumptive, and concise. This is the step in which you demonstrate and provide evidence of the workability of your product or idea.

- Visualization—The visualization section will most likely parallel the need section in breadth and depth. During this portion of a presentation, you must show the audience how the product/service/idea will benefit them if and when they possess it, and/or how they will miss that benefit if they do not possess it. For example, suppose you are in the library and have an appointment that must be kept for a job interview, and an unexpected shower comes up. Reach into your briefcase for your collapsible umbrella as you dash to that appointment in the rain.

Think about what you have done so far. You grabbed the attention of the audience by identifying a problem that they all share. Whether the target audience is housewives, college students, business people, doctors, etc., learn as much as you can about your target audience! Then you extended these needs by creating dissatisfaction with current conditions. You followed this by an introduction of the solution to their problems — your product. Now that the audience is at the edge of their seats, you must show them how the product will work if they possess it.

- Action — No matter how effective your oratory in the first four stages, if you cannot be successful in the last stage, your campaign has failed. The most difficult part of a persuasive presentation is convincing the audience to take action. What you say in the closure may wash out, may turn the tide, or may reinforce what was said earlier in the message. The closure must appeal with all the fervor in language, credibility, and emotion all that you can muster. (Refer to Chapter 11 for seven types of closures often used in sales presentations. These closures can also be transported into different persuasive contexts.)

WHAT MAKES EVIDENCE PERSUASIVE?

What is evidence? **Evidence** is information that is used as proof by someone. Information used as proof is a process in which an individual arranges opinions, hopefully from knowledgeable persons in addition to his or her own personal experience, and provides facts in support of certain claims. This is what is meant by argument and reasoning with evidence.

As we said earlier in this chapter, persuasion is intentional influence. It is selling products and services. It is changing attitudes. It is inspiring loyalty. It is shaping beliefs and getting others to do what you want them to do by means of symbols rather than force. The nickname of "Persuader" for a gun is a misnomer. Guns can force us to do what the holder of a gun tells us to do. That is coercion, not persuasion. Persuasion employs communication and engages people who are free to make choices.

Those who are most informed are the most difficult to persuade to a different belief. One exercise in which each of us should engage before trying to persuade another is to ascertain where that person is with respect to the topic: How informed? How involved? How intense? We each should ask, if I were that person what would it take to change my position?

Just arousing the interest of the uninvolved may be a big accomplishment. For those deeply conditioned to a way of doing or believing, simply to raise consciousness to the fact that others believe differently may be a sufficiently large goal.

When is evidence persuasive? A theory labeled the Elaboration Likelihood Model and conceptualized by Richard Petty and John Cacioppo proposes that there are two paths to persuasion:

- The central route relies on the soundness of arguments, evidence, and substance of the message. This path entails thought and actual modifications in one's beliefs. That's not easy.
- The peripheral route relies on elements outside the message itself, such as the attractiveness and credibility of the advocate and sources, the pressures of the situation, and how different the position advocated is from one's own. The peripheral path requires little, if any, thought about the message itself and does not entail an actual change in one's beliefs as much as it seeks compliance with the desired ends.

The key to whether one is persuasible via the central path or peripheral path depends upon one's motivation. When one is personally involved in an issue, such as a proposal to change another employee's work schedule to suit one's own, then one will be sufficiently motivated to process the information on the central pathway. When we are not involved in an issue, we are unwilling to expend the energy necessary to deal with the central path, and instead tend to rely on the peripheral path.

RESEARCHED VARIABLES

People expect evidence from those who are trying to sell them products, services, and ideas. The use of evidence sells more products and produces more change in attitudes than the use of no evidence.

General Versus Specific

A number of experiments have compared vague or general statements, evidence without its sources mentioned, evidence with sources named, and evidence with sources fully cited. In all cases, messages that used some evidence were more persuasive than vague or general statements; and evidence presented with sources fully cited was most persuasive. Therefore, to be most persuasive, it behooves one when presenting testimony to mention the qualifications of the person quoted, and when and from where the quotation was taken.

Statistics

Studies also have determined that when presenting statistics, to make them more persuasive, one should explain how representative they are for the audience. For example, it is important to explain that one out of 11 women in the United States will get breast cancer rather than to simply give the number who suffer from cancer.

Attorneys know that factual evidence from expert witnesses is more persuasive in their clients' behalf than are character witnesses. This is not to say character witnesses are irrelevant. In nonserious cases, they help. But presenting many character witnesses may backfire by causing the jurors to think something is "fishy" when a lawyer finds it necessary to present a parade of character witnesses. Statistics, to be persuasive, need to be summarized, made graphically vivid, and sparingly used. Statistics generally should be in addition to examples rather used alone. It is important to know the date and to have the full citation for statistical evidence. If the data are controversial, one should be able to describe how the statistics were derived, the sample, and the analysis.

Narratives

Scholars have found and practitioners have intuitively learned that examples and stories are more persuasive than carefully collected statistics. What do you suppose explains this seemingly contradictory finding about evidence? One would think that statistics would be most persuasive because they represent many cases as compared to examples that can represent only a few. But such is not the case. Anecdotal reports have more persuasive impact, with few exceptions. The answer likely lies in the fact that people know more about human-lived experience and therefore find accounts believable of that lived experience in examples, stories and anecdotes. Anecdotes, when well-told, are involving, and enable listeners to ascertain whether they "ring true" with their own experience.

Intelligence

Evidence is particularly necessary for highly intelligent people to change their opinion. But also, for less informed and less intelligent people, evidence lessens their uncertainty.

In trials, jurors are impressed by eyewitness reports and tend to overestimate their accuracy. That is why it is so necessary for an opposing lawyer to cross-examine a witness and to help jurors compare eyewitness perceptions with other evidence. Witnesses who appear confident in tone are more believable than those who are hesitant and unsteady of speech. Witnesses under hypnosis also are considered more believable.

Here are some additional findings about evidence and testimony in trials: Experts have been found to lessen the persuasive effect of eyewitnesses. Jurors appear not to be persuaded of innocence because the accused tearfully deny wrongdoing; in fact, some studies found that the more those accused tearfully proclaim their innocence, the more likely they were to be found guilty. Jurors, however, who see evidence that defendants appear sorry for their crimes, tend to reduce sentences.

<u>WE MEAN BUSINESS</u>

What type of support persuades *you* most: testimony, statistics, or examples/stories?

Congruency

The amount of evidence provided does make a difference, particularly for uninformed and uninvolved recipients of a persuasive message. Increasing the number of prestigious references and pieces of factual information has less impact upon informed than uninformed targets of persuasion. What matters more than the amount is the quality of evidence and its consistency. But evidence is considered to be of higher quality if it comes from several sources. Researchers have learned that people who heard speeches with high-quality evidence attributed to three different experts were more persuaded than hearing the same three pieces of high-quality evidence attributed to the same expert. The principle here appears to be that the congruence of several different experts is more believable than that of one expert.

New Versus Old

That which appears more recent is more persuasive than well-worn evidence. In short, the new is superior to the old. Wisdom tells us that time-tested material should be more believable, and probably it really is. But when an advocate has presented recent research that contradicts older, accepted thinking, that then is more persuasive.

Bias

Biased sources tend to be discounted. It is to be expected, for example, that parents speak of their children as above average, and that students will argue that they deserve above average grades. But when parents reluctantly admit their child is below average or when a student reluctantly asserts s/he deserves to fail, that is persuasive. On the whole, those considering evidence prefer it from unbiased, credible sources.

Source, Credibility, and Trustworthiness

We want opinions from credible sources — those with educational qualifications, those with direct experience, and those who have earned a reputation for their expertise. Source credibility enhances factual data and we tend to believe authorities even without accompanying factual data. When highly credible individuals such as doctors use irrelevant evidence or evidence from other sources that lack quality, listeners tend to change in the opposite direction from that advocated. Persons without particularly good credentials, on the other hand, can stimulate the change desired by employing relevant evidence from highly qualified sources. We tend to believe that knowledge is cumulative, and that new knowledge often proves old propositions untenable. What matters most is trustworthiness of a source. Sometimes we trust what a peer says more than a thousand experts!

Long-Term Versus Short Term

Those messages that take us down central pathways, that engage us in weighing substantial evidence, result in greater conviction. It is then that we like what we buy and that changed attitudes are more lasting. When we buy or change simply to comply because of peripheral cues, such as group pressures, satisfaction may not be as persistent and new conviction may be temporary.

Immunization

In this mass-media age, we are bombarded by tens of thousands of advertisements and appeals for our money and commitment. Evidence helps build defenses or immunity to the persuasive attacks. Knowledge gives one willpower to resist impulse purchasing. Knowledge is a defense against gullibility. Advocates, therefore, want to inoculate their target audiences by providing them evidence and reasoning that enable evaluation of competing appeals.

APPLYING PERSUASION THEORY

We have all encountered the maxim that persons persuaded against their wills are of the same persuasion still. Or perhaps we have seen the cartoon in which the boss says, "No, darn it! You're not going to do it just because I'm telling you to do it, you're going to do it because you believe it!"

Persuasion is not something that one does to another. Rather, persuasion is a process that may be stimulated either externally or internally, that engages reason and feelings of people in change of attitudes, beliefs, or values. This is to suggest that a salesperson or an advertisement does not *cause* but may facilitate the self-persuasion process in a potential customer.

This stimuli–self-persuasion process usually entails five phases: attention-getting, confidence-building, desire-stimulating, urgency-stressing, and response-seeking. Awareness and understanding of these phases may (a) help advocates in being more effective in their facilitation of self-persuasion, and (b) help those targeted in persuasion attempts to be more forewarned and better able to be more discriminating during the self-persuasion process.

Attention-Getting

It has been said that we act based on what captures our attention. Engaging the senses is the surest way to capture that attention. Those who want to win your heart, mind, and/or pocketbook will get you to look, hear, smell, taste, touch, and feel! To engage the attention of these senses notice how colors, music, images, graphic fragrances, exciting action, and thousands of techniques shout "Hi, Look at me. I'm different. Come closer. I'm fun!"

WE MEAN BUSINESS

Wander through a shopping mall or theme park. Gather examples of appeals to eye, ear, smell, taste, touch, and movement designed to get your attention.

Stories, claims, demonstrations, contests, and displays are designed to capture attention. They are starters of the persuasion process.

Confidence-Building

This chapter has examined the many variables that cause the target of persuasion to trust or mistrust. The reason brand names are so valued and protected by law is that reputation is a part of name identity. Holiday Inns for many years used the "no surprise" slogan. They advertised reliability with that motto. "You can count on" is a refrain echoed by almost everyone who seeks to sell ideas, products, or services. Confidence in an organization comes from being represented by trusted spokespersons and/or authority figures. We respect those who are known as experts or especially accomplished. We identify with those who are protective and caring. We like persons we perceive are friendly, attractive, cute, and likeable.

Desire-Stimulating

Value claims come in many emotion-permeated verbal and nonverbal symbols: basic needs, territory needs, belonging needs, and growth needs. Thus we hear words that address these value-engaging terms, such as tasty, protect, exciting, right, popular, hometown, love, mother, respected, discover, and success. Products are sold on the bases of superiority (best), quantity (most), novelty (new), reliability (solid), beauty (lovely), simplicity (easy), utility (practical), etc.

Box 13-2 **Value Added**

Certain language adds value to products, services, and ideas. Notice the appeals used by those selling products and their good name.

SUPERIORITY ("best")   BEAUTY ("lovely")   STABILITY ("classic")
UTILITY ("practical")   QUANTITY ("most")   SCARCITY ("rare")
RELIABILITY ("solid")   RAPIDITY ("fast")   EFFICIENCY ("works")
NOVELTY ("new")   SIMPLICITY ("easy")   SAFETY ("safe")

Basic Needs: **Certitude Needs:**   **Territory Needs:**
FOOD ("tasty")   RELIGION ("right")   NEIGHBORHOOD
ACTIVITY ("exciting")   SCIENCE ("research")   ("hometown")
SURROUNDINGS ("comfort") BEST PEOPLE ("elite")   NATION ("country")
SEX ("alluring")   AVERAGE PEOPLE   NATURE ("earth")
HEALTH ("healthy")   ("typical")
SECURITY ("protect")
ECONOMY ("save")

Growth Needs: **Love and Belonging Needs:**
ESTEEM ("respected")   INTIMACY ("lover")
PLAY ("fun")   FAMILY ("Mom" "kids")
GENEROSITY ("gift")   GROUPS ("team")
CREATIVITY ("creative")
CURIOSITY ("discover")
COMPLETION ("success")

Source: Many of the ideas in this box and in this section of Chapter 13 are adapted from Hugh Rank (1982), *The Pitch* (Park Forest, IL: Counter-Propaganda Press).

Hugh Rank, a scholar of sales tactics, partitions these desire-stimulators into appeals (a) to *keep* (desires for protection) the good, (b) to *get rid* of (get relief) the bad, (c) to *get* (acquisition) the good, or (d) to *avoid* (prevent) the bad.

Urgency-Stressing

Ads may be divided into soft and hard sells. The language attribute that differentiates one from the other often is embedded in the intensity of the words. Scare-and-sell tactics employ terms such as *offer expires, sale ends, deadline, rush, hurry.* If there are no urgency appeals, one can ascertain that the persuasion is soft-sell.

Response-Seeking

As is the case of urgency-seeking, hard-sell employs action trigger words: buy, get, do, act, join, taste. Specific responses are called forth, almost commanded. Chapter 12 discusses a number of close strategies used in sales presentations, some of which the buyer might wisely be aware.

Those who are weighing a decision need to be informed of the actions necessary to get, keep, get rid of, and avoid. Cost and payment plans, for example, are integral to deciding whether to buy or not buy. Those will avoid the hard sell who genuinely want the persons targeted to make decisions in their own and society's best interests, in our opinion. They will help the targeted not to buy products or ideas impulsively. They will caution a buyer to give careful thought and take time to evaluate during the persuasive process.

SUMMARY

Motivation is described in this chapter as the internal impetus to move one toward desired means and ends. Humans strive to satisfy needs. Those needs revolve around existence, relational, growth, and spiritual concerns (ERGS).

Persuasion, therefore, is described as doing or saying those things that stimulate striving to satisfy needs. **Coercion** is forced compliance. To be persuasive is to facilitate another in satisfying her or his needs. Persuasion, from this perspective, is a process that occurs within the target persuadee. A salesperson may influence that process by evidence and source credibility.

Within this chapter, we discussed persuasive strategies such as the motivated sequence and the FAB formula; popular patterns used to design media appeals; and persuasive campaigns and sales presentations. Persuasion is a part of our daily lives, and recognizing strategies that influence others can be a beneficial part of any job we hold.

In this chapter, evidence has been defined as information that is used as proof. The motivational key to whether a persuader's target will follow a central versus a peripheral path is the target's personal involvement. Those who are highly involved will exert the necessary energy to evaluate evidence and test the reasoning presented by an advocate. Those uninvolved will find it easier to make a decision to buy or change belief because of peripheral cues such as credibility or attractiveness of sources of the message, or of social pressures to comply.

Almost any evidence is more persuasive than vague or general statements. But evidence that is well-documented is far more effective than evidence lacking citations. It is also important to establish the credentials of those quoted and of researched material. Studies have shown that statistical data is more persuasive if its representativeness is explained and if it is made vivid. Although contradictory research findings may dispute whether certain types of evidence are more effective than others, a substantial number of studies conclude that anecdotal evidence is more powerful than statistics. The important finding is that people vicariously experience and compare their experience with anecdotal accounts. Finally, those who wish to be persuasive should endeavor to demonstrate their trustworthiness, their immediacy, and their consistency.

SKILL BUILDER: ANALYZING PERSUASIVENESS IN ADVERTISEMENTS

1. Select several advertisements from business magazines. With colored markers, underline the following principles of persuasion.

   Red = Central Route (sound arguments, evidence, and substance)

   Yellow = Peripheral Route (elements outside the message itself, such as attractiveness of people in the ads and their credibility)

   Explain to a classmate how the ads you've analyzed are explained by the Elaboration Likelihood Model.

2. Applying Persuasion Theory: Select a topic such as plant safety. Design a poster that uses at least two of the following persuasion principles:

   - Specific evidence
   - Statistics adapted to a targeted viewer
   - Narrative
   - Source credibility
   - Immunization

RESOURCES

Dresser, William R. (1963). "Effects of 'satisfactory' and unsatisfactory evidence in a speech of advocacy." *Speech Monographs, 30,* 302–306.

Hample, Dale (1979). "Predicting belief and belief change using a cognitive theory argument and evidence." *Communication Monographs, 46,* 142–146.

Infante, Dominic A., Andrew S. Rancer, and Deanna F. Womack. (1990). *Building communication theory.* Prospects Heights, IL: Waveland Press.

Morley, Donald D. (1987). "Subjective message constructs: A theory of persuasion." *Communication Monographs, 54,* 184–203.

Petty, Richard, and John T. Cacioppo. (1981). *Attitude and persuasion: Classic and contemporary approaches.* Dubuque, IA: Brown.

Reinard, Jean C. (1988). "The empirical study of the persuasive effects of evidence: The status after fifty years of research." *Human Communication Research, 15,* 3–59.

Woodward, Gary C., and Robert E. Denton. (1988). *Persuasion and influence in American life.* Prospect Heights, IL: Waveland Press.

Glossary

Accreditation I accept as true; believe; certification.

Acquisition Something that has been acquired; usually referring to recently acquired property or ownership of a new enterprise.

Adaptors Behaviors used to satisfy physical or psychological needs.

Altercentrism Behavior in which the communicator is concerned about the other party's feelings and input.

Ambiguity Double meaning; variable, uncertain meaning.

Apprehension Anxiety or fear associated with a certain activity such as communicating.

Arbitration Settlement of a dispute by lay judges out of court.

Argumentativeness Asserting reason for and/or against policies or practices.

Assertion To affirm or aver with confidence a particular belief or statement of fact.

Attitudes A position or manner indicative of feeling, opinion, or intention toward a person or thing.

At-will doctrine To discharge for any reason or without giving a reason.

Audience-based communication apprehension Anxiety raised by an assignment to speak before a certain group.

Audio teleconferencing The interaction of three or more individuals or groups who use voice communication over telephone lines.

Autocratic leadership Leader takes almost complete control of the group.

Autonomy Self-government; independence.

Axiom A proposition deemed to be self-evident and assumed without proof.

Belief Opinions held that are thought to be true and correct.

Bureaucracy Usually thought of as red tape and control or great influence in government by minor officials; an organization with levels of authority, divisions of labor, rules, regulations, and impersonal policies.

Channels The way a message is transferred from source to receiver.

Chronological résumé Traditional form; you simply list what you have done in the past in reverse chronological order. Most recent comes first.

Chronomics The study of how individuals use time as communication.

Civil Rights Act of 1964 Limited employers on the type and amount of information they could obtain during the job application or preemployment screening.

Clarification Asking "what" and "how" questions.

Clean Indoor Air Act of 1986 Sought to reduce involuntary exposure to tobacco smoke.

Coercion To compel by force.

Cohesiveness The degree of attraction that members feel toward one another and a group as a whole.

Commitment A strong belief in the goals and values of the organization; a willingness to devote considerable effort to the organization; and a strong desire to remain within the organization.

Communication The interactive informational process that links one system to other systems; to make known, impart ideas and feelings, and to give and respond to one another's messages.

Communication apprehension An individual's level of fear or anxiety associated with either real or anticipated communication with another person or persons.

Communication networks The flow of messages between and among people within an organization.

Compact discs Used to store computer software and data.

Conclusion The final part; outcome.

Confirmation Repeating instructions or paraphrasing information to make sure it is understood.

Conflict Differing ideas are put on the table, and discussion determines which of these ideas are best suited for the group.

Conformity The level of a member's acceptance of group norms.

Congruence Agreement; harmonious.

Congruence skills Focuses upon reading the other person and being readable.

Consumer The ultimate user of a commodity.

Context-based communication apprehension The fear of communication in certain types of settings, such as job interviews; being called on in class; public speaking.

Corporate Being pertinent to a body.

Corporation A company or association chartered to act as an individual.

Credibility Perception of another's ability and reliability established by a record of integrity, competence, and goodwill in relationships.

Culture Shared values, traditions, norms, preferences, and practices of a society or a corporate body within a society.

Dead-enders Those who cannot always be relied upon to pass on information.

Decode To translate a message from a code.

Delivery focus Focusing on a person's dress, appearance, or delivery habits instead of listening.

Delta Triangular.

Democratic leadership Leader maintains responsibility for task completion, but invites participation from all task members.

Directive approach The interviewer determines the specific purpose and controls the pace and direction of the actual interview.

Discrimination Any selection or on-the-job practice or communication that has an adverse impact on hiring, promotion, employment, or membership opportunities of members of any race, sex, ethnic, creed, or age group.

Dissonant Disagreement; discord.

Downward communication Messages that often get distorted as they are passed from person to person.

Dyadic Two persons.

Electronic mail The interconnection of computer terminals to which many people have access.

Emblems Signs or gestures that stand alone and are substitutes for a verbalization.

Empathy Putting yourself into another person's shoes and seeing the situation from his/her viewpoint.

Encapsulate Literally to encase in a capsule; symbolically to compact an idea or concept in a short statement.

Encoded To convert a message into code or some other language of communication.

Enterprises Something undertaken; a project, mission, business, etc., especially one requiring boldness or perseverance.

Entrepreneur One who undertakes an enterprise.

Environmental control The ability to handle conflict in a win-win mode (refer to assertion).

Epithet Name or phrase used to characterize a person or thing.

Equity Impartial justice; perceptions of fairness.

Ethical In accordance with accepted principles of conduct.

Ethos Proof that depends on the believability of the speaker and that is generated by the content and manner of delivery of a message.

Expenditures Disbursement.

Expressiveness Emotional tone and style of delivering messages, communicated both verbally and nonverbally.

Extemporaneous delivery The speaker has carefully planned and outlined the presentation and then uses key words to trigger thoughts during the actual presentation.

Evidence Information that is used as proof by someone.

Facsimile (Fax) machines Allow users to send exact images and printed documents over telephone lines, by satellite, or by microwave signals.

Federal Hazard Communication Standard Act Mandates worker training in the hazards faced on the job and a full disclosure of hazardous chemicals used by the company.

Feedback A response or reaction one gets or gives to a message.

Flipchart A large pad of paper that is attached to an easel.

Fog index Level of reading difficulty.

"Foxes" Nations holding values of relatively small power distance and with little uncertainty avoidance—a term used by Geert Hofstede.

Functional résumé The candidate lists abilities and past accomplishments in order of their importance rather than the order they happened.

Grapevine Word-of-mouth transmission of secret information.

Graph A special kind of chart that shows quantitative relationships.

Group A collection of people who frequently interact over time in the hope of achieving interdependently what they cannot achieve singly.

Haptics Relating to sense of touch.

Hierarchy Series of positions of different rank within an organization.

High performers Employees who propose and produce solutions to work out problems.

Icon A sacred image.

Illustrators Used to help describe an event and hold the listener's attention while the speaker paints a picture with his words and gestures.

Immediacy An attitude of mind desirous of connecting with and interacting with others; when communicators send the message to others that they are approachable and available for communication.

Impetus Impulse; incentive.

Impromptu A presentation or remarks done without previous specific message preparation.

Individualism The sense of independence versus collective identity versus interdependence one has with one's group or clan.

Information A process in which an individual arranges data and opinions, hopefully from knowledgeable persons in addition to his/her own personal experience, and provides facts in support of certain claims.

Inevitable Communication of some sort is always occurring.

Inoculate Immunize.

Insubordination Lack of submission to authority.

Integrity Soundness; completeness.

Interaction management Procedural skills that rely on consultation and collaborative decision-making.

Interpersonal communication Face-to-face encounters in which participants sustain focused interaction through the reciprocal exchange of verbal and nonverbal cues.

Interpersonally supportive groups Goal is sharing and growth.

Interview A process of dyadic communication with a predetermined and serious purpose designed to inform or change behavior and usually involving the asking and answering of questions as well as gathering information or securing compliance.

Irreversible When a message has been given, it cannot be taken back or changed.

Investment model Cultivation of good working relationships is viewed as an investment.

Isolates Those who typically ignore grapevine information.

Kinesics The study of face and eye behavior, posture, position, gestures, and physical appearance involving movement.

Laissez-faire The leader does little to lead task completion or provide direction.

Learning group Focuses upon the function of increasing knowledge.

Liaison Contact maintained between independent forces.

"Lions" Nations with both large power distance and large uncertainty avoidance — a term used by Geert Hofstede.

Listening The active process of receiving aural stimuli.

Logos Proof or reasoning used to demonstrate that a thing is so; perceptions of receivers of a message that are traceable to its reasoning and rationality.

Low performers Employees who tend to complain and produce work of inadequate quantity or quality.

Manuscript mode of delivery The use of a script with your entire presentation written out.

Maps Used to show a representation that is dependent on geographic relationships.

Masculinity Defined as the collection of aggressive, performance, object-centered traits in which in almost all societies males score higher than females.

Message Verbal or written communication from source to receiver.

Motivation Internal impetus to move toward desired means and ends.

1935 National Labor Relations Act Guaranteed labor the right to organize and to bargain.

Noise A disruption or something that prevents the message from arriving accurately to the receiver.

Nondirective approach The interviewee initiates and controls the purpose, subject, and pace of the interaction.

Nonverbal communication Involves all uses of our body and voice that communicate a message to receivers.

Nuances A delicate degree of shade or difference.

Norms Rules or standards that determine appropriate versus inappropriate behavior.

Ombudsman A government official who investigates complaints from the public, or a corporate officer independent of management or labor who seeks to resolve complaints pertaining to ethical or relational and personal matters in a confidential, nonthreatening, and conciliatory manner.

Optical character reader (OCR) Scans printed or typed documents and converts them into electrical signals.

Orientation stage Initial phase of interaction; time of defining and testing norms and for securing member commitment.

Orotund voice Energetic, pompous, authoritative, proud, and humorless.

Overhead projector Projects on a screen an image of words or pictures that are printed or may be written or drawn on plastic, transparent sheets.

Panel discussion Informal group presentation in which a moderator introduces the topic and the speakers and directs members of the panel to converse on various aspects of a question or issue.

Paralanguage All behavior that is vocal but nonverbal; all vocal behaviors that complement, accent, emphasize, and contradict verbal cues.

Paraphrasing Restatement of another person's ideas in your own words.

Pathos Proof that is designed to appeal to emotions and sway a listener's feelings; perceptions of a message that are emotionally arousing.

Perception Process of becoming aware of the external world through our various senses.

Peripheral The outer boundary zone.

Persuasion The act of convincing.

Physical noise Some type of outside environmental distraction.

Pictogram Uses pictures or symbols to represent data.

Pie chart Used to show how the parts of a whole are distributed.

Placard A notice posted in a public place.

Power distance The degree to which a society accepts the fact that power is unequally distributed in it.

Prejudge To judge or condemn before proper inquiry.

Proxemics The study of space used to define relationships and power.

Psychological noise Preoccupation with personal problems or being lost in a daydream instead of listening.

Quality A term used by customers to mean fitness for use, exceeding expectations.

Quality control A process that employs precision language and monitoring of operations.

Quid pro quo Something in return; an exchange.

Rebuttal The effort to disprove by argument or evidence.

Receiver Refers to the person listening to the message.

Redundant Using more words than are needed.

Refute To attempt to defeat by argument or proof.

Regulators A gesture that performs a turn-taking function.

Reiterate To repeat.

Reprisal Any act done in retaliation.

Reticent Disposed to be silent, reserved; extreme communication anxiety.

Rhetoric The art of using language to influence; sometimes to talk oneself into something but most often to persuade others; occasionally referred to as lack of action, mere words.

Rudimentary An underdeveloped state.

Sabotage Malicious destruction.

Section 504 of the Rehabilitation Act of 1973 Prohibits any firm or local government that receives federal funds from discriminating against "otherwise" handicapped persons.

Self-disclosure The process of sharing a part of yourself with another person.

Semantic Pertinent to meaning in language.

Semantic noise Problems in understanding due to word choice, articulation, or speech impediments.

Situational communication apprehension When apprehension occurs only for communication with certain persons in certain situations but not in others.

Slide An image that is projected on a screen of a picture that has been taken by a camera.

Social group Helps to fulfill the essential interpersonal needs such as belonging, being with other people, interacting, and receiving feedback.

Social relaxation The level of anxiety that a speaker shows; to be comfortable in a communication interaction.

Source Refers to the person sending a message.

Speech A personal sharing of thoughts and feelings principally via oral and visual channels with another being who for a short time attends to another.

Status report An oral or written presentation that is given to inform the audience about the current condition of a project.

Steering committee Sets policy and procedures for review of and decisions pertaining to designated organizational development efforts such as employee surveys and employee involvement such as quality circle proposals.

Subordination To be submissive to another.

Supportiveness Sending messages to other communicators that you are there for them when needed and value them as individuals.

Symbol That which stands for something else.

Symmetry Excellence of proportion.

Symposium A team presentation in which several individuals each make a presentation on the same or similar topic.

Task competencies The ability to establish operating procedures, analyze problems, generate criteria for good solutions, apply criteria to solutions, and select solutions.

Task groups Have the purpose of accomplishing goals or solving existing problems.

Teleconferencing The interaction of two or more individuals or groups of people in different locations who communicate live via one of several forms of electronic transmissions such as television or telephone.

Thesis statement Declarative sentence that states the main idea of your presentation. Most effective in impelling language.

Trait Characteristic that remains similar over time, such as aggressiveness.

Trait communication apprehension A general fear of oral, written, listening, or singing communication.

Transactional communication Both parties are interdependent; what I say affects you and what you say affects me.

Uncertainty avoidance The extent to which a society feels threatened by ambiguity.

Uncertainty reduction Having enough information about the other person with whom we are interacting that we to some extent can predict the other's behavior; lessening of equivocality.

Upward communication The process of communication with people whose status is greater.

Values That for which something is regarded as useful or desirable; utility, merit, or worth.

Variables That which varies.

Verbal aggressiveness Attacking others' competence, motives, and character by sarcasm, innuendo, insults, or denigrating others' self-worth.

Video teleconferencing Allows audio interaction of individuals and groups, as well as full visual capacities, over closed-circuit television.

Voice mail A form of electronic mail that allows an ordinary telephone to become a small communication center.

Written teleconferencing The interaction of many people using computer terminals.

Credits

Chapter 1: Pages 6–7, excerpt from "The Renaissance of American Quality" by John Bowles. Reprinted from a paid advertising section that was prepared for the October 14, 1985 issue of *Fortune*; p. 17, excerpt from "Conflict at Disneyland: A Root-Metaphor Analysis" by Ruth C. Smith and Eric M. Eisenberg, *Communication Monographs*, 54, December 1987, pp. 367–380. Copyright by the Speech Communication Association. Reprinted by permission of the publisher.

Chapter 2: Page 24, excerpt from *Listen, Management* by William Keefe (New York: McGraw-Hill, 1971); p. 34, adapted survey from "Improving Listening Skills" by Andrew Wolvin. In *Improving Speaking and Listening Skills*, edited by Rebecca Rubin. Reprinted by permission of Jossey-Bass, Inc., Publishers.

Chapter 3: Pages 40–41, excerpt from *Managing the Equity Factor or "After All I've Done for You . . ."* by Richard Huseman and John D. Hatfield (Boston: Houghton Mifflin, 1989), p. 7; p. 52, excerpt from "Hazards of an Open-door Policy" by Everett T. Suters. Reprinted with permission, *Inc.* magazine, January 1987. Copyright © 1987 by Goldhirsh Group, Inc., 38 Commercial Wharf, Boston, MA 02110; pp. 58–59, reprinted with the permission of Merrill Publishing Company, an imprint of Macmillan Publishing Company from *Attention: The Fundamentals of Classroom Control* by Carl Rinne. Copyright © 1984 by Merrill Publishing Company; pp. 59–60, excerpt from *The Interpersonal Communication Book*, 4th ed., by Joseph A. DeVito. Copyright © 1986 by Joseph A. DeVito. Reprinted by permission of HarperCollins Publishers.

Chapter 4: Pages 62–63, adapted from the *Presidential Commission on the Space Shuttle* Challenger *Accident* by the Rogers Commission (Washington, DC: U.S. Government Printing Office, June 6, 1986).

Chapter 5: Pages 89, 102, excerpt from *Nonverbal Communication: The Unspoken Dialogue* by Judy Burgoon, David Buller, and Gail Woodall. Copyright © 1989 by Harper & Row, Publishers, Inc. Reprinted by permission of HarperCollins Publishers; p. 92, excerpt from "Opinions Change as a Function of the Communicator's Attractiveness and Desire to Influence" by Judson Mills and Elliot Aronson, *Journal of Personality and Social Psychology*, 1(2), 1985, pp. 173–177. Copyright © 1985 by the American Psychological Association. Reprinted by permission; p. 110, excerpt from "Waiting Is a Power Game" by Robert Levine, *Psychology Today*, April 1987, pp. 24–33. Reprinted with permission from Psychology Today magazine. Copyright © 1987 (Sussex Publishers, Inc.); p. 114, adapted and redrawn from *Power! How to Get It, How to Use It* by Michael Korda. Reprinted by permission of International Creative Management. Copyright © 1975.

Chapter 6: Pages 130–131, *The Northwestern Endicott Report* published by the Placement Center, Northwestern University, Evanston, Illinois. Copyrighted; p. 132, excerpt from *How You Really Get Hired*, 3rd ed., by John L. LaFevre (Englewood Cliffs, NJ: Prentice-Hall), 1992. Reprinted by permission; pp. 136–137, excerpt from *Communicating at Work*, 2nd ed., by Ronald B. Adler. Copyright © 1986 by McGraw-Hill, Inc. Reprinted by permission of McGraw-Hill, Inc.; p. 140, "10 Surefire Ways to Improve Your Chances of Getting a Turndown" appearing in the 1988–1989 *CPC Annual*, vol. 1, with the permission of the College Placement Council, Inc., copyright holder.

Chapter 7: Pages 147–148, excerpt reprinted with permission from the February 1989 *Reader's Digest*, p. 138. Originally from "Note Pad" by Cheryl Fields, *Chronicle of Higher Education*, January 7, 1980, p. 15. Reprinted by permission of the Chronicle of Higher Education; p. 153, copyright © 1989. From *Introduction to Technical Writing: Process and Practice* by Lois Johnson Rew. Reprinted with permission of St. Martin's Press, Inc.; pp. 165, 166, 167, reprinted from the 1988–1989 *CPC Annual*, vol. 1, 32nd ed., with the permission of the College Placement Council, Inc., copyright holder; p. 181, excerpt from *Marketing and Services News* by IBM.

Chapter 8: Page 196, excerpt from "Towards a Communication Competency Model of Group Leadership" by Kevin Barge and Randy Hirokawa, *Small Group Behavior*, 20(2), pp. 167–189. Reprinted by permission of Kevin Barge; p. 187, excerpt from "You Always Hurt the One You Love" by Mary Anne Fitzpatrick and Jeff Winke, *Communication Quarterly*, 27(1), 1979, p. 7. Reprinted by permission of Mary Anne Fitzpatrick; p. 194, excerpt from "The Seven Keys to Business Leadership" by Kenneth Labich, *Fortune*, October 24, 1988. Fortune, © 1988 Time Inc. All rights reserved.

Chapter 10: Page 238, adapted excerpt from "Memo to Workers: Don't Phone Home" by Jeffrey Rothfeder, *Business Week*, January 25, 1988. Reprinted by permission of Business Week magazine.

Chapter 11: Page 247, excerpt from "Speech Must Grab Attention" by Niki Scott, *Lansing State Journal*, November 2, 1989. Reprinted with permission of Federated Publications, Inc.; p. 254, "What an Audience Likes" from the members' guide to

Speak-Up Jaycee—Lessons in Effective Public Speaking, revised 1967. Reprinted by permission of the United States Junior COC (U.S. Jaycees); pp. 262–263, excerpt from "The Interchange of Technical Information" by Semon Knudsen, *Vital Speeches*, 1973. Reprinted by permission of Vital Speeches, City New Publishing Co.

Chapter 13: Page 298, excerpt from *Basic Speech Communication* by R. E. Busby and R. E. Majors. Copyright © 1987 by Harper & Row, Publishers, Inc. Reprinted by permission of HarperCollins Publishers; p. 305, adapted figure from *The Pitch* by Hugh Rank (Park Forest, IL: Counter-Propaganda Press, 1982). Reprinted by permission.

Index of Names

Index of Companies, Corporations, and Organizations

Index of Subjects

BOWLING GREEN STATE UNIVERSITY
DISCARDED
LIBRARY

A113   0767494 2

HF 5718 .G665 1993

Gorden, William I., 1929–

We mean business